The
Responsible
Administrator

The
Responsible
Administrator

An Approach to Ethics
for the Administrative Role

Fifth Edition

Terry L. Cooper

JOSSEY-BASS
A Wiley Imprint
www.josseybass.com

Published by Jossey-Bass
A Wiley Imprint
989 Market Street, San Francisco, CA 94103-1741   www.josseybass.com

Jossey-Bass books and products are available through most bookstores. To contact Jossey-Bass directly call our Customer Care Department within the U.S. at 800-956-7739, outside the U.S. at 317-572-3986, or fax 317-572-4002.

Jossey-Bass also publishes its books in a variety of electronic formats. Some content that appears in print may not be available in electronic books.

Library of Congress Cataloging-in-Publication Data
Cooper, Terry L., date.
  The responsible administrator: an approach to ethics for the administrative role / Terry L. Cooper.—5th ed.
       p. cm.—(The Jossey-Bass social responsibility series)
  Includes bibliographical references and index.
  ISBN-13: 978-0-7879-7651-4 (cloth)
  ISBN-10: 0-7879-7651-2 (cloth)
  1. Civil service ethics—United States. 2. Government executives—Professional ethics—United States.
I. Title. II. Series.
  JK468.E7C66 2006
  172'.2—dc22   2006014170

Printed in the United States of America
FIFTH EDITION
HB Printing 10 9 8 7 6 5 4 3 2 1

Contents

Preface to the Fifth Edition

As I write these introductory comments for the fifth edition of *The Responsible Administrator,* I am struck by the fact that when I wrote the first edition, I never envisioned that the field of administrative ethics would grow so robustly that there would be four subsequent editions of this book. Indeed, this fifth edition is testimony not only to the growth of the field, but to the continued relevance of administrative ethics and the problem of responsibility. This fifth edition seeks to acknowledge the changes in the field and the advances in research while remaining true to the basic framework of the first edition.

The Responsible Administrator was written for students and practitioners of public administration who want to develop their ethical as well as technical competence. It is for men and women in public service, or preparing for it, who sometimes worry about the right thing to do, but who either have not taken the time to read books on ethical theory or suspect that such treatises would not be helpful at the practical level.

The education, training, and day-to-day practice of public administrators tend to be dominated by the practical problems of getting the job done. Concerns about what should be done and why it should be done get swept aside by the pressures of schedule and workload. Modern society is preoccupied with action, to the exclusion of reflection about values and principles. Theory is diminished to theories that concern means—"how to" crowds out "toward what end?"

Ethical theory, in particular, tends to suffer under the sway of this mentality. Because ethics involves substantive reasoning about obligations, consequences, and ultimate ends, its immediate utility for a producing and consuming society is suspect. Principles and values, "goods" and "oughts," seem pretty wispy stuff compared to cost-benefit ratios, GNP, tensile strength, organizational structures, assembly lines, budgets, downsizing, deadlines, outsourcing through contracts, interest group lobbying, and political pressures. The payoff for dealing formally with ethics is unclear for individual administrators and for organizations as well.

The result is a tendency either to totally ignore the study of ethics or to deal with it superficially. A study conducted by the Hastings Center two years before the first edition of this book was published revealed that "few higher-education institutions offer courses in ethics" (Watkins, 1980, p. 10). The researchers attributed this neglect primarily to the controversial nature of the teaching of ethics. Academicians apparently had difficulty agreeing on who should teach these courses, as well as some apprehension about "the dangers of indoctrination" (p. 10).

Since 1980 interest in administrative ethics seems to have mushroomed. (See Cooper, 2001b, for a review of the emergence of ethics as a field of study.) The demand for in-service training sessions has increased substantially, more articles on ethics have appeared in the professional literature, sessions on ethics have grown in number and attendance at the annual conference of the American Society for Public Administration (ASPA), and in 1989 ASPA conducted its first national conference on governmental ethics in Washington, D.C., with seven hundred participants, including both practitioners and scholars. ASPA now has a standing Section on Ethics (see www.aspaonline.org/ethicscommunity), which boasts a membership of four hundred scholars and practitioners and has hosted a number of conferences, including the first international conference in 2005. It publishes a thirty- to forty-page online electronic newsletter four times annually that has won the Best Section Newsletter Award from ASPA every year since its inception almost ten years ago.

In 1991 the first Conference on the Study of Government Ethics was held in Park City, Utah. The conference was led by George Frederickson and sponsored by the Section on Public Administration Research of ASPA, the Ethics in Public Service Network, the Institute of Public Management of Brigham Young University, and the Public Administration Program at the University of Utah. This two-day event focused on research on public ethics, the fifty to sixty participants consisting mostly of scholars from around the nation. The nine sessions, with a total of twenty-one presentations, covered topics including Ethics and Organizational Controls, Ethics and Independent Controls: The Role of Commissions, Ethics and Professional Culture, Codes of Ethics, Administrators' Attitudes Toward Ethics and Professional Conduct, Legislative and Political Corruption and Ethics, Conflicts of Interest, Policy Ethics, and Organizational Ethics. The range of topics, participants, and research methods reflected in the program indicated that serious research was well under way on public ethics.

The next major milestone was the National Symposium on Ethics and Values at the Public Administration Academy in Tampa, Florida, in 1995, organized by James Bowman and Donald Menzel. This was the first national forum for examining the treatment of values and ethics in curricula, academic professional ethics, the ethical dimensions of faculty-student relations, research ethics, virtue approaches to ethics education, and the role of the academy in educating ethics officials in government. More than a hundred persons, mostly academics, participated in the two and a half days of deliberations, including thirty-one presentations.

The rapid development of research on administrative ethics is reflected in the publication of the first *Handbook of Administrative Ethics* (Cooper, 1994). The second edition of this volume (Cooper, 2001a), an overview of the state of the art in administrative ethics research, contains thirty-four chapters by forty-one scholars from around the world. The first edition of this book would have been inconceivable only ten years earlier; the expansion of the second edition after just six years is testament to the growth and relevance of the field. I have recently examined some of the major research questions before us in "Big Questions in Administrative Ethics: A Need for Focused, Collaborative Effort" (2004a).

Another important indication that administrative ethics had passed beyond the academic fad stage was the 1997 publication of *Public Integrity Annual,* sponsored by the Council of State Governments and ASPA. This book included chapters by both academics and practitioners and focused largely on practical administrative problems and applications (Bowman and Ensign, 1997). It was so well received that it is now a quarterly scholarly journal, *Public Integrity,* currently edited by James S. Bowman. It is currently considered a very high-quality journal on administrative ethics.

In spite of these significant developments in scholarship, the academy nevertheless seemed slow to adapt to these trends in the curricula of professional education for the field. April Hejka-Ekins (1988) surveyed 139 of the more than 200 schools and departments that belong to the National Association of Schools of Public Affairs and Administration (NASPAA) and found that only 66 (31.4 percent) had offered an ethics course during 1985–86 and 1986–87. It appears that academe responded weakly to the emerging interest in ethics; there was a disturbing lag in developing courses as part of the core curriculum of public administration education.

Although it now seems that the treatment of ethics in graduate courses in public administration is growing, there are no current comprehensive statistics on the number of programs offering or requiring ethics courses. Fragmentary data suggest that graduate programs are increasing their emphasis on ethics. Catron and Denhardt (1994) reviewed the thirty-nine NASPAA self-study reports for 1989–91 and found that 18 percent not only offered ethics courses but required them. This amounted to a substantial increase in the number of required courses over an earlier study they conducted. Menzel (1997) indicates that 78 of the 225 NASPAA programs (35 percent) he surveyed in 1996 now offer ethics courses. My own review of the curricula of the twelve programs ranked in the top ten by *U.S. News and World Report* (March 20, 1996) indicates that eight (67 percent) offer an ethics course and four (33 percent) do not. None requires such a course.

The number of freestanding courses devoted entirely to ethics does not really tell the whole tale, however. Catron and Denhardt (1994, p. 52) point out that in 1989, a new NASPAA curriculum standard went into effect mandating that "the common curriculum components shall enhance the student's values, knowledge, and skills, to act ethically and effectively." In the self-study report instructions adopted in December 1996 (National Association of Schools of Public Affairs and Administration, 1996), this was made more specific:

4.21 Common Curriculum Components

The common curriculum components shall enhance the student's values, knowledge, and skills to act ethically and effectively:

In the Management of Public Service Organizations, the components of which include: Human resources; Budgeting and financial processes; Information, including computer literacy and applications.

In the Application of Quantitative and Qualitative Techniques of Analysis, the components of which include: Policy and Program formulation, implementation and evaluation; Decision-making and problem-solving.

With an Understanding of the Public Policy and Organizational Environment, the components of which include: Political and legal institutions and processes; Economic and social institutions and processes; Organization and management concepts and behavior.

This section is followed by a further requirement to indicate how ethical conduct is cultivated:

4.21.B. Ethical Action: Describe how the curriculum enhances "students' values, knowledge, and skills to act ethically and effectively." In the current standards revised in January 2002, the standards concerning ethics education are essentially the same except the 4.21.b requirement to spell out how the curriculum accomplishes the kind of ethics outcomes that are desired has been dropped.

The adoption of curriculum standards and reporting requirements by NASPAA has likely led to some treatment of ethics in all of the NASPAA programs, but that does not mean that all will have separate courses. In many cases, ethics has been integrated broadly into the curriculum by incorporating modules in various courses on management, policy analysis, human resources, public finance, quantitative methods, and research design. Responses to a query sent out on the NASPAA listserv about ethics courses produced responses that suggested that many programs prefer this approach and in some cases are too small to be able to offer a separate ethics course. For a period of about ten years, Robert Cleary, now an emeritus professor at American University, analyzed the NASPAA directory listings every two years and confirmed in a personal e-mail message that integration into courses on other subjects is the predominant mode of delivery. The possibility of requiring a free-standing course in all NASPAA accredited programs has been raised a number of times at both NASPAA and ASPA conferences but has received little support beyond those whose focus is administrative ethics.

At an earlier stage, there seemed to have been an uneasiness with the formal study of ethics rooted in an assumption that ethics is simply a matter of relativity and subjectivity. In a pluralistic society, where no one religious or cultural tradition is dominant, ethics has been viewed as a private, individual matter, not susceptible to the canons of rational inquiry. To address the study of ethics openly in an academic setting was thought to run the risk of either creating unresolvable conflicts among those who hold differing ethical perspectives or unfairly propagandizing for one particular point of view. However, Americans appear to have become more comfortable with the topic of ethics in public life and with offering academic courses on the subject or treatment of it in courses on other topics. One change since the fourth edition is that the role of religious faith and belief in public administrative ethics has become an increasing point of controversy in conferences and on the Section on Ethics "Ethtalk" listserv, although it has not yet surfaced in a major way in publications.

Although significant progress seems to have been made in accepting the legitimacy of studying administrative ethics, it is still true that once students leave school, they are probably not well equipped to think about the ethical problems they face regularly on the job and shape their conduct accordingly. Yoder and Denhardt (2001) argue, "No guarantee exists that even if public administration/affairs schools integrate and teach ethics in the most effective manner, administrators will practice what they have learned and act ethically" (p. 74). The mere acceptance of the academic legitimacy of ethics still sends a clear message to those preparing for careers in public service that it is not a top priority. The essential value-orientedness of the field of public administration remains largely unacknowledged. We should not be surprised, then, to see expedience and technical considerations dominate decision making. Even when ethical issues are recognized, often they are considered hopelessly frustrating and beyond the domain of rational analysis. We can predict that decisions involving value conflicts will not be engaged as systematically, seriously, or openly as matters of economics, politics, and organizational survival. Menzel concludes his 1997 study on the impact of ethics courses with the assertion that ethics instruction has definitely found a niche in public administration schools and that however the topic is handled in the classroom, it seems to be making a difference in the professional lives of the students—but not enough of a difference. So there is still work to be done by those who believe that competence in ethical analysis and decision making are central to the field and should shape administrative practice.

Practitioners, however, do seem to have recognized the importance of ethics in their professional roles. Bowman and Williams's 1997 study of 750 public managers who are ASPA members concludes, "The respondents indicate that ethics is hardly a fad and that government has the obligation to set the example in society. They further hold that ethics in the workplace can be empowering, although not all organizations and their leaders have a consistent approach to accomplish this. The findings emphasize the key role of leadership—both by its presence and absence—in encouraging honorable public service" (p. 525). Their empirical findings reflect a substantial increase in the importance attributed to ethics by public administrators as compared to a similar study published by Bowman in 1990. This is a hopeful sign; perhaps academe will respond to these perceptions of practitioners more forthrightly in the years ahead.

Acknowledgments

Twenty-four years since the first edition of *The Responsible Administrator* was published, my intellectual honesty and humility still require admitting that writing a book is not a task for which an author ought to take sole credit. The more I write and reflect, the more I interact with students in the classroom, and the more I converse with colleagues around the world, the clearer it becomes that scholarship is truly a collective enterprise.

I am indebted to the many undergraduate students who have taken my course in Citizenship and Public Ethics as part of the undergraduate program in the School of Policy, Planning, and Development at the University of Southern California. Their blunt questions and serious challenges have deepened my thinking and forced me to be clearer in expressing my views. Their interest in the subject of public ethics and the intensity of their struggles with their own professional obligations have stimulated lively debates that have caused me to rethink my own perspective.

I express my deepest appreciation to the women and men at all levels of American public service who have shared their struggles, insights, and creativity with me. Their cases and ensuing discussions in ethics workshops I have conducted since 1975, as well as in my graduate course on Public Ethics more recently, are the empirical basis for this book and a major source of any knowledge I may be able to pass along. I have been deeply impressed by their intention to do the right thing in the face of formidable impediments. I hold their contributions to ethics in public administration in respectful trust and pass it along as their gift to the reader.

I thank my colleagues around the world who are teaching and engaging in research on administrative ethics. Our numbers have grown substantially since 1982 when *The Responsible Administrator* first appeared. Through sessions at the annual conferences of

ASPA and at other smaller meetings in the United States, Canada, Hong Kong, France, Belgium, and Australia, I have observed that a genuine community of scholars and practitioners is emerging worldwide that is committed to the development of public administrative ethics. In particular, I thank Terry Lui, formerly on the faculty of the University of Hong Kong, for collaborating with me on two research projects on administrative ethics in Hong Kong during my year there as a Fulbright Professor in 1989, and again during the 1993–1997 period. Working with her has enriched and expanded my understanding of public sector ethics.

My thanks also go to the reviewers, who once again carefully examined the previous edition of this book and gave me their constructive advice, and to Allison Brunner at Jossey-Bass, whose competent editorial guidance has been invaluable.

I express again my continuing gratitude to my dearest and best colleague, my wife, Megan, whose inspiration, insights, writing skill, knowledge of the field of public administration, practical insights, and personal support have been freely and warmly given since the first edition, and again at every stage of this project.

I must also acknowledge a moral guide in my life who has become more insistent and instructive since the previous edition, my daughter, Chelsea. Throughout her twenty-one years of life, she has caused me to take my own ethics more seriously. Her honest and direct questions have called me up short and caused me to reflect. Her "Why?" questions and her observations about the gap between what I say and what I do have deepened my moral life. This book has made its way through four previous editions as she has grown up. Observing her own moral development from infancy to young adulthood has illuminated my understanding of how we humans are most fundamentally valuing creatures.

Finally, I express my deep appreciation to Diane Yoder, whose scholarly knowledge and superb writing and editorial skills have been absolutely essential in getting this fifth edition to press. During the months preceding the publication deadline, I struggled with health problems, and Diane stepped in to handle the final editing process. She is a teacher and scholar of administrative ethics with whom I have collaborated on other work, and I look forward to further collaborative efforts with her.

All of these people and many others have helped to broaden and sharpen my thoughts. I deeply appreciate their gifts to me and hope that what I have done with them in these pages is worthy of their respect.

Los Angeles, California   TERRY L. COOPER
January 2006

The Author

Terry L. Cooper is The Maria B. Crutcher Professor in Citizenship and Democratic Values (Social Ethics) at the University of Southern California (USC). His research centers on citizen participation and public ethics. He is one of the coprincipal investigators in the USC Neighborhood Participation Project (NPP), conducting research on the role of neighborhood organizations in governance in the City of Los Angeles through the system of neighborhood councils established in 1999. Also, he is the director of the USC Civic Engagement Initiative, which is expanding the work of the NPP beyond neighborhood councils and beyond Los Angeles.

Cooper is the author of *The Responsible Administrator: An Approach to Ethics for the Administrative Role* (4th ed., 1998) and *An Ethic of Citizenship for Public Administration* (1991). He is the coeditor of *Exemplary Public Administrators: Character and Leadership in Government* (1992) and the editor of *Handbook of Administrative Ethics* (2nd ed., 2001). His articles have appeared in *Public Administration Review, Administration and Society, International Review of Administrative Sciences, International Journal of Public Administration, Administrative Theory and Praxis, International Journal of Organization Theory and Behavior, Public Budgeting and Finance,* and *The Bureaucrat.* He is a past member of the editorial boards of *Public Administration Review* and *Administrative Theory and Praxis* and currently serves on the editorial board of *The American Review of Public Administration.* Cooper is the editor of the Exemplar Profile series in the journal *Public Integrity.*

Cooper has previously served as chair of the Section on Ethics of the American Society for Public Administration. He has conducted ethics training for many professional groups at different levels of government around the United States and in several other countries.

The
Responsible
Administrator

| Introduction

The Responsible Administrator is one attempt to respond to the need for a systematic treatment of public administrative ethics that is grounded in both the realities of practice and the requirements of sound scholarship. It is important to identify the particular contribution intended here. The conceptual focus of the book is the role of the public administrator in an organizational setting; the central integrating ethical concept used in dealing with that role is responsibility. The central ethical process adopted for addressing ethical problems associated with administrative responsibility is a comprehensive design approach.

What Is Ethics?

Ethics is defined in various ways, some more technical and precise than others. The usual brief textbook or dictionary definitions define *ethics* as "the attempt to state and evaluate principles by which ethical problems may be solved" (Jones, Sontag, Becker, and Fogelin, 1969, p. 1), "the normative standards of conduct derived from the philosophical and religious traditions of society" (Means, 1970, p. 52), or "the task of careful reflection several steps removed from the actual conduct of men" concerning "the assumptions and presuppositions of the moral life" (Gustafson, 1965, p. 113). Preston (1996) becomes a bit more specific by suggesting that "ethics is concerned about what is right, fair, just, or good; about what we ought to do, not just about what is the case or what is most acceptable or expedient" (p. 16). Martin (1995) defines ethics as moral philosophy and stipulates that it includes four main goals or interests: clarification of moral concepts; critical evaluation of moral claims focused on "testing their truth, justification, and adequacy" (pp. 7–8); constructing an inclusive perspective by elucidating the interconnections among moral ideas and values; and providing moral guidance through improving practical judgment.

Gibson Winter (1966) defines ethics more comprehensively by describing the functions it serves in the social world. As an active enterprise, he says, "Ethics seeks to clarify the logic and adequacy of the values that shape the world; it assesses the moral possibilities which are projected and betrayed in the social give-and-take" (p. 218). Anyone engaged in ethical reflection takes on the task of analyzing and evaluating the principles embodied in various alternatives for conduct and social order. Ethics is, according to Winter, "a science of human intentionality" (p. 219).

For our purposes in this book, ethics may be understood as the study of moral conduct and moral status. *Ethics* and *morality* are often used interchangeably, but here I will distinguish them. Morality assumes some accepted modes of behavior that are given by a religious tradition, a culture (including an organizational culture), a social class, a community, or a family. It involves expected courses of conduct that are rooted in both formal rules and informal norms. Morality includes such things as "decent young people do not engage in premarital sex," "family comes first," "one should not conspicuously display one's wealth," "guests in one's home must always be treated with respect," "never drive under the influence," "a day's pay requires a day's work," "follow the orders of those above you in the organization," and similar expectations. Sometimes these are written out in codes of conduct or rules, but at other times they are assumed and taken for granted. Typically they are asserted by a tradition, culture, religion, community, organization, or family as simply what is right.

Ethics, then, is one step removed from action. It involves the examination and analysis of the logic, values, beliefs, and principles that are used to justify morality in its various forms. It considers what is meant by principles such as justice, veracity, or the public interest; their implications for conduct in particular situations; and how one might argue for one principle over another as determinative in a particular decision. Ethics takes what is given or prescribed and asks what is meant and why. So ethics as related to conduct is critical reflection on morality toward grounding moral conduct in systematic reflection and reasoning. It is not without an affective element since ethical reflection often evokes emotive responses of comfort or discomfort, resolution or quandary, and affirmation or antagonism.

Ethics also deals with the moral status of entities such as families, organizations, communities, and societies. Here ethical reasoning is focused on how the characteristics associated with the good family, or the good organization, or the good society are grounded in certain principles, values, beliefs, and logical argument. Ethics weighs the adequacy of these attributes and analyzes how they are justified.

Ethics may be dealt with descriptively or normatively. Descriptively, ethics attempts to reveal underlying assumptions and how they are connected to conduct. Normatively, ethics attempts to construct viable and defensible arguments for particular courses of conduct as being better than others in specific situations. This book engages mainly in a descriptive approach to the ethical situation of public administrators and provides some analytical tools for arriving at normative judgments. It does not describe a particular public service ethic, which I have addressed in another book, *An Ethic of Citizenship for Public Administration* (1991). However, my approach to the normative ethics of the public administrative role is just one among several options under discussion currently.

Ethics may be viewed from either or both of two major orientations: deontological and teleological. Deontological approaches to ethics focus on one's duty to certain ethical principles such as justice, freedom, or veracity without regard for the consequences of one's actions. Teleological ethics, in contrast, involves a concern for the ends or consequences of one's conduct. This is the position most notably associated with utilitarianism and its calculus of the greatest good for the greatest number. This book assumes that most of us undertake decisions using both of these perspectives most of the time. That is, we consider principles that are important to us in a concrete situation and then ask ourselves what the consequences of acting on those principles are likely to be. The decision-making model presented in the next chapter combines deontological and teleological orientations.

Doing ethics, then, involves thinking more systematically about the values and principles that are embedded in the choices we otherwise would make on practical or political grounds alone. As we reflect on these implicit values, we ask ourselves how they are consistent with our duties and toward what ends and consequences they lead. Keeping in mind the obligations and goals of the roles we occupy, we seek to rank-order them for a particular ethical decision we confront in the course of carrying out a specific role.

The relationship between law and ethics often comes up in the discussion of specific cases. My answer is that law is the moral minimum. It is the minimum level of conduct that we as a society can agree to impose on all of us through the threat of force and sanctions. Ethical considerations are often involved in deliberations about proposed legislation, but once crystallized into law, the conduct prescribed is assumed to be backed up by the coercive power of government. However, from an ethicist's point of view, law must always stand under the judgment of ethics. Sometimes laws may be deemed unjust and therefore unethical. Those who believe so may challenge those laws in the courts as inconsistent with the human rights guaranteed by the U.S. Constitution, or they may engage in civil disobedience even to the point of being arrested and going to jail.

Both kinds of challenges occurred during the civil rights movement of the 1960s and 1970s. The NAACP engaged in litigation against unjust segregation laws in the American South. Martin Luther King Jr. and many others employed civil disobedience by sitting in at segregated facilities, refusing to sit in the back seats on buses, and demonstrating against segregated schools even when ordered by legal authorities not to do so. Sometimes laws need to be challenged on ethical grounds. In the long tradition of civil disobedience exemplified by Gandhi and King, the key proviso is that one must be willing to accept the consequences of one's actions in order to demonstrate commitment to ethical principles over what are considered unjust laws. That is, one must be willing to suffer fines and imprisonment in order to evoke a response from the larger society to bring about change in the laws in question.

Responsibility and Role

The terms *role* and *responsibility* are peculiarly modern in connotation. Both suggest a worldview in which the power of tradition is broken and human beings are left to construct a world of their own making. Roles must be devised and responsibility defined as ways of reestablishing obligations in our modern, pluralistic, technological society. Technology is applied not only to production but also to society itself.

Gibson Winter (1966, pp. 254–255) observed: "Responsibility is a relatively new term in the ethical vocabulary, appearing in the nineteenth century with a somewhat ambiguous meaning. The term evaluates action and attributes it to an agent; it does so in lieu of cosmic or natural structures of obligation. The historical awareness of the nineteenth century, the scientific and technological revolutions, and the collapse of metaphysical systems had undermined fixed notions of obligations. The term 'responsibility' was a way of filling this gap by defining the scope of accountability and obligation in contexts of law and common culture."

Similarly, Richard McKeon's study of the emergence of the term in Western thought reveals that *responsibility* first appeared in English and French in 1787. It was used initially in reference to the political institutions arising out of the American and French revolutions, but its use continued through the nineteenth century. When "constitutional government was vastly extended, in scope of operation and in spread among nations, as a result of contacts of cultures and peoples" (1957, p. 23), the concept of responsibility became increasingly significant as a way of defining a common set of values among people of divergent cultures and traditions.

The concept of role then becomes a convenient way to package expectations and obligations associated with the modern world. As we cease to view social functions as received intact from the past and instead to be manipulated and created anew, we take upon ourselves bounded obligation in the form of various roles. People exercise responsibility and are held responsible in society by accepting and carrying out an array of more or less well-defined roles: employee, parent, citizen, group member. The most problematic roles are those not clearly defined, usually because there is little agreement about the boundaries of responsibility associated with them. What does it mean to be a responsible parent in the first decade of the twenty-first century? Or a responsible spouse, responsible citizen, responsible politician, or responsible public administrator?

The problem is that although public administrators are responsible for certain duties (those that constitute the professional role), they sometimes believe they are obligated to act otherwise. This is because administrators, along with everyone else in modern society, maintain an array of roles related to family, community, and society, each carrying a set of obligations and vested with certain personal interest. The quite common result is conflict among roles as these competing forces push and pull in opposite directions. The effects of these conflicts are compounded by the range of discretion administrators must exercise. Legislation frequently provides only broad language about its intent, leaving the specifics to administrators. Consequently, ethical standards and sensitivity are crucial to the responsible use of this discretion.

The Responsible Administrator

The responsible administrator is one who is responsible in the two senses discussed briefly above; the subject is treated more thoroughly in Chapter Four. Responsible administrators must be able to account for their conduct to relevant others such as supervisors, elected officials, the courts, and the citizenry, which means being able to explain and justify why specific actions they took resulted in particular consequences. They must also be able to act in ways that are consistent with their inner convictions as professional guardians of the public good. That is, being a responsible administrator includes both objective accountability for conduct and subjective congruence with one's professional values. Ethics is the most fundamental way in which one satisfies both kinds of responsibility. Responsible administrators must be ethically sophisticated enough to reason with others about how their conduct serves the public interest and have sufficient clarity about their own professional ethical commitments to maintain integrity and a sense of self-esteem.

What, then, is the difference between an ethical administrator and a responsible administrator? A public administrator who has been properly socialized may be able to act in accordance with the common good some or even most of the time, thus being an ethical administrator some or most of the time, but not be able to account for his or her conduct with reasons when questioned or challenged, and perhaps not even be able to understand in a self-conscious way why he or she acted in a particular way. Understanding one's motivations and being able to explain and justify the actions that flow from them are the essential qualities of the responsible administrator. This book seeks to provide the concepts, theories, and techniques for responsible administration.

A Design Approach

All too many treatments of professional ethics stop with a conceptual and theoretical philosophical analysis of typical ethical problems. Some lead to a desired solution or a prescribed set of ethical norms, whereas others elucidate the problem, offer some analysis of various alternatives, and leave the reader with the implication that all are of equal value. Here a design approach is adopted as the central organizing ethical process. This orientation assumes that there is no single best solution to a significant ethical problem, but rather numerous possible solutions, some of equal value but others of greater or lesser worth. The task is to design a response to a problem at hand that addresses the immediate short-term situation but looks to the wider organizational, legal, and social contexts for the longer-term answers.

Practicing administrators cannot live exclusively in the realm of philosophical reflection, but must connect such considerations to action and organizations. As Caroline Whitbeck suggests, "People confronted with ethical problems must do more than simply make judgments. They must figure out what to do" (1996, p. 9). Far from simply assuming that ethics is a matter of looking for an ideal rational solution to an immediate problem, Whitbeck argues that a person confronting an ethical problem should be thinking like a designer. "Design problems," she points out, "are problems of making (or repairing) things and processes to satisfy wants and needs" (p. 10). And this "making" and "repairing" always involves constraints—in time, money, power, ability to persuade, and the strength to absorb consequences. For public administrators, the design of a viable and acceptable solution to an ethical quandary always takes place in the context of organizations that will support some kinds of conduct and impede others. A workable resolution of an ethical problem cannot ignore that organizational context.

Following Whitbeck, the approach developed throughout this book is one of considering the facts of a situation—its social and organizational context, its constraints, opportunities, and implications for all concerned—and then advocating the design of courses of action that may include changes in organizational structure, culture, rules, policies, and procedures. It is assumed that there are several conceivable alternative courses to consider before selecting, not the ideal or perfect solution, but the best among an array of possibilities, some of which may be equally acceptable. This design approach assumes that it is always possible to improve on any solution given moral imagination, ingenuity, and creativity and that one must always bring these qualities to bear on important ethical quandaries. But administrators have limited time to exercise their inventiveness and finally must act in the short run while planning for the future.

Thus, as the chapters unfold, responsibility for the public administrative role will be developed by leading the reader through considerations of the elements involved in designing what to do in the face of ethical uncertainty and challenge. Some of the moral lessons Whitbeck has advanced for design problems include:

- *Begin with a consideration of the uncertainties involved in any ethical problem.* For example, no one should ever assume that appearances are always true. Conduct that may seem to be unethical may not be when it is fully explored and understood. Also, human behavior is not always predictable. A person may decide on a course of action and find out that the key actors respond very differently from what had been expected. As the process of addressing a problem unfolds, the nature of the problem may change. Other problems and conflicts heretofore unknown may be discovered to be involved in the problem.

- *The generation of alternative solutions to an ethical problem is separate from defining the problem and may necessitate gathering additional information.* This is related to the first lesson. Often, in order to reduce uncertainty, it is necessary to find out more about who is involved in the problem, how long it has existed, the characters of the key actors, the implications of various options for action for the larger organization and people within it, and how key actors outside the organization may respond to the proposed courses of action.

- *One is always acting under time pressure.* Busy public administrators do not have the luxury of contemplating an ethical problem until they are fully satisfied that all options and contingencies have been exhaustively considered. Decisions have to be made and things have to get done, always under constraints of schedules and deadlines. Sometimes that means pursuing several alternatives simultaneously or developing a contingency approach with a decision tree indicating what will be done if various things do not happen as initially planned. Not taking this approach may mean that the opportunity to intervene and correct misconduct may be lost. Postponing action may result in a fait accompli. The damage may be done, and irreversibly so.

• *Ethical problems are dynamic.* They change as we begin trying to address them. What one may at first engage as an ethical problem may become also a legal problem. Or, while one is beginning to work through a planned course of action to address an ethical problem, someone else may intervene and resolve it in another way, which may in turn create an entirely new problem.

These lessons are rather abstract at this point, but readers should try to keep them in mind as the chapters unfold. Chapter Nine develops this design approach in summary fashion by applying it to a case.

Overview of the Contents

The first and most basic task of this book is to illuminate the ethical decision-making process. Chapter Two begins with some basic concepts for understanding the levels of deliberation at which ethical problems are addressed. This is followed by a model for analyzing and resolving these problems. The model is partly linear, involving a sequence of steps, and partly nonlinear, requiring a search for integration of several key elements, including moral rules, ethical principles, self-image, and the norms of the political community. It also combines reasoning, emotion, and beliefs. The model presented here is not simply a rationalist approach that focuses on principles, but includes as essential the affective dimensions of ethical decision making and conduct. The logic espoused is not a linear syllogistic calculus, but something more like the logic of aesthetics or the logic of rhetoric. Some readers seem to have missed this essential thrust in earlier editions of the book (Bruce,

1992; Cooper, 1992a; Harmon, 1995; Cooper, 1996). This chapter concludes with a summary of the design approach that is developed through the remaining chapters.

Chapter Three develops the social context within which the public administrator must work and discusses the problem of defining and maintaining the administrator's role in the diverse and relativistic environment of modern society. Without the guidance of a coherent tradition, the administrative role in modern societies is just one more set of obligations and interests that must be managed amid an array of other competing roles. One significant implication of this social context is the inescapably political nature of public administration.

Chapter Four addresses the dual nature of administrative responsibility in modern society: objective responsibility (in which one is held accountable by superiors, the public, and legislation) and subjective responsibility (in which one feels and believes oneself to be responsible). Conflict between these two forms of responsibility seems to be the most common form in which ethical dilemmas emerge.

Chapter Five further develops the conflict between subjective and objective responsibility. Conflicts of authority, role, and interest are reviewed. It is not that these three forms of conflicting responsibility require distinctly different forms of analysis to be resolved. Rather, understanding the different ways we experience conflicts helps us clarify the key actors and relationships that must be examined and dealt with if we are to achieve resolution.

Chapter Six presents two general approaches to maintaining, from a management perspective, responsible conduct in public organizations—internal and external controls. External controls include instruments imposed from outside the individual, such as codes of ethics and ethics legislation; internal controls involve the professional values and standards that public servants have internalized through the socialization process, both personal and professional.

Continuing the management perspective from Chapter Six, Chapter Seven focuses on the importance of establishing congruence among the various internal and external controls. Two examples illustrate what happens when this is not done. Four components of responsible conduct are then discussed: individual attributes, organizational structure, organizational culture, and societal expectations.

Chapter Eight shifts the perspective to an individual who is attempting to act ethically in the face of management that has become corrupt or lost sight of its mandated mission in the public interest. The problem is one of conflicting loyalties—to superiors on the one hand and to the public on the other. Whistle-blowing is recognized as one response to this kind of conflict. Sources of organizational pressure on individual employees are outlined, organizational remedies are discussed, and the ultimate necessity for individual responsibility is asserted. The chapter closes with a treatment of the components required for individual ethical autonomy.

It is important to note that ethical autonomy is not tantamount to ethical individualism but must be seen in the context of the previous chapters and the concluding model. Individual autonomy is necessary to some degree to provide for the exercise of conscience in resistance to corrupt authority, but that always occurs for public administrators in organizational, institutional, and societal contexts. The administrator is not in his or her job simply for self-fulfillment, but to serve the citizenry by enhancing the public good. The public administrator is a fiduciary of the citizens, holding their common good in trust. Thus it is assumed here that women and men entering public service must be prepared to find fulfillment in this pursuit.

In Chapter Nine, I elaborate the design approach and its relevance to significant ethical problems. I restate the approach in terms appropriate for the public administrative role using cases as examples of how the approach would be applied. I conclude the chapter by applying the design approach to a concrete case about contracting for government services.

The final chapter summarizes the argument developed through the previous chapters and presents a model of responsible administration that brings together the components of responsible conduct from Chapter Seven and the components of individual ethical autonomy from Chapter Eight. Illustrative material has been added to Chapter Ten to clarify the practical implications of the model.

The cases in the book are based on reality and fictionalized only slightly to protect the privacy of those who wrote them. In a few instances they are composites of several actual cases. They are intended primarily as illustration, but also to stimulate thinking about the ethical problems they portray. For both reasons, the situations are left unresolved. To indicate an outcome would diminish the experience of dilemma they are calculated to evoke; it would also short-circuit the reader's own reflections. For the same reason, the case narratives are a bit longer and more detailed than usual. Again, the ultimate purpose of *The Responsible Administrator* is to illuminate the ethical situation of the public administrator and cultivate imaginative reflection about it—not to prescribe a particular set of public service values. This is not to suggest that all alternatives are of equal value, but that the focus of this book is not on prescribing particular courses of action.

This book is largely descriptive and analytical; it is only secondarily prescriptive, and even then only in a particular sense. It prescribes a design approach to public administrative ethics that includes techniques that individual administrators can use in analyzing ethical dilemmas they confront, and a combination of organizational and management components for fostering responsible administration.

I do not attempt to develop a substantive ethic for public administrators in this book. That is a necessary and important undertaking, but it is dealt with in another of my books, *An Ethic of Citizenship for Public Administration* (1991). There I develop the argument that normative ethics for public administration is to be found in the ethical tradition of citizenship as it has evolved throughout U.S. history. This tradition has at its core a notion of the common good, the importance of democratic participation by the citizenry, and the ultimate sovereignty of the people. The public administrator is viewed there as taking his or her ethical norms from those of citizenship in a democratic society. The administrator is a fiduciary professional citizen in some sense. For the purposes of this book, some such public service ethic is assumed.

Chapter Two

Understanding Ethical Decision Making

James A. Michener's novel *Chesapeake* (1978) portrays the history of two families who settled near each other on the shores of Chesapeake Bay during the American colonial era. As Quakers, the Paxmores tended to espouse values in both religion and politics quite different from those of the Steeds, devout Roman Catholics. However, in spite of their divergent doctrines and frequent conflicts, the two families managed to live as neighbors with a kind of grudging respect and a willingness to work things out.

In the closing pages is a scene involving the family patriarchs of the mid-1970s, Pusey Paxmore and Owen Steed. The two men are sitting on the porch of the Paxmore house, looking out over the Chesapeake and reflecting on the events of Watergate. Pusey had been a high-level appointee in the Nixon White House, and Owen was one of the oil company executives who had covertly, and illegally, raised money for CREEP, the Committee to Re-elect the President. Both men's careers were seriously damaged by the scandals, and both have returned home to retire and to think. During this conversation, an insightful and pithy exchange occurs:

Steed: How do you explain the corruption, the near-treason?
Paxmore: Men without character slip from one position to the next. And never comprehend the awful downward course they're on.
Steed: Couldn't Nixon have stopped it?
Paxmore:: Woodrow Wilson could have. Or Teddy Roosevelt. And does thee know why? Because they had accumulated through years of apprenticeship a theory of government. A theory of

democracy, if thee will. And they would have detected the rot the minute it started.

Steed: Why didn't the Californians?

Paxmore: For a simple reason. They were deficient in education. They'd gone to those chrome-and-mirror schools where procedures are taught, not principles. I doubt if any one of them had ever contemplated a real moral problem, in the abstract where character is formed [p. 1049].

This bit of dialogue suggests the underlying assumption of this book: *ethical public administration requires a theoretical perspective on the role of the public administrator.* Moreover, this theoretical perspective must be developed by practicing administrators through a combination of professional experience, contemplation, study, and deliberation with colleagues, whether in a structured course or through self-motivated inquiry.

The theories of others, including scholars from various disciplines and historical periods, are essential ingredients in a professional ethic, but a fundamental assumption of this book is that knowing the thoughts of others is only the beginning. Administrators must also develop skill in thinking about ethical problems, toward the end of creating a working professional ethic of their own. Without cultivating this ability to theorize and generalize from experience, no public administrator can transcend the boundaries of particular events to comprehend and assess them. Without the illumination born of the marriage of abstract thought and practical experience, it is impossible to see where we are going. Choice is constrained and freedom is ultimately stunted by the unforeseen consequences of our actions. Without the moral compass created by regular deliberation with others about real ethical issues, whether fellow practitioners, elected officials, or citizens, our ethics may be too narrow and self-serving.

This chapter presents a sequence of steps you might employ in thinking about ethical issues you confront. The goal is not only to develop skills in resolving particular situations, but to help you cultivate a habit of using such instances as opportunities to develop and refine a working "theory" of ethical conduct. Case material (based on actual situations but partially fictionalized to protect the persons involved) is introduced here and throughout the rest of the book to illustrate the treatment of concrete administrative problems. To stimulate your thinking, the cases are generally left unresolved.

Ethical Problems

You were recently hired as the manager of a municipal department of parks and recreation. Soon after you assumed your duties, you discovered that the payroll clerk was falsifying the payroll account by continuing to carry the names of laid-off employees. When the clerk picked up the payroll at city hall, he would pull out those checks, endorse and cash them, and keep the money.

Most administrators would have no difficulty recognizing that this clerk is not only involved in unethical conduct, but he is also clearly violating the law. Both moral and legal sanctions against stealing are well established and generally accepted. You are immediately aware that this behavior is unacceptable and must be stopped, although you would probably pause to think carefully about the best course of action. Your responsibility for the image of the organization may suggest firing the clerk quietly, involving as few other people as possible. However, your responsibility for maintaining the public trust may lead you to consider formal charges and prosecution. Sometimes, as in this case, the ethical situation is quite clear, but the demands of administrative responsibility for resolving it are much less so. More often, however, both the ethical issue and its implications for administrative responsibility are complex and ambiguous.

Consider another situation. You are the director of a unit within a federal regulatory agency that is charged with monitoring the use of potentially harmful commercial chemicals. Linda, a junior project manager under your supervision, is responsible for studying a broad-spectrum insecticide used in agriculture by small grain farmers, large truck gardeners, and cotton farmers, and in the livestock industry as an animal spray. She has been assigned to determine whether this product should be removed from the market. At a party, Linda met a man named George, who she later learned was the Washington representative for the insecticide manufacturer. After several dates with George, she became rather fond of him and wanted to pursue the relationship. However, Linda realized that their professional roles created a potential conflict of interest for her and she decided to tell you about the situation. She intended to continue seeing George, she said; she considered herself mature enough to maintain a separation between her professional and private lives. Linda insisted that her feelings for George would not influence her judgment in any way; in fact, she and George had never even discussed the chemical in question.

In this case, the ethical situation is much less clear. Has Linda done anything that represents a breach of professional ethics? Because of her relationship with George, it might well be difficult for her to maintain objectivity in discharging her duties. But perhaps it might not be. People differ in their ability to manage tensions of this kind. And what is your responsibility? Is it more important to avoid even the appearance of unethical conduct within your organization, or to support an employee's right to freedom in her private life? Should Linda be trusted until her behavior demonstrates otherwise? What are your alternatives?

To intensify the quandary a bit, imagine the following situation. Your spouse works for a contractor that provides support services to your organization under contract. The two of you work in roles that do not require you to deal with each other professionally, nor is there any possible conflict of interest, either real or perceived, under normal circumstances. However, you learn through the grapevine that the contract with your spouse's organization may be terminated in the near future. Because the spouse's organization is small, the loss of the contract is likely to result in budget cuts and, consequently, her termination. Although you are a manager in your organization, you have no direct or indirect decision-making authority over this contract, so there is no legal conflict of interest. However, you know that the contractor is unaware of the possible contract termination, and if that information were divulged, it could erode performance. For that reason, this information is considered sensitive and confidential within your organization. If you tell your spouse in order to give him time to plan for a possible layoff, he will no doubt feel some obligation to tell his employer and fellow employees.

Also, you are painfully aware of two other problems. First, your own financial well-being is tied to that of your spouse; if he is laid off with short notice, both of you will suffer financially. Second, if you remain silent and the contract is terminated, sooner or later your spouse will find out that you knew what was coming and kept it from him. That failure to be honest and forthcoming in a marital relationship will likely hurt your spouse deeply and damage the marriage.

In this case, fundamental loyalties and attendant obligations come into direct conflict. Where do your primary obligations lie: with the employer or with the spouse? Can you trust your spouse not to tell his employer and colleagues? Should you expect that of him? Can you trust your boss enough to discuss this with her and try to work out some kind of accommodation that does not require you to sacrifice either your marriage or your job? Should you expect that of your boss? Does a boss bear any ethical obligation for the well-being of employees beyond the workplace?

Consider yet another situation. A soil bacterium common to warm climates can sometimes be found in the groundwater of such areas. It seldom causes disease in humans, but when it does, the infection is severe. The bacterium enters the body through an open wound and produces infections resulting in a mortality rate of 75 percent.

You are a department manager for a public utility district that produces electricity through steam-driven turbines. The department has constructed a lake for this purpose, which is also open to the public for recreational use. Recently a man was injured in a boating accident that severely lacerated his legs. He developed gangrene and, after a double amputation, eventually died. A technician in your department suspected that the man may have contracted the bacterial infection and decided to run tests. He reported that the bacterium is indeed in evidence throughout the lake, and although he cannot be certain without an autopsy, he believes it was the cause of death. Has the department committed an unethical act by not monitoring the quality of the water more carefully? Does it have a moral obligation to inform the public health authorities, the victim's family, or the general public? What is your responsibility to your organization in the face of possible litigation and public outcry? What is your responsibility to those who have used the lake for recreation and those who may use it in the future?

Here you are dealing not simply with the questionable or clearly immoral actions of a particular individual, but rather a matter of organizational policy. How should the department define its obligations to society? Does it owe something to the deceased man's family and to others who may use the lake? Should it merely try to rid the lake of the bacterium and leave it open to use?

Ethics as an Active Process

As these cases demonstrate, ethical issues arise in many forms for administrators, but they nearly always raise difficult questions of administrative responsibility. The answers we give to these questions over time amount to a de facto administrative ethic. The central thesis of this book is that it is through this process of defining professional responsibility in specific, concrete administrative situations that an operational ethic is developed. Every administrator has such an ethic by virtue of having made decisions about ethical issues, even if the decision is to ignore the problem. A decision to take no action is in fact a decision about personal responsibility.

This operational ethic, hammered out in actual decision making, is the basic concern here. Put into the language of ethics, this working ethic becomes the substance of one's professional character over time. It creates an inclination or predisposition to behave in certain ways, which is one common way of understanding the meaning of character. Many professional associations, business firms, and governmental organizations have adopted codes of ethics. They amount to official statements of appropriate conduct that reflect noble but often general and abstract principles. Formal codes of this kind do serve a useful function, but without the support of other techniques involving day-to-day decision making, they tend to be ineffective as a way of achieving desired conduct. They do not have an impact on the operational ethic of professionals for whom they were written; they never get to the level of internal ethical development where character is formed and integrity of conduct developed. Such codes of ethics serve a needed function of clarifying minimum standards of conduct, much as the law functions for the larger society, but they remain externally imposed controls.

As discussed in the preceding chapter, the focus of this book is ethics as an active process of design, an ongoing process that occurs whenever circumstances force us to deal with conflict, tension, uncertainty, and risk. As administrators define the boundaries and content of their responsibility in resolving specific ethical dilemmas both great and small, they create for themselves an ethical identity and form character traits. Often this is done without consistent, intentional, and systematic reflection, but that need not be the case. Skill in addressing ethical issues can be learned and cultivated if we recognize the importance of doing so. We can view the treatment of ethical problems as an ongoing process of designing the best courses of action for specific situations we face within the constraints of time and information. As an initial step, we must have a framework for understanding ethics in dynamic rather than static terms. The following framework for ethical decision making illustrates this dynamic process.

Levels of Ethical Reflection

Henry David Aiken (1962) constructed a framework for explaining the fluid nature of ethical argument that we can adopt for understanding the process of ordering our values and making decisions about ethical dilemmas. Aiken assumes that in a broad sense, ethics has to do with concepts such as good, right, and ought, but in the arena of everyday life, considering the practical meanings of these abstract concepts causes us to deal with them at different levels of seriousness and systematic reflection. Often we simply express emotion about what is "good" or what someone "ought" to do. Less frequently we face ethical questions that force us to reflect long and hard about our fundamental worldview—even the meaning of life itself.

From this perspective it is possible to identify four distinctive levels at which we deal with ethical concerns.

The Expressive Level

Many times every day, we find ourselves simply venting our feelings about something. When you learned about the misdeeds of the payroll clerk in your department, Linda's involvement with George, the possible contract termination, or the presence of the bacterium in the lake water, you may well have responded first at this level: "That stupid clerk should have known better!" "Linda, this relationship disturbs me deeply." "What did I do to deserve being caught in this bind between my spouse and my organization?" "We must have a bunch of incompetents managing the lake operation!" These spontaneous, unreflective expressions of emotion are perhaps the most common form of value judgment. They neither invite a reply nor attempt to persuade others. They provide neither evidence nor detailed descriptions of a state of affairs. However, depending on who utters them and how intensely, they may be followed by a more rational and systematic treatment of the problem.

The Level of Moral Rules

This is the first level at which serious questions are raised and serious answers are given. We address the problem of appropriate conduct and begin to assess alternatives and consequences. We consider these courses of action and their anticipated outcomes in the light of certain rules, maxims, and proverbs that we hold as moral guides:

- Always be a good team player.
- Loyalty to your clients comes first.
- If you're not part of the solution, you're part of the problem.
- Honesty is the best policy.
- Truth will win out.
- My country, right or wrong.
- Never fight a battle you can't win.
- Take care of number one.
- The public should be trusted.
- Love your neighbor as yourself.
- Do unto others as you would have them do unto you.
- Don't air the dirty linen outside the organization.
- It is easier to ask forgiveness than to ask permission.
- It is better to be safe than sorry.
- Go along to get along.
- If it ain't broke, don't fix it.

Some of the more colorful moral rules emerge around particular roles and reflect the informal moral code of those roles and the organizational culture in which they are enacted. Here are a few from the field of law enforcement:

- It is better to be tried by twelve than carried by six.
- You can't make an omelet without breaking a few eggs.
- What goes around comes around.
- Don't embarrass the bureau.
- Don't rat on a fellow officer.

These are examples of moral rules we acquire through the socialization process from our families, religious affiliations, education, and professional experiences. For better or worse, they provide rules of thumb for appraising a situation and deciding what ought to be done.

Consider the problem of Linda and George. After your initial emotional reaction, you have to think about how to handle this highly sensitive state of affairs. Some alternatives immediately come to mind:

- Order Linda to stop seeing George.
- Transfer her to another task.
- Discuss the matter with your supervisor.
- Trust Linda to do the job without being biased by the relationship.

Then you consider the possible consequences:

- Linda may resign.
- Progress on investigating the chemical may be delayed.
- The media may pick up the story.
- A biased decision may be reached about the chemical, with serious consequences for the public.
- You may be blamed for irresponsible conduct if your superior discovers the relationship without being informed.

As you evaluate the alternatives and their possible consequences, various moral rules and maxims come to mind as reference points for arriving at a decision:

- "You should be fair with subordinates under your supervision." Would I handle this situation differently if it involved a male member of my staff?
- "Avoid even the appearance of evil." Even if Linda performs in an objective, professional manner, will the credibility of my

organization be eroded if this situation is picked up by the press?

- "Honesty is the best policy." If I take any action that Linda perceives as punishment or distrust, am I discouraging honest communication from my staff? Should I tell my boss, or should I maintain Linda's confidence and accept responsibility for dealing with the situation myself?

Most of the time, the problem is resolved at this level. As we review the facts of the case, the alternatives for action, and their likely consequences on the one hand, and associate them with our stock of relevant moral rules on the other, the field of alternatives begins to narrow and one or two rules emerge as crucial. We move toward a decision, with the practical consequences and the moral justification related in some way that is acceptable to us.

Our decisions are not necessarily consistent from case to case. At the level of moral rules, which is where most practical administrative decisions are made, rationality and systematic reflection are involved, but only in a limited, piecemeal fashion. Most of the time, we are ad hoc problem solvers, not comprehensive moral philosophers. However, on occasion we are driven to the next level of generality and abstraction, usually because we are unable to reach a decision by applying our available repertoire of practical moral rules.

The Level of Ethical Analysis

When the available moral rules prove ineffective in a particular case, when they conflict with each other, or when the actions they seem to prescribe do not feel right, a fundamental reconsideration of our moral code may be required. In the normal routine of the administrative role, we do not usually undertake this kind of basic reassessment. However, sometimes an issue is unique, so complex, or so profound in the consequences of its resolution that we have no choice but to reexamine the ethical principles that are implicit in our routine norms for conduct.

A brief but adequate definition of *principle* is "a general law or rule that provides a guide for action." An ethical principle is a statement concerning the conduct or state of being that is required for the fulfillment of a value; it explicitly links a value with a general mode of action. For example, justice may be considered a significant value, but the term itself does not tell us what rule for conduct or state of society would follow if we include justice in our value system. We would need a principle of justice to show us what pattern of action would reflect justice as a value. A common form of the justice principle is, "Treat equals equally and unequals unequally." We might interpret this principle as meaning that if all adult citizens are politically equal, they should all have the same political rights and obligations. If one has the vote, all must have it.

Or if we look at another value, truth, we might start with a general principle to indicate its meaning for conduct and then develop more specific statements for particular conditions. Generally we might support this principle: "Always tell the truth." But when faced with a particular situation, we might revise the principle: "Always tell the truth unless innocent third parties would be seriously harmed."

Defining the ethical dimensions of a problem may require teasing out not only the values that are in conflict but also the unarticulated principles that indicate the mutually exclusive kinds of conduct those values dictate. Otherwise values are far too vague to have much meaning in ethical analysis. To say we believe in freedom or liberty conveys meaning of only the most general sort. If, however, we identify and elaborate principles about liberty, the meaning becomes more specific and ethically useful. We might, for example, indicate that liberty means we ought not to interfere, without special justification, in the chosen course of any rational being or impose on him conditions that will prevent him from pursuing his chosen courses of action. Although this statement does not prescribe precisely what should be done in every situation, it does provide some conditions and qualifications for the range of conduct that falls under "liberty."

There are several ways to train people to clarify this distinction between values and principles and cultivate the skill of thinking in a principled fashion. One way would be to give participants a list of values, or have them make up their own, and then develop these values into statements of principle, varying from brief and general to highly elaborate and more specific. Another would be to spend time developing principles as part of the exercise in defining ethical issues discussed later in this chapter. First, have the participants identify the contending values in a case; then ask them to write statements of principle for each. Finally, when time and interest permit, readings on specific ethical principles might be assigned, such as Sissela Bok (1984) on secrecy and truthfulness or John Rawls (1971) on justice.

To illustrate the use of principle at the level of ethical analysis, let us refer back to the contaminated lake. If you discover that eight other people have developed symptoms suspiciously similar to those associated with the bacterium, the problem will have changed significantly. Now the fate of human lives may clearly and directly depend on what you do; expeditious action is required. Because the consequences for the department will be serious indeed, you go to your supervisor without delay.

You are met with an unexpectedly cool and cautious response. He listens and asks a few questions, but seems not to share your sense of urgency. After a lengthy discussion, during which you become increasingly angry, he finally informs you that he has known about the bacterium for some time. When the lake was built more than two years ago, the bacterium was detected through routine water analyses. Because there was no practical way of ridding the water of this bacterium and because the utility district had needed public support for the project, he had decided to keep the entire matter quiet. He had been advised that at existing levels of contamination, the risk of human infection was low.

The administrator orders you to take no action and instead to leave the problem entirely in his hands. He tells you that there is little likelihood that any of the eight people could be treated effectively at this point and that any action would jeopardize the future of this facility and precipitate serious damage to both the department's public image and its financial well-being.

What do you do? None of your well-worn precepts about loyalty to the organization or social responsibility help here. You are not satisfied to keep quiet and leave it to the boss, but you have no hope of changing his mind. He seems firmly committed to waiting the situation out, hoping it will blow over. And if you go to the public or the local elected officials with the story, you will lose your job and probably have great difficulty finding another one.

Confronted with this kind of dilemma, you begin to reflect on the things you value most. You ask yourself what you are willing to risk and what you want to preserve at all costs. More specifically, you think about your personal integrity, professional reputation, financial security, the well-being of your family, the importance of your career, and the extent of your obligation to the organization, its employees, and management. You wonder what you owe the public; you consider your duty to the local elected officials. Furthermore, you begin to imagine the future consequences of allowing this kind of managerial conduct to continue. As you engage in this inventory and evaluation of your fundamental principles, a kind of rough hierarchy begins to emerge.

This particular dilemma causes you to clarify and reorder your priorities. You realize that if you are to continue in your position, you must maintain your obligation to a central principle—the public interest. You took an oath to uphold the public interest when you accepted the position. All other commitments and values must be viewed in relation to that responsibility to a basic principle. The potential negative consequences for the people of the area are great, and their right to know the risk must be upheld. Ultimately the principle of democracy and the integrity of democratic government are also at stake. If managers like your division chief are allowed to continue, self-government will be subverted; people need to know what is going on in public agencies if they are to truly participate in governing. Information about matters of public safety and welfare should not be withheld from the people and their elected representatives. However, when you took your job, you also accepted another principle: loyalty to the organizational hierarchy of your department. The orderly conduct of the public's business requires that subordinates work through superiors if accountability and efficiency are to be maintained. But this loyalty is not an end in itself; it exists for the ultimate benefit of the citizenry, for the public interest.

Another concern is the service provided by the department. Strong public resistance to building a dam had been overcome by promising the lake as a recreational facility. Closing the lake in the wake of disclosures about bacterial contamination might well result in demands to cancel the department's operating license. If the generating plant were closed suddenly, electrical service would be severely curtailed. Without electricity, industrial firms would have to cut back production and lay off workers. Hospital services might be jeopardized. High-rise office buildings and schools might be unable to function. The public interest would be seriously and extensively damaged.

If the public interest is your fundamental controlling principle, you must weigh the probable public impact for each alternative. Ultimately the health of the citizenry must be protected, but your sense of due process requires that you act in a measured and prudent fashion. You decide on the following sequence of steps.

First, you will approach the general manager of the department, your boss's boss, thus maintaining loyalty to those above you who are responsible for the proper operation of the organization. This provides for the orderly management of the problem without unduly alarming the public.

Then, if the general manager does not act to remedy the situation, you will take your information to the mayor and city council. In this way you prevent the political process from being circumvented when serious public concerns are at stake, although orderly procedure may be sacrificed.

Finally, if the elected officials fail to take action, you will inform the local media. Orderly and efficient resolution of the problem will likely be lost altogether, but the ultimate right of a democratic citizenry to control the governmental bodies established for its benefit will be preserved.

If you are unable to arrive at this kind of ordering of principles and alternatives, it may be necessary to move to the next level.

The Postethical Level

This final point is exemplified by the question, "Why should I be moral?" Most administrators seldom reach this fundamental philosophical level of reflection. Only when pushed by a particularly persistent or cynical adversary, or under the sway of a deeply disillusioning experience, or confronting a profound personal crisis are we likely to function at this level. Here the struggle is to find some basis for valuing those things that were identified at the level of ethical analysis. Why is integrity important? Or truth? Or security? Or loyalty? Or the well-being of others? At this level we begin to question our worldview—our views of human nature, how we know anything to be true, and the meaning of life. Resolution at this level is achieved only when practical indecision has been removed. It may require developing or confirming a worldview grounded in philosophical or religious perspectives. When we have discovered an adequate motive to allow ourselves to "play the moral game," this level is resolved.

A Dynamic Process

This four-tiered framework should be viewed in highly dynamic terms. Only in books or scholarly papers do people move logically through these decision-making steps. In real life we move up and down through the levels as we grapple with what is good or what we ought to do and within the constraints of time and context. We may first engage a problem expressively as we react spontaneously with our immediate feelings, but then move rather quickly to problem solving at the level of moral rules. As we get new information and the situation becomes more complex, we may move back again to the expressive level. Then, having vented our irritation and frustration, we may move back again to the search for appropriate moral rules.

If the issue proves unsusceptible to any of our practical maxims and rules, we may move briefly back to an expression of feelings and then to the level of ethical analysis. After a process of evaluating our basic priorities, we may finally be able to reach an action decision by applying rules that now appear to be consistent with the newly established priorities. Or we may find ourselves in such a profound quandary that we move to the postethical level and ponder why we are so concerned with morality anyway.

This movement among the various levels is usually not a matter of conscious choice, although it may be. The transitions occur because we need to solve a problem, not necessarily because we consciously think about which level is appropriate. In a concrete situation as we attempt to integrate known facts with unknown but possible consequences of action, feelings, and values, we find ourselves moving through these stages with varying degrees of rational reflection and abstraction. In day-to-day administrative decision making, we manage this process without giving it much reflective thought. However, a basic assumption of this book is that the more we consciously address and systematically process the ethical dimensions of decision making when we confront significant issues, the more responsible we become in our work as administrators. It is then that we are able to account for our conduct to superiors, the press, the courts, and the public. This does not amount to finally advocating a simple linear rationality, but rather being self-aware and clear about the bases for our actions.

Uses of the Framework

To design effective responses to ethical problems, it is important to be aware not only of where we are in this framework at any given moment, but also where our colleagues are operating as we discuss issues with them. Often, confusion is generated within a staff because some are venting emotion while others are articulating various moral rules, and still others are reflecting on basic principles. Sometimes everyone is presenting moral rules, but the rules are in conflict and someone needs to move to the level of ethical analysis. Fundamental values, principles, goals, and objectives need to be clarified and ordered, for both the individuals and the organization, before an acceptable rule for action can be identified.

This framework helps us focus our attention on the stages in ethical decision making. It suggests that if we want to become more systematic in handling ethical issues, we need to examine more carefully what takes place at the level where rational reflection is most critical: the level of ethical analysis. This is where skill in decision making can be cultivated. Here we attempt to think about what we should do; there is intentionality and some degree of systematic treatment of the problem. At the expressive level, only emotion is involved; it is not that emotion is bad, but it is only one element of ethical decision making. At the level of moral rules, we are largely reflecting our socialization, which can amount to a set of blinders that are too limiting on our critical thinking. At the postethical level, the considerations are too abstract, too personal, and, in modern pluralistic societies, too varied to be susceptible to any generalized approach. People holding radically different philosophies and theologies are not likely to reach agreement at this level, although they may do so at the second and third levels. Also, public accountability in this kind of heterogeneous society requires reasoned application of ethical principles rather than metaphysical assertions. As public servants, we are expected to explain and justify our conduct, or be prepared to do so when requested.

It is at the level of ethical analysis, then, that we are most likely to be able to account for our conduct publicly in terms that political officials and the citizenry can evaluate. If we proceed with reasoned justification, linking the consequences of our decisions with a tradition of ethical principles, then our conduct is reviewable by members of the political community and our deliberations and deeds are accessible for public debate and logical assessment. The higher we move up the ladder of public organizational leadership, the more important it becomes for us to be able to be accountable for our actions in this way. Therefore, the remainder of this book is devoted to applying systematic reflection at the level of ethical analysis as we design solutions.

This orientation of the book does not assume that ethical decisions are, can, or should be purely rational and principled. *The Responsible Administrator* does not advocate an exclusively rationalist perspective; human feelings are an essential part of our ethical life and inseparable from character. However, the approach adopted here is premised on the fact that in our public service roles, logical, principled, and relatively comprehensive justifications for our actions are expected by the public and elected officials.

A Decision-Making Model

In addressing ethical issues, we want to move from a problem to designing a course of action that will resolve it. This movement involves both description and prescription. That is, we describe to ourselves, and sometimes to others, what we believe to be an objective state of affairs and then attempt to prescribe what specific steps should be taken to change the situation. Between these two steps, we do the kind of reflection involved at the levels of moral rules and ethical analysis. It is far more important that we comprehend these steps for ourselves and develop the required skills than it is to simply read someone else's prescriptions.

Books, articles, and training approaches that attempt to prescribe for administrators may be inspiring or thought provoking, but they are usually so general as to provide little guidance for specific decisions. Although they offer value orientations that readers may find appealing, the link between a value system and a concrete situation is missing. We often refer to this dilemma as the *problem of application.* We may want to apply a set of values that seem compatible with our view of the administrative role, but how to move from general to specific prescription is not clear.

This reflective link between description and prescription has several important steps, and they are represented in the model shown in Figure 2.1. This model represents a framework for arriving at a judgment and then deciding what to do. No model, this one included, can lead you to the one best possible "correct" solution, but it can provide a template for creatively designing the best solutions for a given individual in a specific situation within the uncertainties and time limits of real administrative life. As in any other kind of design process, the course of action should take a contingency approach, providing for the pursuit of several alternatives simultaneously or sequentially until the consequences become clearer. Ethical problems, like transportation problems, architectural problems, or surgical problems, are dynamic in nature, so one must be prepared to alter course as one learns from action and the situation changes over time.

The Descriptive Task

When a problem comes to our attention, it is usually presented in a fragmentary or distorted fashion, often with judgmental language and inflections. Perhaps, in the case of the payroll clerk discussed at the beginning of this chapter, you learn about his conduct from a secretary in the office whom he has treated rudely. Having discovered several suspicious names on the payroll list, she eagerly retaliates by concluding that he is involved in illegal activities. The secretary's report to you includes considerable embellishment of what she actually knows to be true, along with a derogatory appraisal of the payroll clerk's character.

Any experienced administrator would know that such a report does not represent an adequate description of the clerk's activities. The names may appear suspicious to the secretary because she does not know them, but there may be a reasonable explanation.

Figure 2.1. Ethical Decision-Making Model

Maybe he has indeed been sexist in his dealings with her but scrupulously honest in his handling of the payroll. Sexism is a problem to be dealt with, but it must not be confused with the payroll issue. It is clear that you must gather more factual information and sift out unfounded judgments before you have a full and objective description. Without this, you dare not proceed to any kind of prescription.

In this example, it is obvious that the descriptive task is critical, but there are many situations where it is equally important but much less obviously so. If the report comes not from a secretary but from someone above us in the organizational hierarchy, we are much more likely to accept it as an accurate description of events. Howard Becker (1973) refers to this tendency as the "hierarchy of credibility." He suggests that "from the point of view of a well socialized participant in the system, any tale told by those at the top intrinsically deserves to be regarded as the most credible account obtainable of the organization's workings" (p. 7).

Admittedly, under the pressure of life in most organizations, we seldom have the time or resources to conduct a full investigation. However, we must always attempt to ascertain and describe as objectively as possible the facts of a situation. This might include identifying the key actors, the viewpoints of each, the issues, the sequence of events, and the risks.

Although it is impossible to avoid value-laden language altogether, it is possible to resist using words and phrases that blatantly create a cast of good guys and bad guys. This is a useful skill to cultivate in dealing with ethical problems because it helps to push us beyond the expressive level. Whether we are struggling with a decision alone or discussing it with someone else (a staff person, a supervisor), we must force ourselves to describe the situation with more than the influence of our gut reactions. If we are to deal with real people involved in real events, we must first face, to the best of our ability, what has actually happened.

Defining the Ethical Issue

With the necessary details before us, the next step is to define the ethical issue. An ethical issue exists when competing or conflicting ethical principles or values are embedded in a practical problem. Experience with workshops on ethics indicates that public administrators seem to have the greatest difficulty with this second step. It is not that they are unable to recognize an ethically problematic situation; their sensitivity to such matters is encouragingly keen. They know when they are confronted with expectations, demands, opportunities, and conflicting interests that have ethical significance. But many have difficulty in articulating which values and principles are at stake. The tendency is to define the problem in practical rather than ethical terms.

Consider an administrator who is asked by a superior to provide confidential information about a colleague being considered for promotion—someone who is a close personal friend and is not qualified for the job. Workshop participants usually define the problem as keeping the boss happy but not hurting or offending the friend. This is a definition of the practical dilemma, but behind these practical considerations are some conflicting values and principles that need to be identified. There is an ethical dilemma to be defined by reference to certain specific conflicting or competing ethical principles.

"Conflicting loyalties" would be the most general statement of the ethical issue involved here. However, we could go further and consider obligations. On the one hand are the obligations to a friend: to preserve confidentiality, honesty, and trustworthiness. On the other hand are the obligations to a superior: to provide honest and objective information about coworkers being considered for greater responsibility. These obligations contribute to the best interests of the organization. Also, we have an obligation to the citizenry to uphold the public interest. Thus, the problem could be defined as conflicting loyalties or conflicting obligations, depending on the details of the case and our own ethical priorities.

Unless we can focus the analysis on underlying ethical issues of this kind, we may resolve the matter on purely practical grounds. We may make a decision without ever really engaging the important values and principles that are pulling us in different directions. Ethical analysis skills, ethical autonomy, and ultimately our ethical identity are developed through engagement of this kind. It is the process through which character is formed. Without this kind of complex character-forming engagement, the practical demands and exigencies of a situation are likely to whip us around in a manner destructive of ethical judgment and antithetical to personal integrity.

Because this step of defining ethical issues is so difficult, those who conduct training sessions or classroom instruction must spend considerable time working on it in a variety of ways before moving on to the full range of steps leading to final resolution. Some lecturing to illustrate the distinction between the practical and ethical dimensions of a problem is probably necessary at the outset.

The next step should involve the participants, under the instructor's leadership, working through the definitional problem in a case or two. Then it seems helpful to divide the participants into groups of three or four, each group with a different case situation, and ask them to define the ethical issue on their own. During the report-back session, all the participants are then exposed to several different definitional problems.

Identifying Alternative Courses of Action

With an adequate definition of the ethical issue before us, we are ready to move on to identifying alternative courses of action. After describing the situation as objectively as possible and defining the ethical issue, the most difficult requirement is resisting the inclination to view the alternatives in dichotomous terms: you do either this or that. Either you tell Linda to stop seeing George, or you trust her to handle the relationship in a professional manner. Either you tell your spouse about the possible contract termination or remain silent. This either-or view is the most common trap in the ethical process. Rarely does an ethical issue have only two or even three possible solutions, but there appears to be a force within us, as pervasive as gravity, that impedes the spinning out of alternatives.

Use whatever methods or techniques are necessary to move beyond either-or thinking, because until at least the most significant alternatives are acknowledged, we risk overlooking the best solution. A simple grid form can help decision-making groups broaden their perspective. Down the left side, group members list all the alternatives they can think of; on the right side, they write the probable consequences, both positive and negative. First they brainstorm alternatives for ten to fifteen minutes, without evaluating any of them; if an alternative is conceivable, they are required to list it. This may sound like a simple procedure, but experience with a large number of groups indicates that some people have an almost irresistible tendency to reject an alternative as soon as it is uttered.

Projecting the Probable Consequences

Once the range of alternative solutions has been widened, the positive and negative anticipated consequences of each possible course of action need to be projected. If you tell Linda to stop seeing George, what is the likely outcome? What if you transfer her to another position? Ask another member of the staff to work along with her? Tighten your supervision of her work? What chain of events will likely unfold, and toward what end? If you tell your spouse about the potential contract termination, what is he likely to do?

Projecting the consequences of alternatives is a key dynamic in our natural, informal decision making. As we consider what we should do, we usually run out a movie in our minds. For each alternative, we construct a scenario with actors, interaction, and consequences. Here we are attempting to raise this informal process to a more formal, conscious, and systematic level. We begin by intentionally pushing out the boundaries of our range of considered alternatives, and then attempting to be more imaginative in our creation of these projections into the future.

John Dewey described this process as one of "deliberation" in which we experiment with "a dramatic rehearsal," in our imagination, of "various competing possible lines of action" (1922, p. 190; see also Schutz, 1970). A reasonable choice of a course of conduct requires us to consider the full range of alternatives rather than only the one or two that dominate our feelings and imagination.

The skill involved here is moral imagination—the ability to produce a "movie in our minds" with realistic characters, a believable script, and clear imagery. The movies we create tend to be more like slide shows or jerky, black-and-white, silent melodramas rather than epic productions in color with stereophonic sound and complex plots. The more imaginative we can be in projecting the probable consequences of each alternative, the more our ethical decision making is enhanced. This kind of vivid projection of alternatives tests their coherence and plausibility, as well as evoking feelings we can expect to accompany each one. It is a key connection between the rational and the affective dimensions of ethical decision making.

Writing scenarios for each alternative may help you develop moral imagination. Although no administrator has the time to do this with every issue, it may be a worthwhile exercise for particularly complex problems. Groups can use the grid form described earlier. After listing possible alternatives down the left side and the probable consequences for each along the right side, the group talks through a scenario for each one, attempting to refine the projected consequences.

It should be emphasized at this point that considering the consequences of each alternative does not mean that this is the only or determining factor in arriving at a decision. Ethicists refer to deontological (duty-oriented) and teleological (consequence-oriented) approaches to ethical decisions. The former is focused on duty to certain ethical principles such as honesty or justice in a quest for which duty is primary. The latter weighs the consequences of a course of action, as in utilitarianism with its calculus of the greatest good for the greatest number, looking for the best outcomes. The model under discussion here includes both perspectives, as it is never possible to completely separate them in practice. Duty to respect human dignity is inseparable from the harmful consequences of not doing so.

Finding a Fit

The remainder of the process is no longer linear in nature. Achieving resolution involves a search for a fit among the four elements in the circle in Figure 2.1, and that search is not simply a matter of reasoning from one thing to the next. This basis for such a fit is more like the logic of aesthetics; it requires proportion and balance among the four elements.

The first consideration is the moral rules that can be adduced to support each alternative and the projected consequences. Identifying these will tend to happen quite naturally in a group setting as individuals are allowed to opt for a particular decision alternative and defend it. However, anyone engaged in this process alone or leading a group session must be sure that all alternatives are addressed and none dismissed too easily or quickly.

The next consideration is a rehearsal of defenses. This is sometimes called the "*Sixty Minutes* test" or the "*New York Times* test." Here we systematically consider each alternative by asking ourselves, "How would I defend this particular option if required to do so before a broad audience?" This is the test of how well a particular alternative will fit with the accepted norms of the wider professional and political communities of which we are a part. Once again, moral imagination is a critical skill as we try to picture ourselves, as vividly as possible, explaining to a superior, or subordinates, or professional peers, or the press, or a court of law why each possible course of action was chosen. In group situations, this exercise is most useful as the field narrows toward one or two alternatives.

Harlan Cleveland (1972, p. 104) advocates an approach of this kind by suggesting that an administrator ask himself or herself the following key question before getting committed to any particular course of conduct: "If this action is held up to public scrutiny, will I still feel that it is what I should have done and how I should have done it?" Cleveland insists that if those involved in well-known cases of corruption had seriously asked themselves this question and answered it honestly, most of these instances of betrayal of public trust would never have happened. One of the reasons behind the power of asking oneself these questions is that they not only help us to think, but also to feel our way through an ethical problem.

In this process of rehearsing defenses, which ethicists sometimes call "the test of publicity," we may find it necessary to move from the discovery and application of moral rules to the third consideration: an attempt to discern the implicit ethical principles at stake. This occurs when the available moral rules are not sufficiently satisfying to permit resolution. One alternative may tend to maximize the security of the individual or organization, whereas others may promote social justice or enhance democracy. As we consider the hierarchy of basic principles, we again rehearse the justification for each option: How could I justify giving higher priority to social justice than organizational security in this instance? As we engage in this process of arraying alternatives, drawing out the probable consequences in the most realistic terms, and rehearsing the application of rules and principles, both a rational and an emotional search for resolution is under way. But what constitutes resolution?

Resolution is reached when we discover an alternative that provides an acceptable balance of our duty to principle and the likely consequences and satisfies our need to have sound reasons for our conduct and our need to feel satisfied with the decision. Because neither a perfect balance of duty and consequences nor a supremely rational alternative that provides complete emotional satisfaction is often available, resolution is ordinarily an approximate state. What we can expect to achieve is the best balance of duty and consequences and the best combination of reasons and affective comfort under the circumstances. It should be emphasized, however, that the assumption here is that both the combination of reasons and feelings and the balance of duty and consequences involved in this resolution should include the obligations of the public service role. This decision-making process must be informed by education, training, and guided socialization into a public service ethic if the public interest is to be approximated. Ethical decisions must be buttressed by public service character— the inclination to do the right thing as we engage in deciding what that should be. Here we are describing and systematizing the process that needs to be informed by such an ethic rooted in character.

Sorting through and selecting adequate reasons occur through the process just described. Arriving at a feeling of satisfaction with a decision happens during the same process but involves a set of dynamics not yet described. It is time to consider the fourth element in the circle: anticipatory self-appraisal. This is the test of how well a course of action fits with our own self-image. As we imagine ourselves undertaking various courses of action, we may experience self-disapproval in connection with certain alternatives. According to Janis and Mann (1977), these anticipations can arouse guilt, remorse, and self-reproach. When we see ourselves, in our mind's eye, carrying out a decision that is inconsistent with our core values, we do not like the self we envision. When we project ourselves into the future and look back on the act as though it had been completed, we are dissatisfied with ourselves. We anticipate not feeling good the morning after. We experience, in advance, a kind of ethical hangover.

In the same way, other decision alternatives create self-approval. The movie in our minds portrays us acting in a way that makes us feel proud and draws praise, or at least approval, from people whose opinions we value. We are drawn toward these options by the reinforcing power of anticipatory feelings of satisfaction. Acting in ways that evoke this anticipatory approval is the way we develop predispositions to act similarly in the future, which is one way of understanding the essence of character.

These anticipatory feelings are usually not appraised systematically, but they create inclinations either to reject alternatives that seem incongruent with our values or the norms of significant reference groups or to choose congruent ones. To the extent that we are able to relate this emotional process to the rational process, we gain ethical autonomy. To the extent that we cultivate a pattern of consistently acting in ways that combine sound reasons with affective confidence, we develop integrity. We can intentionally and systematically assess decision alternatives in terms of the soundness of our reasons for selecting each one and how we can expect to feel about choosing it. We may also be able to identify the sources of those positive or negative feelings. Are we anticipating approval or disapproval from our colleagues in the local chapter of the American Society for Public Administration? From the boss? Or are long-held personal values involved? How important is the source of those feelings? Are there other persons or groups whose evaluation of the decision is equally, or more, important?

Benefits of Using the Model

In brief, these are the steps in a fully systematic and self-conscious ethical decision-making process. Obviously no practicing administrator could be expected to apply this model to every ethical issue. However, the assumption here is that if this model is used with the more significant problems, administrators will cultivate over time something like an intuitive decision-making skill that will serve them well when there is no time for such explicit and formal exercises. Daniel Isenberg's research on senior managers indicates that the most effective ones systematically develop such intuitive decision models that make possible "the smooth automatic performance of learned behavior sequences" (1984, p. 85). Isenberg maintains that this "is not arbitrary or irrational, but is based on years of painstaking practice and hands-on experience that builds skills" (p. 85). When these skills are used under the pressure of limited time for reflection, "we compress years of experience and learning into split seconds. This compression is one of the bases of what we call intuition, as well as the art of management" (p. 83).

By using the model, we achieve a greater degree of ethical autonomy because we become more aware of both our own values and the external obligations under which we act. Even when we develop intuitive skill, it is possible to raise the grounds for our conduct to conscious consideration when necessary. Janis and Mann (1977) observe that authorities sometimes attempt to elicit obedience by creating the illusion that subordinates have no choice but to follow orders. The power of this manipulation of the perceived range of real choices is vividly portrayed in the experiments on obedience to authority conducted by Stanley Milgram (1974), which are discussed at greater length in Chapter Eight. These studies demonstrated that more than half of a random sample of American citizens were willing to comply with orders that appeared to result in serious harm to another person. One of the critical factors in their decision to follow distasteful instructions was the scientist's repeated statement: "You have no other choice. The experiment requires that you continue." Defining the situation in such constrained terms leaves a decision maker feeling helpless before a single unacceptable option; consciousness of alternative choices is foreclosed. Ethical autonomy is reduced to zero, character is eroded, and integrity undermined.

Although it is easier to conceive of this kind of ethical tunnel vision in cases where we are being manipulated by an authority, it occurs more pervasively. We develop blinders that allow us to see only one alternative, or at most a very few. Until we take the initiative to systematically and aggressively widen the range of conceivable options and assess how they fit both rationally and emotionally with our value system, we are at the mercy of the most obvious courses of action. Developing moral imagination requires discipline and practice as demanding as any other intellectual and creative activity, but its rewards are greater measures of self-awareness, self-control, and decision-making flexibility. These are essential for the strengthening of character that inclines us to act on our convictions and the building of integrity that keeps us from weaving through life like a drunkard, first stumbling in one direction and later in quite another.

Summary

I began this chapter by examining some typical public administrative cases in which an ethical dilemma could be discerned. I then defined ethics as an active process involving the ordering of our values with respect to a particular decision. Next I considered the four levels of reflection at which this process occurs. The chapter concluded with a review of a decision-making model that may be used to systematically and self-consciously move from the description of an ethical problem to prescribed courses of action. This is the first stage of the design approach to administrative ethics—the level of individual decision-making and conduct.

In the next chapter, I step back from particular ethical decisions to look at the social and political setting in which public administrators make ethical decisions. This setting imposes certain conditions that significantly shape the nature of the problems that public administrators encounter. To design effective responses to ethical problems, one must always do so with reference to the context.

Part One

Ethics for Individual Administrators

Chapter Three

Public Administration in Modern and Postmodern Society

The Context of Administrative Ethics

To examine best the ethical dimensions of administration, it is necessary to understand the administrative role as it relates to the social and cultural context in which it functions. This perspective is crucial for both adequately describing ethical situations and developing realistic prescriptions for dealing with them. Designing responses to ethical problems requires adaptation to the characteristics of the situations in which they occur.

The key concepts in a sociocultural perspective on the administrative role are modernization and postmodernization. We are in a time of transition in which the modern heritage of public administration is increasingly in conflict with a postmodern world. The formative concepts and ideas of public administration have their roots in the modernizing world of the late nineteenth and early twentieth centuries, but the society it functions in is increasingly postmodern.

Modern is a global term for describing the social, cultural, and economic attributes associated with urban industrial society. Berger, Berger, and Kellner (1973) argue that the key phenomena of modernity are bureaucracy and technological production. In fact, they contend that these are the carriers of modern consciousness. As we become involved with bureaucratic organization and the process of technological production, a distinctively modern way of thinking about the world and our place in it begins to emerge.

Postmodern is a term intended to characterize a world in which foundational assumptions are being discredited as final and absolute. Assumptions about some kind of objectively real and universal human nature, or natural law, or absolute values and ultimate truths, including those of science, no longer hold sway over the entire society. Fox and Miller have contrasted modern and postmodern views of the world as follows (1996, p. 45):

- Integration versus disintegration
- Centralization versus decentralization
- Centripetal versus centrifugal
- Totalization versus fragmentation
- Metanarratives versus disparate texts
- Melting pot versus salad
- Commensurable versus incommensurable
- The impulse to unify versus hyperpluralism
- Universalism versus relativism
- Newton versus Heisenberg

The most obvious example of these differences is the modern idea of society being a melting pot, in which different people and cultures would assimilate into one, similar society. In the postmodern world, that pot is a salad bowl in which the various elements maintain their distinct integrity and complement each other. As well, although Sir Isaac Newton is considered one of the most influential scientists, the ability of his laws of motion and gravity to predict scientific occurrences was later challenged by scientists like Werner Heisenberg and his uncertainty principle. The significance of the postmodern way of thinking is that the notions of generic fixed ways of living, structuring public institutions, administering public agencies, and establishing professional ethical norms no longer have an ultimate basis on which to stand.

Accepting these attributes as dominant in our society can leave one in a state of relativity reduced to normlessness and a conclusion that anything goes, because no one has a basis for claims to moral rectitude and obligation. Generally consistent with Fox and Miller, the position adopted here is that postmodern society does not leave us without meaning or norms, but that we construct socially our values, beliefs, and ethical norms as we interact with each other over time.

There may not be a universally accepted set of values and norms "lowered down from heaven on a string." Nevertheless, together we craft for ourselves through discourse and deliberation conventions such as values, beliefs, and ethical norms to give meaning and order to our lives. Collective decision making in the governance process, including public administration, works best in a postmodern society when it emerges out of an inclusive conversation about how to create order and meaning in our lives together. Hence, democratic governance provides mechanisms and arenas for this social process. Guttmann (1995) calls this deliberative process "eternal vigilance" and argues that deliberation is the democratic self-constraint through which we ward off tyranny and protect the basic liberties of democracy. (See Dennard, 1997, and other articles in this special issue of *American Behavioral Scientist* concerning the implications of postmodern thought for public administration.)

Our collective agreements arrived at through democratic governance may not have any universal or ultimate foundations in the nature of the universe, but they serve as surrogate or ad hoc foundations for us that change from time to time to fit our changing social agreements. History is the attempt to record the evolution of these collectively adopted conventions.

Agreement on these public aspects of life must be accomplished through broad participation in the governance debate if the institutions created are to have legitimacy. Simply imposing authority does not work in this kind of world. Areas of our lives not lived interdependently, often called "private," are left for various subgroups to fashion diverse perspectives and ways of life.

Problems with Modernity in a Postmodern World

Remnants of modernity still exist in today's postmodern world, and the clash between these two worldviews can create conflict. The modern worldview is characterized by the following traits relevant to administrative ethics.

The Attempt to Apply Scientific Principles to Much of Life

The thought of the late nineteenth and early twentieth centuries was heavily influenced by a belief that science could be introduced into more and more areas of human life (Nelson, 1982). This led quite naturally to an emphasis on instrumental rationality. It was thought that science could provide better methods for everything, from conducting our personal affairs, to managing a family, to running a factory, to providing public goods and services. The tendency was to look to science for one best way of doing things that was consistent with generic scientific principles. Thus we began to think about the need to order and standardize society as well as our own lives.

Under the sway of this scientific approach to life, efficiency of interaction and production becomes a concern, along with predictability of the behavior of others. In modern society, tradition no longer provides stability, order, and consistency of conduct; these things have to be thought about and worked out through organizations, rules, laws, and policies based on scientific principles. Science provides the unifying foundational assumptions for modern society to replace those of tradition rooted in history, custom, and religion, which have become relativized.

However, to the extent that postmodern thought has begun to displace modernity, foundational assumptions, including those based on science, lose their power to define ultimate reality. Science is increasingly seen as another social construct that shapes our perceptions of the world, but with no greater authority than other such perspectives. The use of scientific principles as the sole basis for designing and administering public organizations is discredited (Jun and Rivera, 1997).

Multiplicity and Differentiation of Roles

Social relationships and personal identity become more complex in modern society. People no longer identify themselves with one role or even a few. Our lives become an intricate network of interrelated roles, and we move through these roles without thinking very explicitly about the changes in behavior they require. During the course of one day, we may assume a broad array of roles—parent, spouse, neighbor, administrator, church member, investor, citizen, rowing partner—each with its own behavior pattern and set of obligations. Robert Jay Lifton has described the way we move among roles using the idea of the "protean self" (1993). Proteus was a god in Greek mythology who had the power to change his shape at will—to "morph" himself from a human figure to that of a bird, or a snake, or a lion, or running water, or anything else imaginable. In this way, he could elude anyone seeking to capture him. The protean metaphor was also used in early American vaudeville theater involving traveling variety shows. The "protean act" was one of the standard favorites in the vaudevillian repertoire put on by quick-change artists. Protean actors would move rapidly on and off stage costumed very differently from moment to moment. A knight in armor would suddenly be transformed into a Victorian lady, followed by a cowboy, and then a biblical figure, and on and on to the amazement and delight of an audience. The distinguished sociologist Erving Goffman (1973) similarly employed a dramaturgical approach to understanding the ways individuals in modern society present themselves as different actors as they move from one setting and role to the next. Certainly, in the postmodern world with its complexity and multiple roles, we can all be viewed as "protean" at any given time.

Salman Rushdie has described the extremity of this phenomenon as follows (1997, p. 36):

> In the modern age, we have come to understand our own selves as composites, often contradictory, even internally incompatible. We have understood that each of us is many different people. Our younger selves differ from our older selves; we can be bold in the company of our lovers and timorous before our employers, principled when we instruct our children and corrupt when offered some secret temptation; we are serious and frivolous, loud and quiet, aggressive and easily abashed. The 19th century concept of the integrated self has been replaced by this jostling crowd of "I"s. And yet, unless we are damaged, or deranged, we usually have a relatively clear sense of who we are. I agree with my many selves to call all of them "me."

In this Rushdian world, the very idea of a unitary integrated self begins to fade away into a sequential taking of the various roles which collectively he identifies as himself.

Postmodern views intensify this problem of roles, for without any definitive foundational assumptions about human existence and the world around us, there is no authoritative place to turn for determining which roles ought to have priority. We are left in a state of constant perplexity about how to allocate our attention, time, and effort among the array of competing roles. How do I weigh my family obligations against those of the organization in which I am employed? Which comes first: my professional obligations or those of my organization? What happens when my religious views come into conflict with duties assigned at work? How do I sort out the priority of obligations between those of being a citizen in a democratic society and those associated with being a public administrator?

From Separation to Co-Mingling Work and Private Life

In modern society, work no longer blends easily into our private lives as was true of traditional society. It is separated in time and space from home, family, and neighborhood. In traditional society, the farmer or herdsman lived at his place of work and made no precise temporal distinctions between work and nonwork. The same was typical for physicians, artists, lawyers, shopkeepers, and craftsmen. However, in modern society, work is done in a particular place and during defined hours. Deviations from this norm are viewed as intrusions of work into our private life, or vice versa. This spatial and chronological separation has been conducive to the development of an ethical identity for the employment role that may be quite different from those associated with other roles. While that may threaten one's integrity as a whole person, it may also make it easier to uphold a public ethic without undue influence by the norms of more personal and private roles.

The strict separation of work and private realms begins to blur again in postmodern society. As organizations decentralize and move away from uniform work regimens, as information becomes more and more the means of conducting work, and as technology enhances communication, increasing numbers of people work at least part of the time at home or elsewhere. Being in a specific place to do one's work becomes less and less important. Computers, fax machines, pagers, cellular phones, BlackBerries, and personal digital assistants make space less relevant than time. Some employees work out of cars, airplanes, hotels, and homes and go to the place of the organization only infrequently. These changes may tend to make ethical identities associated with employment roles less distinct and susceptible to influence by other roles. Obligations for public ethical norms such as the public interest may be influenced by the interests of private roles.

Schultz (2004) has noted this blurring of boundaries in the postmodern world and its effects on professional ethics. He argues, "In a postmodern society marked by a blurring of the line between public and private as well as by the greater integration of the three economic sectors, the ethical rules that apply to different facets of life and work are being challenged, necessitating a rethinking of moral boundaries and the rules governing professional behavior" (p. 281). He suggests that we may need to reconceptualize ethics to accommodate the move away from the "ethical compartmentalization" of the modern world.

Relativism

Neither roles nor values are viewed as absolute in modern society. Roles are acquired and given up, and they vary in importance from time to time. Consequently they are often maintained with considerable role distance. That is to say, they are not allowed to comprehend our identity. Roles are relative to particular times and places; they are not inherent in our most essential selves.

Similarly, values within society exhibit enormous diversity. Some people believe one thing and some another. We are not shocked to discover this fact in modern society; instead we tend to acknowledge and emphasize the relativity of values.

Postmodernism furthers the erosion of foundational assumptions as the core beliefs of modernism rooted in science are also called into question as universal and ultimate. The relativity of values threatens to undermine any belief in obligation and duty. Thus, the intentional social construction of public ethical norms becomes even more crucial. In the absence of universally accepted moral absolutes, working out agreements concerning the norms of our interdependent public life is essential as the basis for social stability. In other words, although we may be able to agree on fundamental democratic values, we intersect in our collective or public lives and we may need to deliberate and socially construct a set of norms to accommodate this intersection.

Pluralization of Society

The significant dynamic behind all four of these characteristics is the pluralization of modern society. As people from diverse cultures have moved with great rapidity into urban commercial and industrial centers during the past two hundred years, they have found it necessary to confront one another's differences. The homogeneity of traditional society, with its unifying and stabilizing cultural bonds, has been broken. Very little can be assumed or taken for granted. New forms of organization have developed, and new ways of coping with a broad spectrum of lifestyles, diets, preferences, political philosophies, and modes of exchange have evolved. This "pluralization of life worlds" has led to the segmentation of individual lives as people have attempted to relate themselves to "severely discrepant worlds of meaning and experience" (Berger, Berger, and Kellner, 1973, p. 64).

The early stages of this pluralizing process are vividly illustrated in the musical *Fiddler on the Roof*. In a little Russian village named Anatevka, an orthodox Jewish community lives out a predictable and stable existence through the highly integrated web of tradition, which encompasses daily routines as well as major events such as birth, marriage, and death. The leading figure, Tevye, constantly reminds himself and the audience that tradition is how he knows who he is and what God expects of him. "Without our tradition," he says, "we are as shaky as a fiddler on the roof" (Stein, 1971, p. 64).

And, indeed, in the course of the play, we see the integrity and absoluteness of Anatevka's traditions challenged by the arrival of the czar's troops. Familiar traditions governing courtship, marriage, and family roles are confronted with different traditions from an alien society and robbed of their power. Although in this case it was a matter of modern society invading a traditional community rather than the migration of rural villagers to an urban area, the process of pluralization is essentially the same.

In 1927, in *The Public and Its Problems*, John Dewey described how this emerging heterogeneity gave rise to a multiplicity of "publics." From Dewey's perspective, there is no such thing as a unitary public in modern society. As people pursue their various self-interests through social interaction, there are certain unintended indirect consequences, which may be viewed positively or negatively. Entrepreneurs who establish steel mills to make a profit indirectly create air pollution. However, they may also, without planning to do so, create a market for smaller businesses in the surrounding area. Publics either diminish or enhance these indirect consequences by calling for the appointment of public officials and the passage of laws.

Thus, governmental organizations have served an increasingly pluralized public during the past hundred years. These publics, according to Dewey's thesis, are generated by the heterogeneous composition of modern industrial society. As we attempt to realize our own interests, we invariably find ourselves linked interdependently with others who are different and have different interests. We are sometimes inhibited in achieving our goals by the activities of others and sometimes helped, but whatever the case, we begin to realize that our fate is bound up with the decisions and behavior of other people whose values differ, more or less, from our own.

Postmodern conditions unleash the increasingly assertive expression of this sociocultural diversity. One result is that government based on bureaucratic rationality, attempting to offer standardized services and goods, increasingly alienates a diverse citizenry. Operating with modern assumptions advanced by the American Progressive movement of the early twentieth century, government finds itself in interminable conflict with the people it seeks to serve. The Progressives believed that government should treat everyone the same in order to be fair, a reasonable assumption given the power of political machines in that era. However, now sometimes government is expected to treat everyone equally (voting rights, access to employment, judicial processes) and at other times to treat them differently (handicapped access, Head Start, affirmative action). Standardized policies and programs are increasingly at odds with diverse and vocal publics.

Implications for Public Administration

It appears that modernization has had three major implications for public administration.

The Political Nature of Public Administration

An initial impact of modernization on public administration was the attempt to separate politics from administration to develop a science of administration, a science that was expected to lead to a more efficient delivery of public goods and services. To the Progressive reformers of the late nineteenth and early twentieth centuries, this seemed to offer an advance beyond the highly politicized public administration that had existed under the urban political machines of the nineteenth century and in traditional societies for most of human history. However, the paradox was that although modern thinking emphasized the application of scientific rationality to government, other characteristics of modern society made this no more possible in twentieth-century America than it had been in the traditional societies of the past. The diversification of society produced a more turbulent environment for administrators.

In postmodern society, it has become increasingly clear that attempting to define the administrative role as separated from politics simply isolates administrators from a highly differentiated populace; it removes them from accountability to the citizenry. Furthermore, it discourages administrators from facing the substantive political role they do play. It creates disingenuousness and self-delusion as administrators attempt either to hide behind the facade of political neutrality or remain blind to the real nature of their actions.

The separation of politics from administration may have existed in the minds of Max Weber (1946), Woodrow Wilson (1887), Leonard White (1926), Frank Goodnow (1900), and a generation of other scholars, but almost nowhere else. The notion that politicians make policy decisions involving substantive rationality while administrators simply apply their best scientific instrumental reasoning toward implementation has been sufficiently attacked to require no extensive treatment here (Gaus, 1936; Waldo, 1948). Administrators in the postmodern world are at least involved in politics with a small p, and often indirectly in "capital-P partisan" political activity. Postmodernization creates pressures and dynamics that compel administrators to be involved in decisions about goals and policies and to compete with others for power and resources (Benveniste, 1977; Wamsley and Zald, 1973; Cooper, 1994).

The multiplication and differentiation of roles are the critical phenomena in the politics of the public administrative role. Each of these roles may be understood as a bundle of obligations and interests that any public administrator might have acquired in the course of becoming an adult in modern and postmodern society. That is, each role is constituted by a set of obligations, well or poorly defined, that administrators must carry out to maintain the role, and a set of interests—income, social status, and job satisfaction—that they derive from the role. We must bear the obligations to secure the interests.

Some of these roles belong exclusively to the private life of home, family, and community; some have to do with the world of work; and some overlap the two realms. Together they represent the complex multifaceted identity of a modern administrator (Downie, 1971; Means, 1970).

From time to time these differentiated roles come into conflict with each other; the interests and obligations associated with them compete for our time, attention, and energy. We must manage this conflict effectively to prevent one role from destroying another. For example, the role of investor may create tension with the role of administrator in a public organization if an attractive investment opportunity arises that involves association with organizations regulated by that public agency. Potential conflicts of interest could detract from the administrator's objective judgment, or at least could be perceived that way by the citizenry.

The conflict between these roles arises from antithetical attractions: personal economic interests and the obligation to protect the public interest. The tension between them may be compounded if the administrator facing the investment opportunity has significant financial needs to maintain the roles of spouse and parent. And if this hypothetical administrator belongs to a professional association with a strong position against this type of conduct, the conflict is deepened and the tension increased.

The politics of the administrative role is rooted in this kind of tension (Tullock, 1965; Crozier, 1973; Wamsley and Zald, 1973). Because values in postmodern society are not universally accepted, there are no absolutes to define precisely what ought to be done when roles conflict. Values are ordered and priorities established among roles through negotiation with ourselves and others in each situation, generally along the lines described in Chapter Two. It is in trading off our own varied interests for the interests of the organization we work for, and vice versa, that the political dynamics of the administrative role emerge.

Sheldon Wolin (1960) has provided the basis for a further explanation of organizational politics. His focus is the evolution of communities through the modernizing process. Wolin argues that during the nineteenth and twentieth centuries, the "organic," integrated, tradition-based communities of the preindustrial and preurban era began to crumble in the face of migration to urban and industrial areas. People began to look to organizations to fulfill the needs previously satisfied by their communities. They sought stability, identity, belonging, security, purpose, and power in organizations of all kinds: religious, industrial, labor, reform, political, scientific, commercial, and governmental.

In this process, the "natural" networks of relationships of the older organic communities were broken up. They were transformed by the rationality and intentionality of organization builders into instruments for achieving particular goals. They were designed to refine steel, manufacture automobiles, provide water, reform government, operate transit facilities, and enforce building and safety regulations.

However, contrary to Weber's ideal type, people refused to participate in these organizations in a partial fashion. Although modernization tends to fragment identity among an array of roles and separate work from home, increasingly in postmodern society individuals tend to resist. They tend to want to participate in organizations as wholes; they try to spill over the boundaries of roles in a drive to recreate substitutes for the "natural communities." These unintended communities, described by Selznick (1966), subvert the goals of organizations and divert their resources toward satisfying the personal needs of their members.

This overlay of two sets of conflicting goals creates the motivation to engage in political activity both within and beyond the organization. Members of the organization bring with them the often unarticulated goal of self-fulfillment through social relationships and interaction, but the organization is established to achieve certain specific goals for a public or for the owners of the organization. Negotiating the tension between these goals requires continual political transaction within the organizations and among external forces.

Furthermore, the opportunity to engage in political behavior is heightened by the latitude of discretion granted to public administrators (Nachmias and Rosenbloom, 1980; Rohr, 1989). The growing complexity and technical nature of problems addressed by government have created a tendency in legislators to delegate enormous powers to administrators, who are presumed to have specialized knowledge of particular policy areas. Thus, the implementation of legislation becomes, in fact, an exercise in substantive policymaking. Broad legislative "shells," debated publicly and approved by elected officials, are then filled with a multitude of administrative decisions that are far less visible and far more difficult to monitor. These circumstances are highly conducive to political transactions (Lieberman, 1973; Davis, 1969; Lowi, 1979; Benveniste, 1977).

Consequently, it is not surprising to discover that studies of role overlap between politicians and administrators in Western democracies reveal it to be substantial. Aberbach, Putnam, and Rockman (1981) examined the extent to which administrative and political officials engage in similar activities. They found substantial convergence of the two role types, with administrators significantly involved in policymaking and politicians engaging in administrative matters. The greatest overlap was found in the United States.

If the administrative role in postmodern society is inevitably political and heavily discretionary in nature, significant ethical considerations must be acknowledged. For example, using the two broad categories of internal and external political transactions, we can identify three types of ethical concerns associated with each: corruption, loss of efficiency, and abuse of power. If we look at some typical external political transactions, we find these ethical concerns manifest in the following ways:

- *Agency–political party.* In transactions between a public agency and a political party, the ethical concern is usually for corruption of the agency's legally mandated mission. The party may use its influence with agency employees to circumvent established procedure for the benefit of the party or certain of its members. This corrupts the public interest that all public servants are obligated to uphold.
- *Agency–agency.* When two public agencies become involved in political transactions, the concern is for loss of efficiency. This kind of situation typically involves competition for resources and jurisdiction—that is, a struggle for power. The time and effort expended amount to a waste of the citizens' money as well as a

breach of their good faith. Poor stewardship of public resources is ultimately the equivalent of stealing from those who have entrusted you with their property.

• *Agency–constitutional branch of government.* Political interaction between an agency and members of the executive, legislative, or judicial branches of government produces a concern for abuse of power and for corruption. Abuse of power may occur when members of these branches attempt to use an administrative agency for their own advantage. For example, a president who tries to use the powers of the Internal Revenue Service or the FBI against political opponents is going beyond the appropriate use of his executive power. Conversely, if an agency becomes involved in using its resources in unusual ways to influence public officials, that may also be a matter of corruption. When, for example, a planning department cooperates in bribing members of a city council to gain favors for a developer, that agency's maintenance of the public trust has become corrupted.

• *Agency–interest groups.* Corruption is also the concern when interest groups become involved in efforts to influence a public agency. When labor unions, chambers of commerce, community improvement associations, professional associations, industrial associations, taxpayers' organizations, and lobbies of various kinds move beyond persuasion and begin to offer favors, corruption is imminent. The agency may find itself on the take. Its charge to serve the public interest is then corrupted by the rewards of special interests.

When we turn to the internal politics of public organizations, the primary concern is with loss of efficiency. When individual members or subunits of an agency begin to compete for resources and jurisdiction or build coalitions with others, the resources provided by the citizenry to accomplish a legally established mission are siphoned off. The political gamesmanship of the members of the organization diverts time, money, and effort away from the provision of public goods and services. The taxpayers are deprived of some portion of what government rightfully owes them.

The politics of public administration, then, raises some potentially serious concerns for the ethical performance of administrators. As we all know, politics is unavoidable. Given the dynamics of modern society and the overlay of personal and organizational goals that result from these dynamics, the notion of clearly separating politics from administration is not valid. However, it is possible to identify a spectrum of administrative politics ranging from minimal to pervasive. It also is possible to conceive of approaches to reducing, or minimizing, the clearly unethical manifestations of political conduct. (These are discussed further in Chapters Six and Seven.) The significant question is not how to remove politics entirely from administration, but how to constrain it and under what circumstances. Accomplishing this task or, more accurately, engaging it regularly requires that managers think not in terms of discrete decisions but about how to design processes and structures. Policies, procedures, organizational arrangements, training, and sanctions (both positive and negative) must be crafted to encourage ethical conduct and reinforce its importance.

Separation of the Public Administrative and Citizen Roles

The second impact of modern society on public administration is that there is a tendency to separate the role of public administrator from the role of citizen. The administrator as both employee of the citizenry and member of the citizenry occupies an unusual position in modern society, although it is not unique. Elected officials, government appointees, and other public employees find themselves in a similar situation. All who work for a government bear a dual obligation: they are responsible to serve the public, and they are members of the public they are supposed to serve. Elsewhere, I have argued that the dichotomy or separation of the public and private role of the public administrator is best viewed on a public-private continuum (Cooper, 1991). As one moves more toward the public end of the continuum, civic virtue and the common good become even more critical, as does the need for the responsible administrator to embrace the role as citizen administrator.

These dual roles sometimes create conflicting obligations: a public administrator is not simply a servant at large of the people but rather a public servant within a particular organization. This role as employee of a specific organization, although theoretically only an expression of a larger public servanthood, is far more powerful and concrete in its sanctions and incentives. The role of public servant quite easily becomes limited to, and defined by, the particular organization. When this occurs, loyalty to the organization may become confused with duty to uphold the public interest. This in turn often gets translated into an assumption that carrying out the orders of superiors is tantamount to fulfilling the duty as a public servant.

The tendencies to separate roles and create a demarcation between work and private life encourage this shrinking of obligation to the narrow limits of the work role within an organization. Both of these characteristics of modernization make it possible to remove the tension that should exist between the dual roles of the public administrator. We can settle into a schizophrenic pattern of expressing concern about civic virtue and exercising the rights and duties of citizenship away from the office, while thinking only of our personal advantage and that of the organization when involved in the world of work. The building and safety administrator who is paid off regularly by building contractors can be a faithful, informed voter, an active member of a church, a doting parent, and a supporter of his neighborhood burglary prevention group.

Weber's emphasis on functional rationality for administrators (1946), which is also a reflection of modernization, encourages the bifurcation of these two critical roles. We think substantively about the goals and ends of government only in the private sphere of citizenship. In the role of public administrator, however, we are encouraged to think only of the best means to accomplish the goals predetermined by superiors or elected officials.

The dichotomization of citizen and administrative roles is seldom complete; however, the pressure to move in this direction is strong in modern society, and the outcome amounts to an unknown number of public administrators who have given up some measure of their citizenship at the workplace. This role schizophrenia may be less and less comfortable in postmodern society as the foundational nature of employment identity and organizational loyalty weaken and as the diverse citizenry becomes more assertive of its rights to participate in governance. Indeed, one might well understand the blurring of the neat separation of work and other roles as a major factor contributing to the sensitivity of ethics in public life in recent years. It may be increasingly difficult for the citizenry to accept the notion that conduct in private life can be unethical without affecting that of the public role.

Only by devising ways of encouraging public administrators to maintain a linkage between these two roles can we sustain a broader view of the role of public servant than simply loyalty to a governmental organization. The tension provided by the citizenship role stretches the boundaries of the administrative role to include the hierarchy of law and the democratic tradition. Doing so redefines the public administrative role in a way that is appropriate for an increasingly demanding citizenry in postmodern society. It positions the administrator to engage citizens in the process of socially constructing a political order rather than seeking to impose authoritatively expert solutions. (In my earlier work, I have argued that the public administrator should act as a fiduciary administrator. For a more complete discussion of the fiduciary administrator, see Cooper, 1991, particularly Chapter Five.)

The ethical significance of these dual role characteristics should be clear, at least in broad outline. One of the reasons civil service positions are generally available only to citizens is the assumption that they will carry into public organizations a primary loyalty to the people. This loyalty, which should precede loyalties to any particular agency or government official, will enhance the trustworthiness of their service (Stahl, 1976). Because public service is a fiduciary role, anyone who accepts such employment is ultimately bound by an obligation to the public of that jurisdiction. This bond of trust is maintained only if one acts within a public organization as a citizen with certain added responsibilities—as a citizen first, and as one citizen among others who agrees to do work on behalf of all second. Paul Appleby (1965, p. 335) has characterized the occupants of this dual role as "the especially responsible citizens who are officials."

This is particularly critical for those who assume administrative roles, for they take on themselves even greater fiduciary responsibilities. They agree not only to perform work on behalf of the people of a governmental jurisdiction, but also to assist in structuring, coordinating, supporting, supervising, and evaluating the work of others who have chosen to serve the collective weal. In the words of Michael Walzer (1970, p. 216), "They are citizens in lieu of the rest of us; the common good is, so to speak, their specialty." They bear responsibility not only for their own use of public resources but also for achieving the most efficient and effective expenditure of those resources by others.

This compound fiduciary responsibility of public administrators suggests that it is of critical importance that those who occupy these roles maintain a lively awareness of the primacy of their obligations as citizens. Whenever an employing organization is found to be carrying out its mission in a fashion not in the best interests of the citizenry, all public administrators, and indeed all public employees, should feel duty bound to take action on behalf of their fellow citizens. The failure to do so represents a breach of trust and a denial of the responsibilities of citizenship. This is an ethical concern of the most fundamental sort.

The responsibility associated with the role of the citizen is admittedly problematic. For most of us, there is no formal statement of what that responsibility entails, as only naturalized citizens are required to take an oath to uphold the U.S. Constitution. However, it seems reasonable to argue that what is required for those seeking citizenship is implied for those who are citizens by birth.

Another kind of problem is raised by Walzer, who suggests that some people seriously question the moral priority of citizenship in the mid-twentieth century because of the alienation and powerlessness that many feel. He argues that "they experience a kind of moral uneasiness; their citizenship is a source of anxiety as well as of security and pride" (1970, p. 204).

Nevertheless, Walzer and other citizenship theorists assert the importance of the concept and the functions it suggests. The actual state of the citizenship role may be one of disarray. Dennis Thompson (1970) argues that normative citizenship theory functions as an ideal and pictures a desirable state of affairs that is not yet realized. We might argue that rehabilitation and enhancement of the meaning of citizenship are of crucial importance in the modern democratic administrative state. If democratic citizenship continues to wane in meaning and diminish in reality, democratic administration would seem to be impossible. The responsibility of the public administrator must be grounded in an understanding of the responsibility of the citizen.

As well, the meaning and significance of national citizenship may be less meaningful and useful as a distinction through which we categorize our public obligations in the transnational world (Cooper and Yoder, 1999). As the boundaries of the nation-state are increasingly blurred and the nations around the world become increasingly interdependent, the task of redefining citizenship and even considering "denizenship" may be necessary.

Although not all the citizenship literature projects the same ideal, two threads seem to run through those theories that are democratic in orientation. One of these is, of course, participation of some kind in the making of political decisions. The other, which is more directly relevant here, is an obligation to consider the opinions and wishes of other members of the citizenry along with one's own. In Pranger's words, "Incumbent upon the good member, the virtuous citizen, is the ability to make political decisions which at once protect his own integrity and take cognizance of the integrity of others" (1968, p. 102).

Similarly, Walzer (1970) maintains that unless citizens have "a sense of the whole over and above their sense of themselves as particular persons," they will have little interest in participating in politics. He concludes that "it is upon some such sense of the whole that the ideal of citizenship rests" (p. 215). As we will see in Chapter Four, the position taken here is that the notion of the public interest, which public administrators are charged to uphold, involves this concern for inclusiveness, a fundamental obligation of citizenship in a democracy.

Does this primary obligation to the citizenship role suggest that public administrators should run to the press, or an elected official, or a prosecutor every time something occurs that is not totally consistent with the legislative mandate for their organization? Certainly not! It is important to assess the seriousness of a situation, consider the full range of values at stake, and then act in proportion to these circumstances. There is nothing to be gained and much to be lost by overreacting to a perceived problem. A press conference is hardly warranted the first time the boss asks you to hire a friend who does not rank as highly as other candidates for a position. A talk with the boss to express your disapproval of the request might be more appropriate. George Graham (1974) proposes a series of steps that are generally consistent with this "proportional" approach. His prescriptions are founded on the concept of due process, which requires "all administrators in exercising the power and discretionary authority with which they are entrusted to be informed, to be fair, to be rational, and to be reasonable" (p. 9). However, in the face of persistent and egregious misconduct, the primary obligation to the citizen role may ultimately impel an administrator to resort to activities generally characterized as whistle-blowing in which appropriate elected officials, prosecutors, or even the press may be sought out in an effort to bring intervention or remedy the grievance at hand.

Maintaining a citizenship role while serving as an administrator of the public's business requires a healthy sense of critical perspective about an agency's conduct, but it does not necessitate disproportionate responses to misdeeds that may do more harm to the organization than good. The organization itself is a piece of the public's property. Attention to the double obligations of being a citizen-administrator implies the careful adjustment, repair, or on occasion major overhaul of the public's machinery. Moral imagination is the requisite skill, and ethical autonomy is the quality of character necessary for such stewardship.

The normative basis for viewing the administrator in this way is not to be found in some foundational source of ultimate truth, but in our historical tradition of ethical citizenship. This tradition is not simply received as a given from the past, but rather it is a social construct that we ourselves have consciously created over time through deliberation and the weaving together of several strands of political thought: Antifederalism, Jeffersonianism, Puritan democratic ideas, and our understanding of the importance of voluntary associations. This historical social construct serves the function of a foundational source in the absence of one. (See Cooper, 1991, for an elaboration of this normative argument.)

Managers of Diversity

The third implication of modernization is that public administrators must be managers of diverse interests. This necessity grows out of the relativity of values and the pluralization of society, which is accelerated and intensified to the extent that postmodern conditions prevail. In the absence of any unitary value system with absolute authority in postmodern society, both the political and the administrative processes of government become the focus of diverse interests. As the citizenry attempt to construct socially a set of institutions and policies to serve the functions previously provided by received tradition, or subsequently by the scientific perspective advanced by modern progressive reformers, administrators find themselves besieged by an assertive citizenry.

The administrative arm of government becomes significantly involved in managing these interests because, even with the complex political representation provided by the federal government, people still do not feel that their preferences, needs, and problems are cared for adequately. They tend to organize in groups with others who have similar interests. These voluntary associations, some of which are single-interest groups, can be seen asserting their proposals and demands at every point in the policymaking process, from electoral politics to the legislative process to the implementation stage. Kenneth Meier (1979) points out that most of these groups have long since learned that administrative agencies are key leverage points because most legislative proposals originate there and are shaped by these agencies in significant ways during implementation. (See also Lowi, 1979.)

Interest group theorists such as Calhoun (1953), Bentley (1949), and Truman (1951) have argued that these citizen organizations are essential for democratic representation in the modern state. The formal machinery of government could not possibly be designed to represent the changing spectrum of interests in a pluralistic mass society like the United States with sufficient particularity. It is far more efficient and effective to allow these groups to form themselves and project their own demands into the governmental process (Ornstein and Elder, 1978).

However, Parenti (1970) has identified a serious problem with this theoretical perspective. It assumes that all significant interests can be represented in this fashion. In his case study of efforts to organize a low-income community in New Jersey, Parenti concludes that only those with the necessary economic resources can make themselves heard effectively by government through interest group activity. The impediments that citizens must surmount in order to influence public decision making have been conceptualized as "participation costs" by a number of scholars, including Buchanan and Tullock (1962), Warren and Weschler (1975), and myself (Cooper, 1979).

The greatest leverage for reducing or subsidizing these costs lies with public administrators. They and their organizations deal with a defined set of public services. Administrators have great potential for influencing policy developments about these services, and often considerable discretion in their actual delivery. Administrative initiative in managing the plural interests of modern society is essential for effective government. Representation of interests in this kind of society, particularly at the scale of contemporary industrial urban society, necessitates active involvement of public administrators. They can provide a link between citizens and elected officials that is vital in the national, state, county, and even city governments whose populations have expanded substantially during the past fifty years.

However, the tendency of public administration during the first three-quarters of the twentieth century was to place a high value on standardized services and respond to the pluralization of society with reluctance (Caro, 1975). From Weber to Wilson to Goodnow to White to Gulick and Urwick, we find a rather consistent development of the notion that the chief task of public administrators is to implement policy efficiently by applying generic scientific principles. This perspective eschewed notions that social and cultural variation might significantly affect administrative principles. A generic approach to administration, combined with an emphasis on efficiency, gave rise to a tendency to standardize public services. Something like an assembly-line concept of economies of scale seemed to be operative: "If you can determine the one best way to educate children, then the more children you can educate within a single administrative structure, the more efficiently public education can be provided." This hypothetical statement exemplifies the kind of thinking that characterized public administration's approach to the provision of public services. Centralization, of course, has been one of the logical concomitants of standardization, particularly during the New Deal, World War II, and the postwar years.

Another factor contributing to the tendency to standardize services is the bureaucratic assumption that equality is the equivalent of equity (Cooper, 1979)—that if everyone is treated the same, then everyone will be treated fairly. This assumption appears to have gained dominance through the American Progressive movement of the late nineteenth and early twentieth centuries. Reacting against the special favors, patronage, and nepotism of corrupt machine governments, the Progressives called for equal treatment of all citizens and government employees. "Without fear or favor" was the way public administrators were to perform their duties. Good government was understood as standardized government, which would in turn yield efficient government.

Both standardization and bureaucratic organization are manifestations of a certain understanding of rationality in modern society. To manage society rationally has implied uniformity and order as requisites for efficiency. However, in a diverse society with minimal shared assumptions about values and lifestyles, this kind of rationality no longer works for many administrative functions. Hugh Miller (2002) notes that in a postmodern view of the world, the very notion of rationality is viewed as more limited than modern society has assumed. Attempts to carry forward in the old way the rationalization of the world are ultimately seen to be self-defeating. Miller asserts that "our attempts to be ever more rational seem to get in our own way. Rules pile up on rules. . . . Rules are intended to be neutral, perhaps, but they favor some individual or group in spite of the best intentions. . . . Continued attempts to be a more rational society bring about rationality's own corrosion" (pp. x–xi). What seems to be required is a new understanding of administrative rationality that is rooted more in notions of diversity, complexity, turbulence, and disorder and where rationality is not strictly linear.

We are now realizing that the old approach is unworkable and impractical. A more systemic view of the relationship between public agencies and the citizenry is required. If administrative agencies of government are to remain effective and viable, they must view themselves as open systems in turbulent environments. The citizenry, the most important component of the environment, must not be ignored or even yielded to reluctantly under the pressure of interest groups. Rather, those who direct and manage these systems must act with initiative to be certain that input from the societal environment is being sought and encouraged and that participation costs are reduced or subsidized as much as possible.

This kind of dynamic interaction with the social environment may trade off some measure of production efficiency for a varied array of service types and delivery modes. It may even lead to the devolution of service provision or delivery to lower levels of scale such as neighborhoods. (See Berry, Portney, and Thompson, 1991, for research on neighborhood governance.) All this may look less orderly and therefore less efficient in the short run but may represent a more effective adaptation to the pluralistic environment of modern society. It may be a matter of giving up a limited kind of efficiency, which suboptimizes the production at the level of single agencies, for the sake of the broader efficiency of the entire democratic governmental system (Bennis, 1966).

The ethical concern related to this third proposition is for social equity. The assumption that equal treatment is fair treatment needs to be reexamined. If in fact members of a population are not the same and are quite varied in their tastes, needs, preferences, and backgrounds, then treating them as though they were the same is not fair.

Inequity has often been institutionalized in the practices of public agencies under the banner of standardization. This is because the standards adopted have tended to be the key attributes of one population group—often those of the majority. Consequently, so-called standardized civil service exams have often assumed the attributes of white, Anglo-Saxon, Protestant males as the norms. Public education has been built around curricular assumptions that favor the offspring of middle-class English-speaking nuclear families. Housing codes have been standardized around ideal, newly built structures and contain a bias against the varying conditions and needs of older neighborhoods.

Achieving social equity requires a response from public agencies that seeks to approximate the needs, preferences, and demands of the citizenry. Because everyone is not the same in these respects, public administrators need a set of techniques for generating citizen input into organizational decision making, and the skills to use them, to maintain an accurate assessment of the social environment. This kind of intelligence would make it possible, then, to consider the array of services and means of service delivery congruent with that organization's constituent groups.

This is not simply a pragmatic attempt to achieve greater client satisfaction. Although it is concerned with providing public services in a more satisfying fashion, it is more fundamentally a matter of equitable treatment of the citizenry. Furthermore, from one perspective, in a modern industrial society, the full realization of citizenship involves the ability to consume public services. According to Warren and Weschler (1975), citizenship in such a society requires more than the legal constitutional rights normally assumed to be the privileges of citizenship. They argue that people are deprived of their full citizenship if services are provided in such a way that they are too costly to consume.

Warren and Weschler define "consumption costs" as increments of time, effort, and money that must be added by a citizen-consumer to a public good or service to make it consumable. If one has to walk or drive three miles to reach the nearest bus stop, those travel costs must be added to the fare to ascertain the true cost of using bus service. Thus, if services are standardized, the costs of consuming public services will be distributed disproportionately to resources. Justice in the distribution of public services will not be achieved or even approximated.

A parallel ethical concern has to do with the distribution of the "participation costs." If public administrators are to develop a more accurate assessment of citizens' needs, preferences, and demands, it has been argued that active pursuit of citizen input is necessary. To achieve that goal, participation costs must be low enough to allow the full population spectrum to participate. Again, this is not only a matter of practical necessity but also an ethical consideration. Citizens should not be deprived of the right to participate in public decision making because it requires a greater expenditure of time, effort, and money than they can afford or than the anticipated benefits seem to warrant.

Public administrators in modern society need to be effective managers of diverse interests. As both Ostrom (1974) and Waldo (1965) have argued, if democratic administration is to take place, public administrators must abandon their almost exclusive preoccupation with the costs of providing and producing public goods and services and begin to balance these costs against those that must be borne by citizens. Waldo states the case thus: "It has long seemed to me that our approach to administration is far too much 'producer oriented,' far too little 'consumer oriented.' . . . But if we value not only efficiency and productivity, but also seek to increase human equality and the values of participation, do we give these the attention they deserve in and relating to the administrative process?" (p. 45).

Political Theory and Administrative Ethics

Since the first edition of this book was published, it has become increasingly clear that an adequate normative theory of the public administrative role, including a normative ethical theory, must be developed within the context of a larger political theory of public administration. Such a theory lies beyond the scope of this book, but it seems appropriate to indicate at this point some of the ethical issues that will need to be dealt with in such a theory.

The diversity of modern society, the tendency to separate the administrative role from the citizenship role, and the demise of the modern notion of separating politics and administration, with its ensuing recognition of the unavoidability of administrative discretion—all these forces pose some serious problems for a definition of the administrative role. It is now clear that public administrators make political judgments that range from timing of policy proposals, to budget strategies, to extensive rules and regulations pursuant to laws that legislators intentionally made vague. Public administrators exercise discretion, and they do so politically with both legislators and clientele groups. Administrators seem to be firmly ensconced within the policy "iron triangle" as key participants in the political process of public policy formation and adoption (see Smith, 1988, for examples of this). However, although we acknowledge this fact and find no dearth of descriptive analyses of the dynamics involved, we have nothing approaching an adequate prescriptive political theory of the administrative role that would define the obligations of the administrator in the politics of the policy process (Fleishman, Liebman, and Moore, 1981).

From this lack of normative clarity, ethical issues emerge around three related aspects of the democratic public policy process: representation, education, and implementation.

Representation

In modern democracies, it is assumed that the people maintain political sovereignty but that their interests, demands, and preferences are reflected in the public policies that are adopted. This has been understood as occurring through the process of representation, which, until recent years, has been assigned entirely to the political role. However, if we have now discovered that administrators also act in politically significant ways in the policy process, then it is unclear whether in so doing, they also incur obligations for representation. It seems plausible to argue that in a democratic polity, representation of popular preferences, demands, and interests must operate in some fashion whenever substantive policy decisions are being made. If this proposition is valid, public administrators bear an obligation to represent the citizenry whenever they are influencing or determining the substantive content of policies (Chandler, 1984).

Should we accept the representative obligations of public administrators, there are only more questions to be answered. We must then ask to what extent and in what ways administrators are so obligated. How must their exercise of discretion be informed by the people? Is some kind of regular and systematic accounting to the public required, analogous to the electoral process, or is accountability maintained through elected officials? In other words, should administrative representation involve a direct relationship with the people, or one that is indirect? If it is direct, systematic and regular citizen participation seems an essential function for the administrator. If indirect, then elected officials and administrators bear responsibility for discovering ways of acknowledging and carrying out a shared obligation.

Furthermore, if public administrators are obligated to represent the citizenry in some fashion, the classic debate over "trustee" versus "delegate" definitions of representational obligation must be addressed once more, this time in the administrative context. Are public administrators trustees of such normative goals as the public interest, social equity, or regime values? Should it be their responsibility to advocate such values and principles, even if the people do not clearly support them?

Or are administrators more like delegates of the people, whose primary concern should be discerning public preferences and demands and responding to the public will? How are professional judgment and popular sovereignty reconciled with each other? If they are irreconcilable, which should receive priority (Grunebaum, 1981)? Of course, the very nature of professionalism for public administrators turns on the answer to these questions.

Is professional judgment fundamentally oriented toward technical expertise or popular will? Which takes priority?

We might be tempted to conclude too quickly that the trustee definition is more appropriate for the administrator, as that is a nonelective role. It might appear that representation through delegation occurs only through a specific overt act, such as election. We might assume that unless the people engage in an act of choosing some individual to represent them, delegation of political responsibility cannot occur. This is not necessarily the case, however. Delegation of authority and responsibility to organizations and categories of personnel also occurs through legislation, including the normal process and, in some states, the initiative of citizens. These are acts of general delegation. Presumably persons who then accept positions within those designated organizations are agreeing to bear responsibility for carrying out the public will expressed in the law. If that will is not clearly defined in law, we might conclude that there is an implied obligation to discern it through whatever means possible.

Of course, the problem with carrying out the delegate role in many such cases is that all too often the legislation, of necessity, does not spell out the public's will with great clarity. Thus, the administrator is left with a delegation of public authority and responsibility that does not specify in much detail what is expected. Political conflicts avoided and technical questions unaddressed in the legislative process are passed along to administrators for resolution.

The quandary over delegate versus trustee obligations is embedded in these characteristics of much of our legislation. On the one hand, unresolved political issues call for administrators to act as responsive delegates in arriving at some publicly acceptable actions. On the other hand, technical considerations seem to require trustees who exercise the best professional judgment in getting the job done while serving the broad normative goals of the polity. Consequently, the question still remains: Which of these aspects of public policy should take precedence? Should the public administrator be obligated to represent the citizenry primarily as a delegate or as a trustee? Is the answer variable, and if so under what conditions should one or the other become dominant?

Education

It is generally assumed in democratic theory that not only do the sovereign people vote but they cast a more or less informed ballot. One justification for political debate is its educational value. When points of view are exchanged, reason is put to the test of opposing ideas, perception is broadened, information is acquired, and self-interest is tempered by the interests of others. It is through this process of talking to one another and to their political leaders that a public is formed and public opinion is transformed into public judgment (Yankelovich, 1981). Yankelovich (1991) argues that public officials and other experts have paid too little attention to the development of mature, informed, consistent public judgment from reactive, emotional, ill-informed, and inconsistent public opinion. On the basis of experimental research, he prescribes the necessary stages of this process in ways helpful to administrators.

In the classic democratic formulation, the key actors in this educational process of debate and deliberation are the citizenry and their elected representatives. However, in the modern administrative state, the role of the career public administrator must be accounted for in some way. Some administrators are close to the problems, possess specialized knowledge and technical expertise, have ongoing relationships with their clientele groups, and tend to maintain longer tenure in government than most politicians. These appear to be essential participants in the democratic educational process, and their contributions seem necessary for the full development of public judgment.

However, the obligations of this aspect of the administrative role—teaching and learning through public deliberation—are neither clearly defined nor generally acknowledged. For example, one can read the entire winter 1985 issue of the *Kettering Review* (devoted to exploring how the public learns the public's business, with articles by thoughtful individuals such as Derek Bok, Daniel Yankelovich, Robert MacNeil, Geraldine Ferraro, and David Mathews) and be left with the impression that public administrators have no role to play in this process. This journal—generally insightful, sophisticated, and "dedicated to improving the quality of public life in the American democracy"—makes no mention of public administrators as significant participants in the public dialogue. The classical assumptions focusing exclusively on the citizens and their political leaders seem not to have been revised here for the modern administrative state. The media and the university are acknowledged, but not the bureaucrats who run our governments on a day-to-day, year-to-year basis.

However, if the obligation of public administrators for a key educational role in the public policy process is to be established, there are difficult questions to be answered and issues to be resolved. The obligation for informing and educating elected officials behind the scenes is generally accepted. Analyzing data, conducting research, preparing briefing papers, providing evaluation studies, and developing cost estimates for elected officials on request are all well within the classical view of public administrators as nonpolitical instruments in the hands of politicians. But once we move away from that view, how do we redefine the obligations and responsibilities of administrators for educating politicians and learning from them? How should we understand the educational relationship between administrators and politicians in the policy process?

For example, is there an obligation to go beyond the reactive mode of providing information only when requested? Should the administrator role include preparing and disseminating information not requested? Should an agency administrator feel obligated to plan and conduct a systematic educational process, formal or informal, for politicians? Should this include a deliberate challenge of political positions that do not appear to be well grounded in factual knowledge, or values and principles that are inconsistent with the American political tradition, or proposals that rest on faulty methods? Public administrators use these approaches from time to time, but should we now include them among the defined professional obligations?

Furthermore, should we sometimes expect administrators to carry on this educational process not behind the scenes but out on center stage, in full public view? If politics and administration cannot be neatly separated, does it make sense to think in terms of the total subordination of the administrative role to the political one? Or should we understand administrative obligation as including the chastening of political whims and passions with information, expertise, and experience? If public administrators are "citizens in lieu of the rest of us," should we not hold them responsible for publicly asking the hard questions and articulating the counterarguments that expand and balance political debate so that their fiduciary obligations are visibly executed?

Likewise, how should we understand the obligation of the public administrator to learn from elected officials? The professional perspectives of the administrator, rooted in specialized knowledge, technical expertise, and clientele relationships, may need to be leavened with political knowledge of particular constituencies and the ways of legitimate bodies. Administrative specialists can become narrow and isolated from the texture of the political community. They may be overly influenced by client groups and too firmly convinced of the "one best way" of getting the job done. They may forget the importance of political support, not only in adopting policy but also in carrying it out. Legislative proposals, administrative rules and regulations, and agency implementation plans may need to be informed regularly by political realities.

In addition to a mutual obligation for mutually educative interaction between administrators and elected officials, we must also think through a similar relationship between citizens and public administrators. Perhaps administrators who cultivate the kind of relationship with politicians just outlined should be prepared to offer two kinds of knowledge to the citizenry. The first is their own substantive knowledge of particular policy arenas and issues, and the second is procedural knowledge about how government works. If public administrators are indeed "the especially responsible citizens who are officials," should not teaching their fellow citizens these things be among their central responsibilities? If the rest of us are to be able to carry out our citizenship obligations, is it not essential that citizen administrators provide us with their best technical information and judgments, in an understandable form, as well as a more effective understanding of how both the bureaucracy and the legislative process work?

Communicating substantive information to the public is essential if self-government is to be even approximated. Should not public administrators understand this as an ongoing primary role obligation that cannot be set aside or curtailed in order to get on with the job? Is that not the most fundamental job, apart from which administrative efficiency is shortsighted and doomed to failure?

Should we not also agree that career public administrators are likely to be the best civics teachers available to the citizenry? Experience with students, especially undergraduates, suggests that one of the weakest links in our democratic process is teaching young people how their government really works. Somehow they arrive at the university with a wooden, oversimplified conception of the way public policy is formed and implemented. This caricature, acquired in textbooks, is carried over into adult life. Quite reasonably, then, most of our citizens either have little or no interest in government because it appears boring in the extreme, or they become quickly disillusioned over the gap between the world as it is and the world as they would like it to be. In either case, they remain aloof and disengaged from activities that appear to be either dull or beyond their powers.

Administrators engaged with the governmental process on a daily basis may be the best sources of a richer and more interesting knowledge of its practical workings. How can we best conceptualize a public educational obligation for administrators? Might it call for an expanded understanding of how administrators are involved in policymaking, perhaps as procedural coaches or tutors for the citizens, as well as substance experts? Yankelovich's work (1991) suggests that administrators have a potentially significant role to play in helping citizens move from public opinion to public judgment.

Now let us turn to the reciprocal aspect of the educative obligation between administrators and citizens. Is there not the responsibility to learn from citizens as well as teach them? If administrators stand in a representative relationship to the citizens, is it not essential that they understand the perspectives, problems, perceived needs, and priorities of citizens? Because administrators control focused public resources, are they not obliged to reach out beyond their clientele groups and political allies to help cultivate a public conversation? David Mathews (1985) argues persuasively that a democratic public cannot form and act on its own behalf without such ongoing conversation. It cannot move beyond public opinion to public knowledge, and finally to public judgment, without this communication. Mathews insists that "a democratic community begins with—in fact, is—a conversation of people talking to one another. If the public is not talking, there is no democratic state" (p. 60). Unfortunately Matthews's assumption seems to be that only elected officials and the media bear the responsibility for this communicative process. Does that not amount to the omission of an enormous set of actors with knowledge, experience, and resources? Should we not agree that the administrative role also carries with it a central obligation to stimulate this conversation among citizens and to learn from it?

Moore (1995) refers to this kind of engagement as "public deliberation" in which citizens must come to grips with conflicting viewpoints expressed by others and in the process seek some kind of accommodation, some form of "public value." He views this kind of "social learning" as a key responsibility of government leadership.

We tend to assume that public deliberation can occur only at a relatively small scale, but we have seen the emergence of various techniques for conducting large-scale deliberation. One excellent example is the work being done by America Speaks under the leadership of Carolyn Lukensmeyer. The organization has conducted deliberative exercises for as many as five thousand people using a combination of technology and skilled human facilitation. The assumption underlying their work is that public officials and the public can learn from each other in complex ways. (Specific projects are described on the America Speaks Web site: http://www.americaspeaks.org/.)

Implementation

Finally, the third aspect of the policy process that gives rise to ethical issues about the administrative role in a political environment is implementation. In the classical paradigm, this was the administrative area of responsibility. It was assumed that administrators receive policy decisions adopted by the politicians and then apply their best functional rationality to putting them into practice. Administrators were expected to use their professional judgment about the most efficient means for achieving the purposes defined by the legislative process.

However, once we acknowledge the inescapably political nature of the public administrative role, the obligations of the administrator in implementation are no longer so clear. For example, as legislative proposals often originate through administrative initiative, what obligation should the administrator bear for specifying at the outset how a proposed policy would likely be implemented? Should tentative rules, regulations, standards, and time schedules be considered along with the policy statement during legislative debate, rather than be left until later for administrators to handle, as is typically the case now? Would this serve the purpose of making administrative action more visible, and therefore more politically accountable?

Also, we face again a problem raised in the earlier discussion of the representational obligations of the public administrator. How should we expect administrators to balance professional expertise with representation of the citizen during the implementation phase? Aside from whatever is currently required by law for citizen participation in the implementing of policies, should public administrators bear an ethical obligation for representing the interests, preferences, and demands of the people throughout this process? If so, is the trustee or the delegate perspective more appropriate here at the implementation stage? Should we understand the administrators' best professional judgment as tantamount to the trustee approach to representation, and therefore sufficient? Or should we expect administrators, in implementing policies, to think of themselves as delegates in need of regular instructions from the people? Is there an appropriate shift from delegative representation in the adoption stage, as policy is being formed, to a trustee perspective in implementation, as technical judgments are most prominent at that point? Or, again, is the appropriate perspective variable from policy to policy, depending on complexity, specificity, scope, significance of probable impact, and other factors?

Conclusion

From these three aspects of the public policy process—representation, education, and implementation—a plethora of ethical issues emerges concerning the proper definitions of the administrative role in an unavoidably political context. No answers have been provided, but the questions raised begin to sketch out an agenda for normative theory development.

These attributes of the administrative role in modern and postmodern society and the ethical concerns that emerge from them lead quite naturally to a consideration of administrative responsibility. The next chapter begins this consideration with a discussion of the origins of the term *responsibility* and two ways of conceptualizing it.

Chapter Four

Administrative Responsibility
The Key to Administrative Ethics

Responsibility is the key concept in developing an ethic for the administrative role. Frederick Mosher (1968, p. 7) once observed, "Responsibility may well be the most important word in all the vocabulary of administration, public and private." Two major aspects of that concept, as defined by Mosher, are used here: subjective and objective responsibility.

When you are confronted with a problem over what you should do in a given situation, you are experiencing the need to define your responsibility in the administrative role. For example, assume that you are an administrator in a federal agency that allocates funds to state agencies for highway construction. Your organization's mission is to review proposed highway routes for their anticipated environmental impact. Highway projects that significantly affect the environment require an environmental impact statement (EIS); others do not. One section of a federal law mandates that highways constructed with federal money may not have an impact on or use public parkland, unless it has been determined that there is no feasible and desirable alternative—a question that is normally determined in the EIS.

A member of your staff comes to you with a problem. She has recently met with officials from a certain state to discuss a proposed highway improvement. The existing highway is narrow, with no shoulders, and is heavily used by elementary school students on bicycles and on foot. It is extremely unsafe, as the number of accidents clearly indicates. The school board, the parents' association, the local newspaper, the council of churches, and state highway officials are all calling for immediate action to widen the highway and alleviate these hazardous conditions. The problem, according to the state highway planners, is that widening the road sufficiently would require taking a strip of land five feet wide by one hundred feet long from a fifty-acre municipal park. This can be done within the law, but an EIS must be prepared to identify and justify the environmental impact. This process typically takes two years to complete.

You are responsible for complying with the law under which your organization operates, but you also believe your responsibility is to help reduce the hazardous road condition as quickly as possible. Two types of responsibility can be identified in this case. They are sometimes referred to as objective and subjective responsibility (Mosher, 1968; Winter, 1966). Objective responsibility has to do with expectations imposed from outside ourselves, whereas subjective responsibility concerns those things for which we feel a responsibility. As we shall see, this is not to be understood as a difference between real and unreal; subjective responsibility, as an expression of our beliefs, personal and professional values, and character traits, is just as real as the more tangible manifestations of objective responsibility. These concepts are the main focus of this chapter, as they seem to represent the most common ways in which administrators actually experience problems in defining their responsibility in concrete situations.

Objective Responsibility

The specific forms of objective responsibility discussed here include two dimensions: accountability and imposed obligation. All objective responsibility involves responsibility to someone, or some collective body, and responsibility *for* certain tasks, subordinate personnel, and goal achievement. The former is accountability and the latter is obligation. Accountability and obligation, responsibility *to* someone else *for* something—these are the dual dimensions of objective administrative responsibility.

Principal-agent theory, in its current use drawn largely from economics, attempts to describe and explain objective responsibility in terms of relationships between those with the primary right to exercise authority (principals) and those charged with carrying out their wishes (agents). Sappington (1991) identifies the central concern of this perspective as "how the principal can best motivate the agent to perform as the principal would prefer, taking into account the difficulties in monitoring the agent's activities" (p. 45).

The limitations of this perspective for use in administrative ethics are that it oversimplifies the principal-agent relationship; it focuses on the single value of efficiency and fails to deal with the ethical dimensions. The public administrator's role as an agent is complicated by responsibility to multiple principals, including organizational superiors, political officials, professional associations, and the citizenry. Although efficiency is highly important in administrative work, it is not necessarily the most important value; justice, rights (such as privacy), honesty, and a whole host of other values must also be considered. The need to deal with conflicts among principals and competing values, and between accountability and obligation, requires ethical reflection and analysis generally ignored by principal-agent theory (Dees, 1992; De George, 1992).

In terms of relative importance, obligation is the more fundamental; accountability is the means for ensuring the fulfillment of obligation in a hierarchical structure. Accountability implies superior-subordinate relationships and the exercise of authority from the top down to maintain the flow of work toward the achievement of mandated goals. If we explicate these two aspects of objective responsibility in the organizational and political contexts of the public administrative role, we can clarify the relationship of responsibility among the key actors in the policy process. These will be ordered from more to less proximate relationships of accountability, and from less to more fundamental relationships of obligation.

First, public administrators are most immediately responsible to their organizational superiors for carrying out their directives or mutually agreed-on goals and for the conduct of their subordinates. They must be able to explain their conduct and allocation of time and other resources as consistent with the work plan and objectives of the organization, whether these result from orders originated in a strict hierarchical fashion or from some collaborative decision-making process. This is the most proximate relationship of accountability, involving a regular reporting process. However, the relationship of obligation here is the least fundamental. The organization's work plan, specific objectives, and task assignments are simply instrumental in nature. They are pursuant to policies established in the political arena.

Objective responsibility also for the actions of subordinates is essential to the Weberian bureaucratic ideal type. Superiors must direct the activities of those under their supervision, provide resources for accomplishing the work, delegate adequate authority for assigned duties, and monitor performance. They in turn are held accountable for how their subordinates use the resources provided and exercise delegated authority toward the fulfillment of an assignment. This assumes, of course, that superiors are also accountable for clearly defining the assigned duties in the first place and, wherever discretion is allowed, delineating its boundaries. Subordinates are instructed to refer to their superiors any decisions that exceed the stipulated bounds of discretion, and thus the superiors maintain ultimate responsibility.

Second, public administrators are responsible to elected officials for carrying out their wishes as embodied in public policies. Such policies are collectively determined for legislative acts, singly determined for executive orders. As we have seen previously, this obligation includes both preparing policy proposals and implementing legislation and executive orders. Administrators must be able to explain their actions and use of resources as consistent with legislative intent or the intent of executive orders. This relationship of legal accountability is less proximate than the first because it involves relatively infrequent reporting, but it is a more fundamental obligation. As public policy is the basis for the organizational mandate and mission, obligations to those who establish policy supersede obligations to organizational superiors.

Finally, public administrators are responsible to the citizenry for discerning, understanding, and weighing their preferences, demands, and other interests. They may respond by changing programs within existing law or recommending new legislation to elected officials. Administrators must be able to explain their conduct to the citizenry as consistent with either the wishes of the citizenry or the larger public interest. This is the least proximate relationship of accountability, with only very infrequent and often indirect reporting of conduct and achievements. It is, however, the most fundamental relationship of obligation, because the citizenry are sovereign and public administrators are their fiduciaries. Sharing representative and fiduciary functions with elected officials in modern democratic society means that this relationship of obligation is also shared. For both groups, this is the source of role ambiguity and conflict.

One final word about the nature of accountability in all three relationships is in order. Accountability may be understood in both practical and ethical terms. The responsible administrator must be prepared to answer for conduct from both perspectives, but ethical accountability must finally prevail. Generally we should assume that an administrator will be expected to explain actions from a practical perspective in terms such as cost-effectiveness, efficiency, economy, feasibility, and productivity, and from an ethical perspective according to values and principles such as equity, equality, freedom, truthfulness, beneficence, human dignity, privacy, and democracy. The practicality of conduct is never sufficient in and of itself. Unless a course of action can be adequately explained on ethical grounds, it is not a responsible act. The full meaning of responsibility requires ethical as well as practical accountability. To illustrate these concepts, think back to the federal highway case described above.

Responsibility to Elected Officials Through Support for the Law

Your responsibility to elected officials through compliance with the law is a matter of objective responsibility. You are expected to behave according to the wishes of those set in authority over you. Here the expectations are those of duly elected legislators expressed in a legally codified statement. That legislation prescribes how you shall conduct yourself when the construction of highways affects public parkland, apart from your own feelings about the matter.

Objective responsibility involves accountability to someone else and obligation for a particular standard or category of performance. It is objective in that the source of accountability and obligation lies outside yourself. Objective responsibility is not the result of a series of decisions you made about what ought to be done. Rather it flows from the decisions of others about what someone occupying your administrative position ought to do. Your decision to accept the position is understood to be tantamount to accepting these expectations and constraints. Objective responsibility projects generalized obligations for all who fill this type of position without any attempt to acknowledge the individual needs, limitations, preferences, or predilections of a particular incumbent. It is through these external generalized obligations that the role is structured, given its distinctive content, and maintained through changing times, incumbents, and situations. It is through hierarchical arrangements that accountability is maintained. The stability and continuity of the role are rooted in these two aspects of objective responsibility.

Responsibility to the laws governing your organization and your conduct within it is one form of objective responsibility for your role as a public administrator. Ultimately, of course, legal responsibility includes an obligation to uphold the Constitution. Through the Constitution and specific pieces of legislation consistent with it, the intentions of the citizenry for those employed in the public service are presumed to be formally expressed. Inherent in the fiduciary nature of the public administrative role is the objective responsibility to the law. Legal mandates for public agencies are a manifestation of primary obligation to serve the public's interests, not those of the people employed by the agencies. Responsibility to the law is a constant reminder that public organizations and their administrators exist on behalf of the public.

Thus, in the highway-widening case, you are held accountable for acting consistently with your obligations under the law that governs the use of parkland. Your own personal opinion about the relative importance of highway safety versus park space is not the controlling factor, but rather the course of action that the law requires of you as an agent of the public. In accounting for your conduct and justifying your decision, it will not be sufficient to explain that you "have loved that park since you were a kid and just couldn't stand to see it whittled away for a highway." This would likely be viewed as irresponsible conduct.

Responsibility to Superiors and for Subordinates

In addition to law, there are numerous other objective sources of responsibility for public administrators: organizational rules and policies, official job descriptions, and professional standards. However, alongside law, the most prominently experienced objective responsibility is to the hierarchical accountability structure of the organization for which you work: your responsibility to organizational superiors and your responsibility for the conduct of subordinates.

Paul Appleby (1952) has argued that hierarchy is "the formal structure and instrument of responsibility" (p. 340). The chain of command, with its successive delegations of responsibility, is the means by which the generalized intentions of the law are approximated in concrete programs and services. Successive approximations of general legal intent are achieved by specifying accountability for particular aspects of the total task. Particular organizations and individuals are held responsible for implementing specific portions of the legal mandate or providing support for others in fulfilling their responsibility.

Whatever individuals working within the hierarchies of governmental organizations may feel about them, they are the formally accountable means of maintaining conduct that is consistent with the wishes of the citizenry. Appleby insists that only through "loyalty upward disciplined by the sanctions of hierarchy" (p. 228) can the public be maintained at the highest level in democratic decision making. Public servants may very well feel constrained and limited in their range of discretion by the chain of command, but that is one of the intended functions of organizational structure. The personal preferences of individual public employees must be subjugated to the popular will, presumably as communicated through the organizational chain of command.

From Appleby's perspective, this is accomplished by making officials at the top of the hierarchy responsible for the conduct of those below. Then, as diverse public preferences and demands are introduced at various subordinate levels of the organizational structure, they are pushed upward for resolution. Those with greater objective responsibility for conformity to law and popular will are held accountable for reconciling these multiple, often conflicting, demands. According to Bailey (1965, p. 283), this view of the objective responsibility of hierarchies assumes that "the basic morality of the system is in its forcing of unitary claims into the mill of pluralistic considerations," as they move upward.

Once again, the case of the highway and the park exemplifies this process. The member of your staff who laid the problem before you recognized that there were conflicting public demands that she was not competent to resolve at her level of responsibility. The law, expressing the presumed intent of the citizenry of the nation, clearly required an EIS, but the local public, as represented by the newspaper, churches, school board, parent associations, and state highway officials, was primarily concerned about the expeditious widening of the road. Her only responsible option was to carry the problem up the chain of command to the next level.

Authority and *politics* are the key concepts for understanding this upward movement. The pressure of political conflict, combined with insufficient authority to resolve it at any given level in the hierarchy, creates the necessity for moving the problem up the ladder of responsibility. When it reaches an organizational level at which there is both responsibility for resolving the conflict and authority to do so, then a decision can and should be made. If, for example, you have been delegated the authority to make exceptions to the legal requirement for an EIS, then you are obligated to decide whether to do so in this case. However, if you have not been authorized by your superiors to grant exceptions, the problem will need to be pushed upward until it reaches someone with that authority and obligation.

Or, if you have the authority to resolve the issue and attempt to do so but some significant actors in the political arena are not satisfied with the outcome, they may appeal to those higher in the chain of command to review and override your decision. In matters of serious consequence, this movement up the hierarchy may reach the top of the organizational pyramid without being settled and eventually find its way into the judicial system for resolution.

One of the pathologies of bureaucratic organizations is a failure to exercise responsibility when you are in fact authorized and obligated to make a given decision (Barnard, 1952). Passing the buck up the chain of command because you do not want to bear your obligation for deciding is just as irresponsible as acting when you are not authorized to do so or allowing subordinates to engage in misconduct. This reluctance to accept the share of the responsibility delegated to you results in superiors' being inundated with decisions they should not have to make, thus leaving subordinates without adequate direction. It distorts the organizational structure and impedes the flow of work.

However, the objective responsibility that an administrator experiences from the organizational hierarchy must not be viewed as the rigid one-way process exemplified by the strictest interpretation of the Weberian ideal type (Weber, 1946). Carl Friedrich (1952) has criticized Weber's model precisely at this point; it does not sufficiently acknowledge the possibility of consultation and cooperation between levels of the organization. The exercise of objective responsibility to the hierarchy should not involve a simple flow of directives from top to bottom; it should be far more complex and dynamic. The apparently fixed subordinate-superior relationships should be more fluid because of the need for consultation and sharing information up and down the hierarchy. Superiors in any bureaucratic organization are highly dependent on the specialized knowledge and experience of subordinates. Subordinates, in turn, need to consult regularly with those above them about legal requirements, clarification of agency regulations, and political considerations. Appleby's normative view of this process has been described by Egger (1965, p. 307) as "the structuring of a network of intelligence and communication which provides a matrix of abundantly diverse and catholic values and influences for the decisions of a pluralistic society."

Hugh Heclo (1975) has described the responsibility of individual public administrators in terms that are generally consistent with those of Appleby. It was Appleby's belief that, far from being the docile submissive implementer, "the function of an administrator was to complicate the lives of his political masters at least to the extent of assuring that they did not resolve complex issues on the basis of disingenuously simple criteria" (Egger, 1965, p. 307). Heclo referred to this active, even aggressive, role of the administrator as one of exercising "neutral competence." By that he meant not the conduct of a docile and simply compliant automaton but "a strange amalgam of loyalty that argues back, partisanship that shifts with the changing partisans, independence that depends on others" (p. 82). Both Appleby and Heclo were describing the responsibility of the top levels of administration to political officials; however, the mode of conduct they suggest seems generally appropriate for all levels of the administrative hierarchy.

The objective responsibility of any public administrator to the chain of command does not imply a passive acceptance of directives from above or the unilateral issuance of orders to those below.

It includes the systematic filtering upward of information that will complicate the lives of superiors in the sense of providing a more accurate representation of issues and the regular clarification downward of acceptable norms for conduct. If democratic government is to be maintained in a modern pluralistic society, those with authority and responsibility for making decisions should do so with full knowledge of relevant technical information, public opinion trends, positions of interest groups, interpretations of the law, past practice, the views of interested elected officials, the perspectives of other governmental agencies, and the best informed judgment of subordinates, both practical and ethical. Those in subordinate positions should act with clear directives from above about the publicly mandated mission of the organization, and these directives should be based on full knowledge of all relevant factors.

When your staff member came to you with the problem of the highway and the park, she was acting responsibly from the perspectives of Appleby and Heclo if she complicated your life with relevant information about a decision she did not have authority to make. If, for example, she informed you that in addition to support of the project from the churches, school board, parent association, newspaper, and state highway officials, there was also opposition from other quarters, she would be carrying out her objective responsibility. She might have told you that the state environmental agency, the municipal parks and recreation commission, the local chapter of the Sierra Club, a home owners' association in the area surrounding the park, and a city council member from that district were strongly opposing the highway project and threatening litigation. Also, she should have apprised you of the possibility of a more expensive alternative course of action that would involve a realignment of the highway but would permit the use of industrial property on the opposite side of the roadway instead of the parkland.

The objective responsibility of public administrators to the hierarchy of an organization includes not only taking decisions up the chain of command when their authority has been transcended by the magnitude of an issue, but also passing along as much information as needs to be considered in arriving at a decision. This is not only a matter of individual responsibility, but when summed throughout an entire organization or an entire government, it amounts to the responsible conduct of the public's business. Wilensky (1967) has demonstrated that the flow of intelligence through an organization is essential not only for the organization's survival but, more important, for achieving democratic values.

The dysfunctions of this hierarchical system are well documented (Merton, 1952). With particular concern for the flow of information, both Tullock (1965) and Perrow (1972) identify two different types of problems. Tullock describes the tendency for subordinates to withhold or distort information, whereas Perrow argues that superiors often receive appropriate information but are unwilling to use it. The common motivation in both cases is the desire to protect self-interests. Subordinates tend to filter out information that may upset the boss and create problems for themselves, and those higher in the chain of command tend to suppress information that is not favorable to their positions.

The difficulty here is centered in a lack of congruence between subjective and objective responsibility. We will return to the problem of incongruity between these forms of responsibility in Chapters Five and Six. For now, suffice it to say that the assumption here is that it is not necessarily bureaucratic organization itself that gives rise to these problems. Based on years of experience in applied research on hierarchical organizations, Elliott Jaques (1976, p. 2) argues that bureaucracies are "dependent institutions, social instruments, taking their initial objectives and characteristics from the associations which employ them." Jaques insists that bureaucratic organizations can be effective and humane tools for a democratic society. We will return to his prescription for "requisite" organizations in Chapter Seven.

Responsibility to the Citizenry

A third form of objective responsibility is an obligation to serve the public interest. Whether by formal oath, governmental code of ethics, or legislative mandate, all public administrators are ultimately responsible to measure their conduct in terms of the public interest. However, it is impossible to identify any definition of "the public interest" that would receive widespread support among either scholars or practitioners. The public interest has been examined by political theorists like Richard Flathman (1966), but in 1990 Charles Goodsell commented that there had been no serious treatment of the concept in the public administration literature since 1957. That situation has improved only slightly since 1990 with a recent treatment of the concept by Douglas Morgan (2001). However, it remains true that public administrationists have shown little sustained interest in public interest theory. The result is that public administrators are confronted with an array of alternatives for conceptualizing the public interest, left to fend for themselves, and expected to serve this confusing idea even though it is a far less specific and concrete form of objective responsibility than either the will of elected officials embodied in law or the organizational chain of command (Held, 1970).

The confounding paradox is that it is assumed that an indefinite concept of this kind should guide our judgment in responding to these two far more definite and proximate sources of obligation. It is not surprising then that as a practical matter, we either treat it as the object of lip-service, along with the flag, motherhood, and apple pie, or we reduce it to balancing power in a political struggle along the lines of the pluralist tradition, with its interest group theory, as discussed in Chapter Three. In the former case, we may have been exposed to abstract philosophical treatises that have convinced us that the public interest is impossible to define and has little to do with the realities of life in a governmental agency (Friedrich, 1962). In the latter instance, we may have internalized the pluralist notion that balancing organized interests is the way democracy in a mass society approximates the general well-being of the citizenry (Harmon, 1969).

The public interest is clearly a problematic concept. None of the attempts at defining it has been very useful in providing guidance for the practicing administrator. And yet it remains in our political tradition, our legislation, our official codes of ethics, our political debates, our campaign rhetoric, and our deepest reflections during times of profound crisis such as Watergate and the Vietnam War. It remains a part of our thinking about the ends of public policy and the responsibility of public servants—and rightly so.

The function served by the concept of public interest is not so much one of defining specifically what we ought to do or even providing operational criteria for particular decision-making problems. Rather it stands as a kind of question mark before all official decisions and conduct. The primary obligation to serve the public interest as a member of the citizenry should cause the administrator to ask whether all relevant interests have been considered, whether "the interests and welfare of more inclusive populations than self, family, clan, or tribe" are accounted for in the decision (Waldo, 1974, p. 267).

Has the range of viewpoints represented in the development of your policy recommendations, program implementation plans, or service delivery guidelines been too restricted? Are you and your staff listening to opinions that run contrary to your own or to those that would not benefit the organization politically? Have you seriously considered the gains and losses of those not represented in the hearing room, or the advice of experts, or the lobbying process?

The obligation to serve the public interest should always cause administrators and elected officials to feel a little uneasy, not quite sure that everyone worth hearing has been heard. That is its most practical function. The fulfillment of this objective responsibility is to be found neither in adopting a Benthamite utilitarian formula nor in a universal blueprint for society, but in a mind-set. It is a matter of carrying out your duties as though you might be required to stand before the assembled populace and explain your conduct.

Walter Lippmann's oft-quoted words are appropriate here (1922). He observed that the public interest is "what men would choose if they saw clearly, thought rationally, acted disinterestedly and benevolently" (as quoted in Held, 1970, p. 205). Admittedly this is an extremely general statement with a significant *if* in the middle. However, it does suggest an attitude in dealing with the public's business that is more than rhetoric. It is not unlike the conditions stipulated by John Rawls (1971) as the necessary prerequisites for arriving at principles of justice that could be defined as "fair."

Rawls insists that anyone who attempts to reflect on this problem should do so from the "original position," that is, without consideration for one's own social, cultural, economic, or biological circumstances. We should attempt to reason about the requirements of justice as though we did not know our own social class, natural assets and abilities, intelligence, strength, or even the political and economic characteristics of our society. He terms this perspective "the veil of ignorance." One of the basic conclusions Rawls reaches by reasoning from this assumed vantage point is this: "All social primary goods—liberty and opportunity, income and wealth, and the bases of self-respect—are to be distributed equally *unless an unequal distribution of any or all of these goods is to the advantage of the least favored"* (1971, p. 19, emphasis added). In other words, if none of us actually knew what our situation in society might be, according to Rawls, we would all think it just to distribute these goods equally unless we could increase the advantages of those who turn out to be among the least favored. We would do so because from behind "the veil of ignorance," it would be in our interest to do so; none of us would want to run the risk of winding up among the disadvantaged without these provisions.

This very limited treatment of the complex and carefully reasoned philosophy of John Rawls is included only to suggest the attitude required of administrators in serving the public interest, an attitude built on rationality and benevolence, both inclusive and projected over the long run. It is an attitude that attempts to eschew short-run personal gains and resists immediate pressures. It is a frame of mind that struggles to maintain a commitment to an evolving social system, a vision of the distant future, and a sense of equity that excludes none. It assumes that public servants can realize that they are primarily members of the public, whose fortunes will rise or fall with the concern and fairness exercised in the conduct of the public's business.

Subjective Responsibility

Externally imposed obligations are only one dimension of responsibility. Alongside these are our own feelings of, and beliefs about, responsibility. Objective responsibility arises from legal, organizational, and societal demands on our role as public administrator, but subjective responsibility is rooted in our own beliefs about loyalty, conscience, and identification. Subjective responsibility in carrying out our administrative role reflects the kind of professional ethic developed through personal experience that was discussed at the beginning of Chapter Two. We believe in being legal, and so we are compelled by our conscience to act in a particular way, not because we are required to do so by a supervisor or the law but because of an inner drive composed of beliefs, values, and character understood as predispositions to act in certain ways. These internal sources of responsibility may begin as external standards and expectations that become internalized over time through training and socialization.

Faced with the highway problem, for example, although you may have no specific objective responsibility for reducing hazardous conditions, nevertheless you may have an intense concern for the safety of children. All the law requires of you is to prepare an environmental impact statement when parkland is involved. That is also what the hierarchy of your agency expects of you. The one source of objective responsibility that may require more of you is the obligation to serve the public interest. However, that is such an abstract and elusive notion that it may not serve even the purpose of expanding the perspective of the decision maker, unless there is a strong sense of subjective responsibility. Sometimes subjective responsibility reinforces a person's objective responsibilities, and sometimes not. Sometimes it moves the public interest obligation to the forefront, and at other times it obscures it altogether.

Our feelings and beliefs about responsibility to someone or for something emerge from the socialization process. They are manifestations of values, attitudes, and beliefs we acquire from family, school, religious affiliation, friends, professional training, and organizational involvement. Through these experiences, we begin to perceive patterns in physical nature and in the behavior of others that become a part of our cognitive system.

According to Rokeach (1970, pp. 112–113), these beliefs may be descriptive ("I believe rain is a form of water"), evaluative ("I believe rain is good for the earth"), or prescriptive ("I believe experiments to increase rainfall should be encouraged"). These beliefs, Rokeach explains, are organized into attitudes as they become oriented around types of situations. They are relatively enduring and tend to create within us predispositions to respond in a consistent fashion to these situations—another way of saying that they contribute to the development of both character (predispositions) and integrity (consistency of conduct over time).

Values are types of beliefs more basic than other beliefs we may hold; they are central to our belief systems and thus to our attitudes. They are beliefs about how we ought to behave and about the desirability of certain end states. Figure 4.1 shows three concentric circles: values are located in the innermost circle, indicating their fundamental relationship to the more specific beliefs one holds; beliefs lie in the middle ring; and attitudes are placed in the outer circle to suggest that they are generalized composites of values and beliefs (see also Wright, 1971).

Figure 4.1. Beliefs, Attitudes, and Values

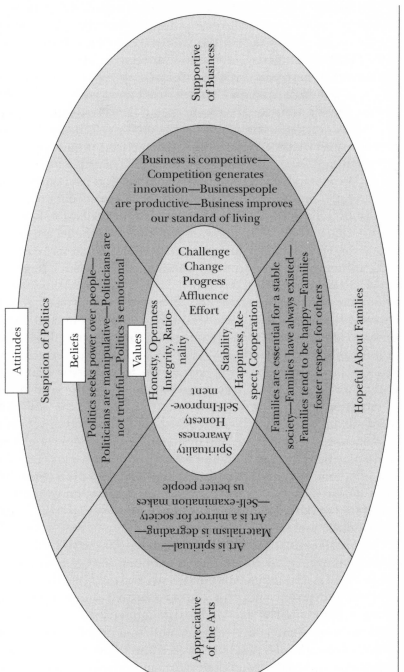

Supportive of Business

Business is competitive—Competition generates innovation—Businesspeople are productive—Business improves our standard of living

Attitudes

Beliefs

Values

Suspicion of Politics

Politics seeks power over people—Politicians are manipulative—Politicians are not truthful—Politics is emotional

Challenge
Change
Progress
Affluence
Effort

Honesty, Openness Integrity, Rationality

Stability Happiness, Respect, Cooperation

Spirituality Awareness Honesty Self-Improvement

Families are essential for a stable society—Families have always existed—Families tend to be happy—Families foster respect for others

Hopeful About Families

Art is spiritual—Materialism is degrading—Art is a mirror for society—Self-examination makes us better people

Appreciative of the Arts

Source: Rokeach (1970).

Values are powerful influences in human experience. Although we have referred to subjective responsibility as involving feelings, it is important to note that the values from which this kind of responsibility emerges are not simply emotional expressions. They have three components, which affect the way we live: cognitive, affective, and behavioral. Values not only emerge from our cognitive interaction with our environment, but they also shape our perceptions as we continue to experience the world. Values also evoke emotional responses to what we perceive; we have positive and negative feelings associated with what we believe about what we perceive (Drews and Lipson, 1971). This combination of cognitive and affective responses to the physical and social environment creates predispositions within us toward certain kinds of behavior. In other words, what we believe and how we feel about that belief affect our character, which shapes our conduct. A value functions as a powerful imperative to action; it is "a standard or yardstick to guide actions" (Rokeach, 1970, p. 160).

As a federal administrator considering the hazardous highway, you may have formed an *attitude* of support for any effort that proposes to alter highways for the increased safety for children. This attitude may be composed of a number of *beliefs* about the accident rate on narrow highways, the best means for reducing that rate, the vulnerability of pedestrians and bicycle riders, the special vulnerability of children traveling by these means, and the desirability of walking and riding bicycles instead of driving motor vehicles. At a deeper and more determinative level in your cognitive system, there may be some fundamental values about preserving the dignity of human life and the particular importance of protecting children. These values motivate you to feel responsible for expediting the widening of the highway. They cause you to want to take action in that direction.

These sources of subjective responsibility may be rooted in one or more of our other roles, such as member of a professional or religious association, citizen, or parent. For example, our membership and involvement in the American Society for Public Administration (ASPA) may create, through the experiences it provides, a sense of subjective responsibility that influences our conduct in our work roles. This may arise from ASPA's de facto ethical standards expressed through the informal norms of its culture. We acquire these through participation in its activities. Note that these may be more or less consistent with ASPA's espoused ethics set forth explicitly in its code of ethics.

Subjective responsibility is rooted in these basic determinative beliefs that we refer to as values, which become more or less elaborated as principles. These principles connect values to broad criteria for conduct. As we confront problems and issues, our values, and the principles associated with them, give rise to feelings and inclinations to behave in a certain way or to seek the fulfillment of a particular goal.

Chester Barnard, in *The Functions of the Executive* (1964), has argued that these values and principles are organized into various constellations, which he terms private, unwritten "codes" governing the conduct of an individual (p. 262). His notion of codes suggests that values and principles are not merely ranked hierarchically but also are structured into subsystems. These normative subsystems are functionally related to the various types of activities in which we are involved. They serve as unwritten, internal codes of conduct for particular aspects of our lives. Although Barnard does not relate these internal codes specifically to the roles we occupy, it is generally consistent with his conceptual scheme to do so. Identifying internal codes with roles helps to clarify both how they are organized and how they are linked to behavior. Values that are appropriate for defining and structuring a given role function as a subsystem of our total value system, functionally oriented around conduct in a particular role but related also to other value subsystems for other roles.

Roles were described generally in Chapter Three as bundles of obligations and interests. Now the description needs to be elaborated in a more complex fashion. There are two components in the enactment of a role: the objective and the subjective. The objective component consists of those external obligations that were discussed under objective responsibility. They give to the role a structure, stability, predictability, and continuity that approximate the will of the citizenry. The subjective component consists of a subsystem of values and principles that we construct in the process of responding to those objective obligations and expectations. As we assume the role and begin to act it out in making particular decisions, we organize a set of values and principles that guide our specific, personal, individual responses to the generalized objective definition of the role. In this process, elements of a role that

began as external expectations may be internalized through socialization and become part of our system of subjective responsibility.
The more we internalize the values and principles of a role, the
more our behavior is guided by our subjective responsibility and
the less we depend on external structures.

In other words, we develop a structure of subjective responsibility that is the counterpart of the objective responsibility imposed
from outside ourselves. This is the way we mesh our own needs and
idiosyncratic perspectives with the demands of the role. A role
evokes within us a need to create a value subsystem, a code for living out its objective responsibilities in a way that is compatible with
our own inner inclinations.

This inner code may or may not be significantly informed by
some professional consensus about the responsibility of public
administrators. Sometimes when an administrator has not been
socialized by a professional community, idiosyncratic personal values derived from other roles provide the only source for subjective
responsibility; no identifiable public service ethical norms shape
the conduct of the administrator. In these cases, the public role is
carried out on the basis of personal values that may or may not be
consistent with public expectations. Inconsistency may be discovered only when some significant action by the administrator is
found by superiors, political officials, or the public to be at odds
with public service norms.

Barnard (1964) also makes a useful distinction between moral
status and responsibility. Moral status has to do with the attributes
of the inner code for a particular role: "simple or complex, high
or low, comprehensive or narrow." Responsibility is "the power of a
particular private code of morals to control the conduct of the individual in the presence of strong contrary desires or impulses" (p.
263). Thus we may have a clearly worked out code for any given
role, but may not behave consistently in a manner that is congruent with the code. To the extent that our codes do not consistently
control our behavior, we may be described as irresponsible. A
responsible person's conduct is not at odds with his or her code
for that role.

Sometimes we say that those whose actions are in conflict with
what they believe are lacking in integrity. They cannot be trusted
because their inner controls are so weak that their behavior is

unpredictable and inconsistent. Maintaining a high degree of subjective responsibility is important not only for the sake of our sense of wholeness, self-esteem, and identity—essential as these are to mental health—but also for the fulfillment of our objective responsibility. As Srivastva and Cooperrider (1988) suggest, integrity involves wholeness, not only within ourselves but in our relationships. They maintain that integrity is not a single character trait and not limited to particular roles, but rather "a sophisticated state of processing experience in the world that encompasses moral judgment, creativity, and intuitive capability, as well as rational-analytic powers" (p. 5). They further assert that executives who have this kind of integrity "invite trust from others" because they are "consistent in word and deed" (p. 5). More essentially than organization charts and procedures, it is this trust that actually integrates the organization.

Egger (1965, p. 303) cautions us to be suspicious of the notion that an administrator can function "as a sort of ethical automaton." He argues, in effect, that the need for logic and consistency in our administrative behavior requires a developed subjective responsibility. The range of administrative discretion that the objective sources of responsibility allow must be structured by "possession of some of the impediments of reflective morality" (p. 303). An administrator needs "some bench marks for relating the various and frequently conflicting claims of competing values which enter into his official actions" (p. 303). These will not be provided by the law, the courts, or delegated authority; they are too general in nature. According to Egger, sources of subjective responsibility are the means for "the maintenance of a consistent and perhaps corrective ethical continuum to the administrative process" (p. 304).

Consequently, subjective responsibility is not only an unavoidable fact of human experience, growing out of our socialization and our other roles, but its conscious and systematic development is essential for carrying out objective responsibility in a consistent, rational, and dependable fashion. Consistent and powerful internal controls allow administrators to exercise discretion in a pattern that is relatively predictable and therefore engenders trust among associates. The ethical process is the means by which these internal sources of responsibility are related to external demands. Moral imagination is the requisite skill for meshing the two without a loss of integrity. The reflective decision-making approach discussed in Chapter Two outlines the steps for maintaining congruence between values and external obligations associated with the administrative role.

Now let us turn to another case situation and attempt to apply some of these concepts and distinctions related to subjective and objective responsibility.

"What to Do About Mrs. Carmichael"

The Municipal Redevelopment Agency (MRA) is involved in a project in Victoria, one of the older communities in Urbopolis. Because most of the turn-of-the-century housing is in a seriously dilapidated state, the Urbopolis City Council has declared Victoria an appropriate area for redevelopment.

You have been appointed assistant project director, with primary responsibility for determining which of the houses should be rehabilitated and which must be demolished. You have a staff that includes two specialists in municipal building codes and housing construction. You have assigned them to conduct on-site inspections of the residences in the first project area and prepare a draft report with their recommendations. They are nearing the completion of their fieldwork; another two or three weeks should do it.

Harmon, one of the two specialists, buzzes you on the intercom to say that he and Franklin, the other specialist, need to talk with you as soon as possible about Mrs. Carmichael, who lives in project area 1; in fact, she has lived there for thirty years. Mrs. Carmichael is now eighty-two years old, her husband is deceased, and her income has been so battered by inflation that it barely meets her basic living expenses. The mortgage has been paid off, but there have been taxes and maintenance costs. Some time ago Mrs. Carmichael began to neglect repairs on her home as her money shrank in value. "Now," Harmon says, "her house is in pretty bad shape." He sums up the condition of the house by admitting that according to the standards they have been applying elsewhere in the first project area, Mrs. Carmichael's home should be demolished.

However, Harmon cannot bring himself to recommend the destruction of the old woman's home. This is his fourth redevelopment project and he has seen it happen before: "Elderly people, whose homes cannot justify rehabilitation loans, are relocated into apartments, or board and care homes, only to lapse into senility and sometimes death." Harmon never felt very good about it before, and he just cannot stand to do it again. He tells you that he knows what the law requires and what the MRA project guidelines specify, but it seems wrong. He argues that "the government has no business treating decent people who have worked hard all their lives as though they were disposable trash."

You feel moved by Harmon's concern for Mrs. Carmichael, but you are unsure about what it means for you and the project. It occurs to you that Franklin has said nothing, so you ask if he agrees with Harmon.

No, Franklin does not agree. He feels as strongly as Harmon but not in the same way. "It is too bad about Mrs. Carmichael, and all the Mrs. Carmichaels who get caught in her predicament, but there is nothing *we* can do about it," says Franklin. He tells you that the MRA's job is to rehabilitate when it can and demolish when it cannot, and there are laws and rules and standards that must govern those decisions.

Franklin insists that you cannot go around making exceptions; you have to be fair with everyone, and that means treating everyone equally. There must be no special favors, or the entire project will be jeopardized. Everyone will demand an exception, and nothing will get done. The only way to deal with this case is to go by the book. "Let the relocation unit find her a satisfactory place to live—that's their problem," Franklin maintains. "Our problem is to make a decision about whether to fix up her place or tear it down." He knows that the house is beyond repair according to the standards employed by the MRA for all other similar projects.

The tension has been rising between Harmon and Franklin, and at this point a heated argument breaks out between the two men. You try to calm their tempers, and as they settle back into their seats, you express appreciation for both men's concerns. You assure them that you respect their judgment and indicate that you would like to give the matter some thought and discuss it again later. Harmon and Franklin thank you for hearing them out and then leave your office.

It is not our intention to attempt to resolve the issue of Mrs. Carmichael's house, but to use this case to illustrate some of the concepts just discussed in this chapter and indicate ways of clarifying the situation that will be helpful in arriving at a decision.

First, consider the facts concerning your objective responsibility. You know, for example:

1. The laws related to this redevelopment project clearly authorize the condemnation and demolition of substandard structures. If the owner cannot or will not make the necessary repairs, the building may be torn down.
2. A long series of court cases have upheld this kind of action.
3. The criteria for determining substandard buildings are well defined in the agency guidelines for such projects and in the Urbopolis building and safety code.
4. You are responsible to Bronson, the Victoria Redevelopment Project director, for recommending which buildings should be demolished and which rehabilitated. If it looks as though this case will be a matter of dispute or if you cannot resolve the issue in your own mind, you may have to discuss it with him.
5. You are not sure what your responsibility for upholding the public interest requires of you in this case. You need to ascertain how the public, at least in the Victoria area, feels about it.

Then you review in your mind what you know about Mrs. Carmichael's case and what essential information you need to obtain. You feel reasonably confident about the following:

1. From Harmon's description, the house probably falls into the demolition category. Harmon did not try to soften the hard realities of its condition, and Franklin concurred.
2. Because the house is in such bad shape, it will not qualify for a federal grant or loan large enough to do the work required to avoid condemnation.
3. Mrs. Carmichael could not qualify for a loan from a private lending institution, and she would be unable to make the payments if she did.
4. If demolition takes place, Mrs. Carmichael could not afford to rebuild on the present site.
5. If the agency condemns the house for demolition, Mrs. Carmichael will receive market value for it.

You feel much less certain about several other aspects of the case. You believe that you need to clarify the following:

1. How does Mrs. Carmichael feel about the situation? Harmon is deeply concerned about saving her house, but not once in his presentation of the problem did he report *her* viewpoint. It would be a good idea to stop by and hear her reactions first-hand. Maybe she would like to move into a place that she could manage better.
2. Can she handle a change in residence? What are her mental, emotional, and physical states? Is she in reasonably good health? You know that Harmon is right about the serious negative impact of moving on some older people.
3. What are some options if her house is demolished? Will she have enough money from the agency's purchase of her house to buy another house elsewhere, or perhaps a condominium? Maybe she could invest the proceeds and produce enough additional income to afford a nice apartment.
4. Is Mrs. Carmichael truly an exceptional case? Are there other elderly people in the project area who face the same threat? Maybe they should be considered as a group.
5. How do people in the community feel about Mrs. Carmichael's case? Without violating her privacy, is it possible to assess how others believe their interests might be served or subverted by the way her case is handled?

Finally, you reflect on your own personal inclinations. You attempt to clarify in our own mind what your subjective responsibility is with respect to Mrs. Carmichael. After mulling it over for a while, you realize the following:

1. Your general *attitude* toward older people is one of deep respect. Since your boyhood days with your grandparents, you have felt almost a reverence for those who have survived the vicissitudes of the modern world. They evoke within you a deferential feeling.
2. This attitude is composed of a number of *beliefs*. You view them as having "paid their dues," as having worked hard and deserving our esteem for having done so. You believe young people

often do not recognize the valuable knowledge and experience that older people have accumulated. You believe that the elderly are often ignored and mistreated. They generally do not receive what is coming to them.

3. Behind these beliefs are some *values* you have long recognized within yourself. Wisdom about life in the world, based on knowledge and experience, is important to you. Getting the most out of the time allotted to you is something about which you feel deeply. Perseverance in the face of hardship is a significant virtue in your value system. Fairness, or equity, is one of the most essential principles of all. Sensitivity to the feelings of others is another of your values.

On the basis of these reflections, you conclude that your strongest sense of subjective responsibility leads you in the direction of trying to resolve the problem without harming Mrs. Carmichael in any way. You do not want to disturb her life. However, you have other obligations too. You are the administrator responsible for making a recommendation about Mrs. Carmichael's house. You are paid to do that by MRA, and you made a commitment to carry out that responsibility when you accepted the job. It is your objective responsibility, and as long as you hold this position, you may not ignore it.

Also, you have other subjective responsibilities associated with your administrative role. You feel responsible for maintaining morale and a cooperative team spirit among staff members. You value efficiency, and you believe these qualities are essential for an efficient organization. You also feel responsible for avoiding conflict with the residents of Victoria, both because that would upset the orderly schedule of work and lead to reduced efficiency and because you value the esteem of others. You want the residents to feel that you have been fair with them. Furthermore, you feel responsible to Bronson, the Victoria Project director, and Markham, the executive director of MRA, for maintaining the image of the agency. Loyalty to the organization is important to you.

In determining the best course of action, you may simply respond to the strongest and most definitive sources of objective responsibility—perhaps your superior, the law, or both if they coalesce. Or you may allow deep-seated feelings to function as the decisive factors.

The perspective outlined in Chapter Two assumes that if we want to make ethical decisions in a more intentional and rational manner, we must be more systematic. Working through the steps of the process outlined there is a way of accomplishing this task. As we consider alternative courses of action, their probable consequences, and how each might be defended, we are seeking an acceptable fit among the facts of a situation, our values, and our external obligations. Resolution is achieved when we are able to imagine an alternative that satisfies the need for consistency in our fundamental self-image. This allows us to maintain our sense of integrity, a feeling of being an identifiable whole, someone whom we and others will recognize as the person we imagine ourselves to be. Needless to say, this self-image and sense of integrity should be shaped to a large extent by a normative public administrative identity, by an internalized public service ethic.

Conclusion

Fulfilling our responsibilities is a stressful, complex task in modern society. As should be obvious from this chapter, the management of the administrative role with its dual components is a difficult task in itself. Any reader with administrative experience will realize by this point that it is much more complicated than suggested here. If we begin to consider, for example, the multiplicity of roles that must be maintained by an individual in the urban world today, the thought and energy required can be overwhelming. Conflict among responsibilities related to a single role, compounded by conflicts among several roles, is a regular, even daily experience for public administrators. In the next chapter we examine these conflicts.

Chapter Five

Conflicts of Responsibility
The Ethical Dilemma

Confronting conflicting responsibilities is the most typical way public administrators experience ethical dilemmas. We may feel torn between two sets of expectations or inclinations, neither of which is without significant costs. "Damned if you do, damned if you don't" is a common way of expressing this feeling of being caught between incompatible alternatives. Frequently we do not identify this dilemma as an ethical issue, only as a practical problem. However, at base, these situations involve ordering our values and principles, consciously or otherwise. They are therefore problems of ethics as well as practical problems. They are occasions on which we run the risk of violating one or more of what Banton (1965) calls "the social bargains which underlie cooperation." He argues that they involve "moral as well as legal customary requirements" (p. 2).

It is not surprising that conflicts of responsibility are so common when we look at the nature of roles in modern and postmodern society reviewed in Chapter Two and at the dual meanings of administrative responsibility discussed in Chapter Three. Because the administrative role is only one among a whole repertoire of roles we might occupy in modern and postmodern society, the possibility of role conflict is always present. Each role consists of sets of obligations and interests that stand a high chance of being at odds with those of one or more other roles. Furthermore, because the role of public administrator is sometimes in tension with the citizenship role, there is the potential for recurring conflict among these two in particular.

Also, as I argued in *An Ethic of Citizenship for Public Administration* (Cooper, 1991), the fiduciary character of public service employment, involving responsibility to act on behalf of the citizenry, and the fact that it occurs within organizational settings, establish the possibility of two types of conflict: *conflict among interests* (such as personal interests, those of the organization, and those of the public) and *conflict among various sources of authority* (such as organizational superiors, political officials, and laws).

Before we examine each type of conflict, it might be useful to remind ourselves that in this book we are dealing with administrative responsibility, so our attention is focused on the conduct of an administrator within an employing organization. Thus, we will not examine here activities of family, community, and voluntary associations unless they directly relate to the administrative role within the organization. However, we should not be oblivious to the ways those other sources of responsibility affect administrative conduct. Although roles such as mother, spouse, or investor are not enacted within the organization, these sources of obligation and interest nevertheless are carried with the person who functions as an administrator during working hours.

It is important to emphasize that the different kinds of conflict discussed here are not classified according to some universally accepted categories inherent in the nature of things. Instead, they are simply ways of perceiving and experiencing a conflict that have emerged from our previous experience and peculiar cognitive style.

Three of the most common ways of experiencing conflicts of administrative responsibility are conflicts of authority, role conflicts, and conflicts of interest. We will consider each of these and illustrate the first two with cases. Because conflict of interest includes a number of legally defined types, it will not be possible to provide a single extended case illustration; brief examples must suffice for that category.

Conflicts of Authority

In the previous chapter, we discussed the difference between objective and subjective responsibility. Here we are examining conflicts between two or more objective responsibilities imposed on us by two or more sources of authority, such as the law, organizational superiors, elected officials, and the public. In these situations, we feel torn between two sources of authority that demand incompatible actions from us. The law mandates one course of action, but the boss orders you to do something else; or the boss instructs you to move in one direction, but an elected official tells you otherwise; or your superior gives you an order that conflicts with one you have received from her boss. Let us look at a case in which this kind of ethical dilemma is confronted.

"The Major, the Captain, and Corporal Montague"

You are a first lieutenant in a military organization responsible for maintaining and providing a wide range of supplies for the larger unit of which you are a part. You report to a captain, who reports to a major. You have been in this job for about a year and have developed positive working relationships with both of these senior officers.

An office manager position, involving the supervision of two secretaries and three clerks, opens up in your office. Both the captain and the major come to you independently and encourage you to request that a particular woman, Corporal Montague, be transferred from her present post to fill your open position. They both acknowledge that although this position would normally be filled by someone at the rank of sergeant, they believe she is very competent and would serve your office well.

You do not know Corporal Montague, but after reviewing her personnel records and conducting an interview, you are not impressed. She has performed adequately as a senior secretary, but there is no indication of the level of excellence reported by the captain and the major. Your interview left you feeling that she seems unmotivated and somewhat lacking in the communication and interpersonal skills needed for a supervisory position.

After thinking it over, you decide to put in a request for Corporal Montague. Although you see no evidence of a level of competence that would justify hiring a corporal for this job, you decide to trust your two superiors, who have always demonstrated good judgment in the past, especially concerning personnel matters.

After Corporal Montague has been on the job for a month, it is clear to you that your own judgment was correct and your two superiors were wrong. Her productivity is adequate but certainly not exceptional. The quality of her work is generally acceptable but highly uneven. Although she is developing better supervisory skills, she precipitated some problems in the office at the beginning by her inept treatment of the clerks and secretaries under her supervision, and the atmosphere is still a bit chilly. You see her as someone who was promoted too soon but who can now probably develop her skills, given some time in the position, some coaching, and formal in-service training.

However, the situation has become extremely complicated in unexpected ways. Soon after the corporal came to work in your office, you received some alarming information: Corporal Montague had been having simultaneous affairs with the captain and the major, but neither knew of the other's involvement with her. To make matters worse, you learned during the last month that Corporal Montague and your immediate boss, the captain, have had a lovers' quarrel and have broken up. She is still seeing the major.

Even more disturbing, the captain and the major are now sending you conflicting signals. The captain recently has commented that Corporal Montague does not seem to be working out in her new job after all and strongly suggests that you review her performance early and transfer her out. The major, for his part, has urged you several times to write an early, highly positive performance evaluation for Corporal Montague. This would, according to the major, provide a basis for then applying for a promotion to the rank of sergeant for her. It seems likely to you that Corporal Montague has been encouraging her remaining lover, the major, to offer this suggestion on her behalf. Finally, because you have not yet acted on their "suggestions," both senior officers have issued oral orders to move ahead with Corporal Montague's evaluation and then to take the action they recommended.

As with other cases we have considered, the point here is not to arrive at a solution but to stimulate thought about the nature of one kind of conflict of responsibility. We are attempting to cultivate a way of thinking about the conflict of authority that this case represents.

When you begin to reflect on your dilemma over Corporal Montague, you realize that you are faced with a conflict among three authorities: your boss, his boss, and the personnel regulations. The regulations specify a performance evaluation at the end of the first three months in a new position, but Corporal Montague has been in your office for only one month. Furthermore, the regulations require you to provide regular evaluative comments and constructive advice during the probationary period and objectively evaluate her performance on the various aspects of her work specified in the job description at the end of the period. If she is to be retained, you are to recommend steps to improve her skills wherever necessary. If you comply with the requirements of this source of authority, you will undertake an evenhanded review of Corporal Montague's performance two months from now, not now, as your superiors are urging.

Hiring Corporal Montague was a mistake, but you want to try to redeem the error. You hope that with your counsel and guidance, she will have developed her skills significantly by the time of the scheduled review and that her motivation will have improved as she feels more competent in the position. You anticipate a report that will find her acceptable for the job but needing training in supervisory skills and time management, and advanced training in the use of computers.

You also know that compliance with the personnel regulations will place you in conflict with the authority of your two superior officers. Generally you are required by basic military rules to carry out the orders of superiors, but in this case, if you obey one, you will disobey the other. And if you follow the orders of either the captain or the major, you will be violating the personnel regulations because neither wants to wait out the probationary period and neither wants an objective evaluation.

As you consider possible courses of action, you define these alternatives:

1. Discuss this problem with the personnel officer, and ask her to intervene.
2. Confront the captain with your knowledge, and try to get him to withdraw his order.
3. Confront the major with your knowledge, and try to get him to withdraw his order.
4. Inform Corporal Montague of your knowledge, explain the problem, and ask her to request a transfer.
5. Go to the colonel, next up the chain of command, and ask him to intervene.

CONFLICTS OF RESPONSIBILITY 111

6. Ask both the captain and the major to put their orders in writing.
7. Simply refuse, in writing, the orders of both superior officers, with references to Corporal Montague's performance, progress, and promise, and to appropriate sections of the personnel regulations and procedures.

You are painfully aware that each alternative will almost certainly produce intense conflict, with potentially dire consequences for your own future.

Faced with this kind of conflict of authorities, which reflects objective responsibilities, you realize that you must clarify your own subjective responsibility and consider any broader or more fundamental objective responsibilities. Because you cannot escape conflict in this situation, you must first turn to your own beliefs, values, and principles to decide which conflict to engage, which course of action would be best, and how you could justify your conduct.

As you do so, it is clear that although you are accountable to your superior officers, you do not feel responsible to follow the orders of either of them. The sources of that feeling require some reflection, which leads you to thoughts about your deep sense of loyalty to the military service, to the nation, and more concretely to the Constitution. You took an oath to uphold and defend the Constitution. To you, taking that oath meant more than simply meeting a legal requirement to join the military service. It was an overt manifestation of the value of public service you had grown up with. Your parents had always involved themselves in service activities for the community and had encouraged you to do so.

Taking that oath not only reflected your commitment to serve the nation, but also your belief in the fundamental importance of the rule of law. The Constitution is the basic law of the land, and anyone who vows to uphold it must also uphold specific laws that proceed from it and are consistent with it. It is true, however, that you believe that there are some rare circumstances when specific laws must be broken in order to challenge their consistency with the Constitution and fundamental ethical principles. But that does not seem to be the case here; the personnel regulations seem fair and consistent with constitutional values like due process and equal protection under the law, as well as with basic ethical principles like justice.

As you consider your devotion to the rule of law, it occurs to you that the legal structure of the nation, including military laws, rules, and regulations, represents a source of authority and objective responsibility that supersedes the authority of your superior officers. In fact, no member of the military is required legally to obey an illegal order; the authority of law is higher than the authority of any military officer.

You reflect on the importance of being fair with your subordinates. You recall your military academy training: one of your instructors in leadership stressed the cardinal importance of officers' "taking care of their troops." He used to argue passionately that the authority delegated to an officer must not be abused by using it to exploit and manipulate subordinates for the officer's own ends.

Also, you think about what is best for your organization. Because its management is your responsibility, you feel the need to do that which will make it function most effectively. That is what gives you professional satisfaction and meaning. If Corporal Montague is transferred for other than job-related reasons or unjustifiably promoted before she has earned it, will that serve the organization's best interests, or will it have destructive consequences? What if you keep her for the full three months and she does not improve or even becomes increasingly destructive?

Through this kind of assessment of your subjective responsibility and identification of more fundamental objective responsibilities, you attempt to move toward an alternative that will fulfill both objective and subjective responsibility. Following the line of reasoning developed here, this will necessarily require subordinating, although not abandoning, some objective responsibilities to others—probably your responsibility to superiors to your responsibility to the regulations. Also, it will likely require subordinating your objective responsibility to your superiors to your subjective responsibilities rooted in your long-standing beliefs.

You may resolve the ethical conflict through this process, but it should be clear that ethical resolution does not resolve the practical problems. It only helps you identify your primary obligations and establish a basis for explaining your behavior to yourself and others. In other words, it is a way of establishing a perspective on the problem, a place to stand in dealing with the captain, the major, Corporal Montague, or other higher authorities in the government.

In situations such as this, you are likely to suffer in one way or another, but it is still important to be clear about what you will suffer for, and why. It is important to have a means for maintaining accountability for yourself in the midst of intense and hazardous conflict. In the most basic sense, it is through this kind of analytical and normative reflection that we create an operational ethic, develop integrity, and maintain responsible behavior.

Role Conflicts

The key attribute with this type of conflict in responsibility is the concept of role. Here, a public administrator experiences values associated with particular roles as incompatible or mutually exclusive in a given situation. Generally, however, we do not simply experience the values themselves. Rather, we feel the collision of roles governed by those values. We may be confronted with an expectation in our work that we believe to be inconsistent with being a good mother, a good Catholic, or a good member of the American Society for Public Administration. In these cases, the conflict is between the administrative role and one or more of our roles outside the work organization.

Sometimes we may also feel that we are being asked to do something as a fiscal manager that does violence to our ability to function effectively as a supervisor, or asked to behave as a subordinate in a way that jeopardizes our ability to be a good fiscal manager. These are examples of conflict among our roles within or inside the organization. To be more precise, we might refer to these as conflicts among subroles of the larger administrative role, or conflicts among components of the administrative role.

Inside Roles Versus Outside Roles: "Politics and Toilets"

Imagine that you are the public health officer for the municipal health department of the city of Micro. Your professional training was in public health, but you have been in administrative positions for the past ten years. You are now at the second level of the department, reporting directly to the director. You supervise eight professionals and an office staff of six. Most of your unit's work involves inspecting restaurants, food markets, food processing plants, and sanitary facilities for large public buildings.

The city of Micro has been experiencing severe financial pressure for a number of years as a result of a tax limitation measure adopted by the state more than a decade ago. Some traditional sources of revenue have been lost, and the city council is having to cut the budget wherever possible, as well as search for new revenue. One of the more progressive members of the council observes that rock concerts often attract large crowds willing to pay high prices for well-known entertainers. He argues persuasively that Micro might be able to raise much of its lost revenue by sponsoring one big event of this kind each year. After conducting lengthy debate extending over several council sessions, a coalition of citizens forms to support this proposal. For the most part, they are consumers of services threatened by the loss of revenue and property owners who fear new forms of taxation such as garbage collection and sewer fees.

The council finally approves the idea and signs a contract with a concert promoter. He arrives in town and begins meeting with appropriate city officials to make the necessary arrangements. He contacts you to discuss the requirements for public health services: toilet facilities, water, food vendors, and emergency medical care. Because the concert is to take place in a city-owned field on the edge of town and there are no utilities of any kind at the site, temporary, portable equipment must be provided. Also, because there are no existing city or state laws establishing public health standards for events of this type, you have been given the responsibility for determining what should be required.

When you meet with Ripley, the promoter, you are astonished to learn that he expects a crowd of about five hundred thousand people for a fourteen-hour concert. As you begin to talk with him about the necessary public health services for such a large number of people, it soon becomes clear that your standards are much higher than he expected. In the absence of legal requirements, you have resorted to the recommendations for large outdoor events approved by the National Public Health Association (NPHA) some years ago. After Woodstock and several attempts at imitating it, the NPHA had appointed a committee, of which you were a member, to study public health conditions at these events and propose a set of guidelines for sanitation, water, food, safety, and medical standards.

The further you go in discussing the plans, the more incensed Ripley becomes. He argues loudly that one toilet for every fifty people is absurd and impossible. He insists that if he provided ten thousand portable toilets for the anticipated half-million people, the rental costs would be prohibitive, and space for paid attendees would be reduced. The ratio he had in mind was more like one toilet per three hundred people. Ripley's reaction is much the same for the number of medical tents and personnel, the amount of food, and "all of those damned tank trucks full of water." He finally refuses to comply with your standards, informs you that he will take the matter up with the city council, and storms out of your office.

Later that same day, your boss, Harley, the director of the city health department, asks you to come to his office. It seems that he has received a call from the president of the city council reminding him of the financial exigency that Micro faces. The council president had suggested that Harley have a chat with you about the importance of the rock concert and then send you over to meet with two members of the council the next morning. The council president had expressed confidence that reasonable requirements could be worked out to the satisfaction of all parties involved. Finally, he had observed that "it would be detrimental to all of us if we frightened Mr. Ripley away."

After relating this conversation, Harley urges you to be cooperative and to acknowledge the practicalities of the situation. There are no legally prescribed standards, and this is only a one-day event, which should make it possible for you to live with less stringent requirements. Harley reminds you that there is a lot of support for the concert among the citizens of Micro and that anyone or any agency that complicates the success of this important event might "feel the wrath of an unforgiving public." He assures you that as a member in good standing of the NPHA, he is concerned about maintaining public health standards, and he believes in supporting the recommendations of the association. "However," argues Harley, "we mustn't be rigid or foolish about such things."

He assures you that he will not resolve the matter bureaucratically by exercising his authority as your superior, but he hopes you will keep uppermost in your thinking what is best for the department and the city of Micro. He respects your professional judgment and autonomy, but he reminds you that your responsibility as an employee of the health department and the city is to support the efforts to solve the serious fiscal problems.

You leave the boss's office and return to your own. You are uncertain about your responsibility in this matter and need to think it through.

First, you are accountable to Harley, your superior in the chain of command. Ultimately he is to be held accountable by the city council for accomplishing the mission of the department. However, he is not threatening you with his authority as your superior; he has indicated his willingness to let you do what you feel must be done. But he has requested you to cooperate with Ripley and the council by relaxing the standards for this brief and unusual affair. And you know from five years of association with Harley that he has both personal and professional integrity. He has backed you on some tough cases: the market chain with the filthy meat department and a council member who was a partner in the corporation that ran that chain. Harley withstood a lot of heat on that one.

Furthermore, Harley is right about the standards: they are not required by law. Their only authority comes from the professional prestige of the NPHA. Maybe the most important consideration is the long-term effectiveness of the department and your position within it. If you insist on maintaining the standards, the council may hold a formal hearing on the issue and inflame the public. You, Harley, and the department could get hurt if that happened. You might be fired or eased into a dead-end job. Your reputation might be irreparably damaged if they made you the butt of a joke about ten thousand toilets. The headlines would be brutal. Besides, you might at least be able to negotiate Ripley down from his position of one toilet per three hundred persons if you are willing to be flexible. But if you are discredited or fired, the council will probably give Ripley a free rein to do as he pleases.

Even if you are not attacked, the department could lose the support of the public and the goodwill of the council. The next budget cycle begins soon, there is enormous financial pressure, and the department is requesting approval for a bond issue to expand its facilities. Does not the daily routine work of the department contribute far more to enhancing public health than this transient issue over a rock concert?

Your role within the city of Micro Health Department gives rise to these concerns. Loyalty to Harley, based on your esteem for him personally as well as on your professional esteem, has created a bond with him. The way he carries out his job provides a model that gives definition and integrity to your role as a member of the department. Another factor is trust in his good judgment and sense of proportion. Furthermore, you value the well-being of the people of Micro; your role is to protect and enhance their health. Also, the department has an instrumental value in serving that goal; its long-term effectiveness and continuity are important to you. As an administrator, you have learned to value the efficient operation of your unit. One aspect of your role is to seek more efficient ways of fulfilling your mission, particularly with the recent decreases in revenue. These are some of the values that constitute your internal code, or subjective responsibility, for your role inside the organization.

However, your role as a member of NPHA is influenced by a different cluster of values. Because you have been involved in that organization for about fourteen years and recently served as a member of the national executive board for four years, you are well known as an active leader within its ranks. You greatly value the respect and esteem of your NPHA colleagues. Because you were a member of the committee that developed the guidelines for these unusual large outdoors events and argued for their approval at the annual meeting, you are particularly concerned about how you will be perceived by the members of NPHA. Your professional integrity is at stake.

Also, you have taken unpopular positions on issues before the NPHA in the past and insisted that courage and commitment to high standards for the health of society are essential for public health professionals. There was the time a large fast food chain violated a number of generally accepted requirements for sanitary food handling. Some of your colleagues were reluctant to openly support a resolution calling for action against this company, for fear of political repercussions. You told them that an effective public administrator "can never bend to political pressure on things that count."

Now how will you look if you do not uphold the association's guidelines that you helped write? What if you give in to the pressure from the city council and there is an outbreak of botulism? Or influenza? Or some other contagious disease among five hundred thousand people? What if there is a riot and hundreds of people require emergency medical care in a remote area such as this?

Ripley dismissed such specters as the "fantasies of an all too fertile imagination." He pointed out repeatedly that this is a one-day event and asked rhetorically, "What is likely to happen in one lousy day?" But you now realize that it is not really a one-day event. The police department has estimated that it will take a full twenty-four hours just to park the cars for that many people. They indicate that you can expect arrivals during the three days before the concert, and hangers-on who will be around for a day or two after it formally concludes. That amounts to a five-day span during which concert goers will pose a public health concern for the city of Micro. You must provide for very large numbers of people for approximately three of the five days. A lot can happen in that amount of time.

If this thing blows up in your face and it gets into the press, will you ever be effective again in calling for progressive action by NPHA? You have always felt that it was important to be an agent for change within any organization, and you have especially valued that image of yourself in the association. What will happen to that image? Will anyone take your crusades seriously in the future? Will you?

Your role within NPHA has been shaped and defined by these values. Your colleagues in NPHA have come to expect you to behave in certain ways. They know you value your personal integrity and the respect it evokes. They think of you as one of the courageous administrators in the public health profession. Whenever the question of public health standards arises, they know they can count on you to push for the most. Similarly, they expect you to be one of those people in the association who is never willing to stay with the status quo just because "it has always been done that way"; they look to you to make the case for shaking things up and experimenting with new ideas, techniques, and procedures. The members of NPHA expect you to be this kind of person, but it is not they alone who have cast you in this role. You have cultivated these expectations. You have carved out this kind of role for yourself because you have wanted to be this kind of person. These are some of the elements that constitute your inner code, or subjective responsibility, for your role as a member of the NPHA.

This is an extreme case of tension between a role inside the public organization for which you work and an outside role—in this case, between two kinds of subjective responsibility. The values that shape and direct the enactment of each role are pulling you in two different directions, motivating you toward two mutually exclusive alternatives. You are confronted with one kind of ethical dilemma rooted in the roles we occupy. Let us now look at a case in which you experience the other common kind of role conflict.

Inside Roles Versus Inside Roles: "Raising Salaries or Raising Hell?"

The Rancor County sheriff's department is a large law enforcement agency with about three thousand sworn deputies. You are the lieutenant in charge of the research and planning unit (RPU); you were appointed to the position three months ago after two years of service within the organization. You previously have worked alongside four of the five deputies in the unit and know them well; in fact, you have often socialized with them. You do not know well the new woman who was just assigned to RPU as a replacement, nor are you well acquainted with the new civilian statistician whom you have just hired.

You are in the midst of your first salary review process as supervisor of the unit. All the supervisors meet with Assistant Sheriff Dutton, who is in charge of the personnel and training division. Dutton briefs the group on departmental procedure, the required forms, and the time schedule for completing the process. The department, along with all other departments in Rancor County, conducts merit reviews for step increases and promotions at the same time each year that the across-the-board cost-of-living increase is negotiated with the county board of supervisors. Dutton reminds you that your role in the process has to do only with the merit review. The cost-of-living raise will be discussed and negotiated by the sheriff and his staff; it is a given over which you have no control.

Someone asks Dutton what the across-the-board percentage is likely to be for the coming year; the department grapevine is beginning to float rumors about a low figure. He is evasive at first, but finally admits that it is likely to be lower than recent years—probably about 2 percent. Before the scattered mumbles can erupt into disorder, Dutton rushes on to explain.

Several members of the board of supervisors are running for reelection and are facing stiff opposition from a slate of "cut the fat out of government" candidates. They realize that any new tax measures adopted this year to fund the county budget would be extremely risky for their futures. After consultation with the county administrative officer, the board members have indicated they will not support across-the-board wage increases of more than 2 percent. Merit raises must come from department funds already budgeted for that purpose.

After hearing this, a captain from the juvenile division asks how the board can get away with only 2 percent when there is a clause in the county charter establishing pay levels for law enforcement and fire service employees comparable to those paid to the state troopers and other counties of similar size. The captain points out that a study conducted by the local unit of the Law Enforcement Professional Association (LEPA) concluded that 5 percent would be necessary to meet that charter requirement. Dutton's response is that statistics are easy to manipulate. He firmly suggests that all of you stay out of this matter and pay attention to your particular duties. When a lieutenant asks how to handle any complaints from the rank and file, Dutton reminds him that he is to support the sheriff and demonstrate loyalty to his position at all times. He terminates the discussion by saying, "Some of you are going to have to absorb a little flak over this, so be prepared to put some iron in your spines."

You leave the meeting feeling perplexed. There have already been several bull sessions around the RPU offices about the salary situation. You know the people on your staff are expecting more than 2 percent and have been expressing their feelings about the "gutless brass in this department," who they fear will not stand up to the politicians. Two of them have been members of LEPA for a year now; you know it is not a docile professional association but a militant police union. If the department gets stuck with a low percentage for salaries, LEPA will gain a few more recruits from your unit. You realize the sheriff pays attention to units in the department where LEPA is growing in power. He tends to view increases in union membership in a unit as a sign of weak or inept management.

The merit review process will not help this highly volatile situation. You recall your own feelings about the small 2 or 3 percent raises for good performance. When the blanket cost-of-living increase was decent, the merit raise evoked a feeling of satisfaction, even though it was not very large. However, it seemed to have the opposite effect when the basic increase was inadequate. You tended to resent something called a "merit increase" when in fact the total amount hardly met the rise in the cost of living. With only 2 percent across the board this time, you anticipate some bitter feelings from deputies in RPU who have a higher level of education than the median for the department and view themselves as generally underpaid.

You feel caught between your staff and the departmental hierarchy. Because you are new to the supervisory position, you are still establishing your credibility as an administrator. The members of RPU feel that you are one of them, but you have sensed a degree of benign suspicion about how long you will remain so. You are attempting to overcome those feelings while at the same time redefining your role. You do not want them to stop trusting you or feeling friendly with you, but your duties have changed. You want to be accepted as the supervisor of the unit, but you do not want to create a gulf between yourself and the staff.

Still, you need the trust and support of the sheriff and his staff. At the time of your promotion, Dutton expressed concern about your ability to meet the demands of the administrative role after having worked so closely with four of the five members of RPU. He feared that this might create problems for both you and the RPU staff. The sheriff had discussed this potential pitfall with you and encouraged you to pay attention to it. He had told you that he expected loyalty to the chain of command and had reminded you that as the supervisor of RPU, you would become a member of the management team, accountable for carrying out the policies of the department.

You are still being watched and sized up. You do want to support the sheriff. He is the boss, and his negotiations with the board of supervisors are too sensitive to tolerate dissension in the ranks. He will expect you to exercise your authority, as he will exercise his. You have to trust his judgment about what can be gained in the short run against the long-term future of the department. He is the only one with the information and position to deal with that kind of decision.

And yet you feel the need to let the department brass know how it looks from your vantage point. The county charter provision does seem to call for more than a 2 percent raise. If the raise is not larger, the department may wind up with far more members in a very tough union. Can you present these concerns without appearing to abandon your management responsibilities? Will this confirm the suspicion that you could not make the transition from rank and file to supervisor?

You feel caught because this salary issue could destroy your relationship with both your staff and the hierarchy of the department. This is not just a practical management problem. It is also an ethical dilemma involving a conflict between objective and subjective responsibilities. You are experiencing conflict between the subjective responsibility of your role as the supervisor of a unit on the one hand, and both the objective and subjective responsibilities of your role as a member of the sheriff's management team on the other. Each role evokes feelings of obligation rooted in sets of values (subjective responsibilities) that influence your behavior, and you are formally held accountable (objective responsibility) by the sheriff for fulfilling your obligation to stand behind his decisions.

If we examine your role as the supervisor of RPU, we see that you are viewed by your staff as their channel to the hierarchy. They expect you to take care of their interests and to look out for their needs. They cannot hold you formally accountable, but in a tight chain of command, such as in a law enforcement agency, the implicit bargain is acceptance of the hierarchy as the means for communicating with the organization in exchange for an acceptance of responsibility by the hierarchy for those below. The members of your unit see you as their spokesperson, their voice, to those above. They expect you to stand up for them when their interests are at stake. They project these expectations on you, and your role as supervisor within the unit is partially structured by them. You empathize readily with these expectations because you recall having shared them so recently.

A set of values emerges in response to these role demands. These values are internalizations of expectations. You find yourself valuing the loyalty and trust of your staff because both are necessary for your function as their spokesperson. If they do not feel bound to express their concerns to you, believing that you will not take them seriously, your role will be truncated. You will be severed from your subordinates. This creates pressure from your staff to value the narrow interests of the unit above those of the whole department. Loyalty to RPU means to them that you support their needs and preferences above those of others.

Furthermore, you value being perceived as a fair person by your staff, one who will hear them out and speak on their behalf in an honest, even-handed fashion. You also value credibility as a spokesperson. You want to be viewed as one who conveys their views accurately to those above. Another related value is integrity. Your staff expects you to behave with consistency and with some degree of independence and courage in dealing with management. Responsiveness is another value that you draw from their expectations. They not only want you to listen, but they also expect you to do something consistent with their wishes.

Those above you in the chain of command give primary definition to your other role as an administrator. In your capacity as a member of the management team, they expect you to communicate the wishes of top-level management to your staff. More important, they expect you to gain compliance from the members of your unit, and they hold you accountable for doing so (objective responsibility). Behind these expectations there are also values that you must internalize in order to conduct your managerial role (subjective responsibility). Cooperativeness, for example, is likely to be a significant value for this role. Those above you in the chain of command expect that you will generally go along with their decisions. In other words, they expect compliance from you in the same way that you expect it from your staff. In response to this expectation, you are likely to value being perceived as a cooperative person.

Primary identification with the management team is probably viewed as a necessary concomitant of cooperativeness. Cooperation is strengthened and enhanced when people internalize a belief in the importance of management solidarity. You are encouraged to see your interests as identical with those of the departmental hierarchy.

Maintenance of authority is, in all probability, another value associated with this role. Your ability to direct and, ultimately, to command is likely to be highly valued. Being cooperative and viewing yourself as a member of management will come to naught if you are unable to control the behavior of those in your unit. This requires the ability to exercise authority in its various manifestations. Comprehensiveness is another management value. You are expected to take into account the needs and interests of the entire organization, not just those of your unit alone. You learn to value the well-being of the whole rather than that of a part. You value the larger perspective of the organization and learn to place your unit's needs within that perspective.

The value subsystems associated with these two roles are not always in conflict. In fact, values such as trust, credibility, and responsiveness are generally viewed as necessary attributes of an effective manager by those above as well as those below in the hierarchy. However, in specific situations, such as this matter of salary increases, there may be conflict. In this case, you are torn between loyalty to staff and solidarity with management, between responsiveness to staff and the authority of management, between the interests of the RPU and the interests of the department as a whole. The impending conflict between employees and management creates tension between two of your organizational roles, which are structured around responsibility to one of these groups and responsibility for the other. You face the risk of neglecting one role for the sake of the other, or failing in an attempt to serve both.

The members of your unit will not be satisfied when you explain that the matter is out of your hands. They will want you to be loyal to them; they will appeal to your ability to identify with their point of view. Your staff will expect you to respond to their interests and stand up to the sheriff and Assistant Sheriff Dutton. They will want you to insist on more than a 2 percent raise. But it is clear that Dutton expects you to represent management and support the sheriff's position. He will expect you to exercise your authority in dealing with the dissension of your staff. Dutton will want you to defend the interests of the organization as a whole and not capitulate to the short-range immediate needs for a larger raise. Furthermore, he will evaluate your performance and your retention in the role of supervisor accordingly. He will quite specifically hold you accountable for maintaining that role.

We experience ethical dilemmas in ways portrayed in these two cases—as conflicts between the roles that present us with formal obligations (objective responsibilities) and the underlying values (subjective responsibilities) that tend to motivate us in incompatible directions. Barnard (1964) argues that these conflicts become more frequent as our array of inner codes, or subjective responsibilities, increases. The more of these codes we have to respond to, the more likely it is that situations will occur in which two of them pull us in different directions. Furthermore, he notes, we are likely to have more of these unwritten inner codes if we are associated with many organizations.

Another way of explaining the same phenomenon is to suggest that value subsystems emerge around our roles; therefore, the more roles we adopt, the more value subsystems we need to maintain. Because the multiplication of roles is inherent in modernity, so is the management of multiple value subsystems. According to Banton (1965), people in modern urban society are far more likely to experience conflicting inner codes than those who live in traditional settings.

This perspective is helpful in understanding Barnard's claim that executive positions involve a complex morality. It is the role complexity of high-level executive positions that leads to a complex interaction of often conflicting values. As we move up the organizational ladder, it becomes increasingly difficult to behave responsibly, to respond consistently and dependably to the multifarious demands of the many roles involved.

In the face of such conflicts, what do we do? Barnard (1964, pp. 271–272) suggests several possible consequences:

1. General moral deterioration as manifested in frustration and inability to make decisions
2. A diminution of the sense of responsibility demonstrated by a tendency to allow incidental or external pressures and chance determinants to make decisions for us
3. Withdrawal from active involvement in the arena of decision making, such as resignation, a leave of absence, or retirement
4. Development of an ability to avoid responsibility by steering clear of conflict situations that may require difficult decisions
5. Development of the ability to construct alternative measures that satisfy immediate desires or requirements without violating any codes

It is clear that Barnard prefers the fifth alternative. He believes that any of the others involves a neglect or sacrifice of one or more codes. This would amount not only to dereliction of duty but a degradation of character. A failure to respond positively to a role and its value subsystem would weaken both. Their power to determine behavior in the future therefore would be diminished. Behavior would become less consistent with espoused values, less dependable, less responsible. Because Barnard regards responsibility as essential to effective executive leadership, he views its erosion as a serious matter indeed.

Although Barnard does not dwell at length on how we acquire the ability to develop alternatives that do not violate any of our codes, it seems certain that he had in mind a quality called "moral creativity," something he experienced in himself and others but does not discuss in any detail. Moral creativeness is understandably difficult to explain or teach, but one of the assumptions of this book is that, like any other acquired skill, it can be cultivated as part of the design approach to administrative ethics. The thesis here is that moral creativity requires the following:

1. A clear understanding of the obtainable facts relevant to the situation
2. An understanding of the roles involved, including the codes, or value subsystems, that guide their enactment
3. A consideration of all possible alternatives
4. A projection of the consequences of each alternative, as imaginatively as possible, or how your role and the roles of others would be affected
5. An attempt to anticipate how you would feel about yourself if you adopted each alternative
6. A consideration of how you would justify each alternative to a broad public audience—on what moral rules and principles you would base a choice of each alternative and its consequences

As we pursue this reflective process involving moral imagination, sometimes it is possible to conceive of ways of inventing what Barnard (1964, p. 279) calls a "moral basis for the solution of moral conflicts." This may involve redefining the values that govern a role's enactment; it may call for renegotiating the expectations and obligations that give it structure; or it may necessitate "a bargaining process which decides how much attention" will be given to any one role (Banton, 1965, p. 209). In short, it requires thinking about how one designs or redesigns roles, relationships among roles, and organizational structures and cultures—all within given constraints and opportunities.

For example, in the case of the city of Micro and the rock concert, you might decide to adopt a more flexible attitude that would permit you to negotiate arrangements that are as close to NPHA guidelines as possible. One of the conditions for such flexibility might be a formal written agreement with the city council that would phase in the NPHA standards through a series of city ordinances during the following two years. Because there is no such legislation at present, this would be a chance to initiate it. Also, the council would be given enough advance notice about the requirements to determine whether to continue holding such events in the future.

Using this strategy, you would not subvert your role as a progressive public health professional, but neither would you maintain a position that would jeopardize your role with the Micro municipal health department. You would have an opportunity to test the effectiveness and practicality of NPHA's guidelines, which you might consider writing up for the association's journal. You might be able to recommend changes that would improve the association's guidelines and offer suggestions about the politics of implementing them. A critical case study of your own efforts would be a way of maintaining your bargain with NPHA.

In the Rancor County sheriff's department case, you might need to take this opportunity to define your role further—for your staff, your superiors, and yourself. Meeting with your staff to clarify the limits of your role as their representative to the hierarchy might be in order. Perhaps you would want to assure them of your willingness to go to bat for them in situations where you believe they had a legitimate case and when you had a chance to influence decisions on their behalf. You may want to be sure that they understand, however, that you had no intention of going down in flames over battles you could not win. The 2 percent salary increment for the cost-of-living raise appears to be one of those instances. In dealing with your staff in this way, you reinforce your role with them and add to it the necessity for some degree of autonomy in dealing with the hierarchy.

As to the department, you may want to prepare a well-thought-out memorandum assuring the sheriff and Assistant Sheriff Dutton of your loyalty but suggesting a broader definition of loyal behavior. You might indicate that your understanding of loyalty includes the obligation to inform your superiors of the impact of certain decisions. You might feel obligated to express your concern about the effects of a small raise on the unionization of the department. You might also include your own analysis of the LEPA study of the comparable salaries included in the county charter provision.

The kinds of responses suggested here are attempts to rationally and actively maintain responsible conduct in conflicting role situations. They seek to confirm and preserve the values associated with these roles. Sometimes you will be successful, and at other times you will fail miserably, but being aware of the dynamics involved and dealing with them intentionally and systematically is likely to enhance your overall administrative responsibility.

It is difficult enough to manage your own role conflicts in this way, but the administrative role often calls for more. Barnard (1964, p. 279) observed that those with executive positions are expected to assist others with their ethical dilemmas. Borrowing language from jurisprudence, he described this as the "judicial function," "the appellate function," or "handling the exceptional cases." One of the tasks of management is this "inventing of a moral basis for the solution of moral conflicts."

When one of your subordinates is faced with a decision that seems right from one perspective but wrong from another, you should take the matter with the utmost seriousness instead of dismissing his or her concern as only a moral issue that is irrelevant to the business at hand. The employee wants to maintain congruence between values and conduct—to maintain a high level of responsibility. That impulse should be reinforced. Help the person clarify the objective conditions, and seek alternative courses of action. You may even need to redefine the code to account for special circumstances. According to Barnard (1964) this creative judicial function is the "highest exemplification of responsibility" and "the essence of leadership." He explains:

It is the highest test of executive responsibility because it requires for successful accomplishment that element of "conviction" that means identification of personal codes and organization codes in the view of the leader. This is the coalescence that carries "conviction" to the personnel of organization, to that informal organization underlying all formal organization that senses nothing more quickly than insincerity. Without it all organization is dying, because it is the indispensable element in creating that desire for adherence—for which no incentive is a substitute—on the part of those whose efforts willingly contributed constitute organization [pp. 281–282].

Dealing with these conflicting role demands and the values associated with them is a matter of ethics that, if not justified by our philosophical or religious views, is most certainly essential to maintaining an effective organization. Orders, edicts, rewards, human relations training, and organizational development strategies are not likely to accomplish much if we do not encourage and systematically develop responsibility by addressing ethical dilemmas that arise from role conflicts. It is unfortunate but true that many members of public organizations have never learned to understand these conflicts and cope with them effectively, whereas others have become so inured to the pressure to be practical and political that they no longer think about these experiences very seriously.

Conflicts of Interest

Another way we experience conflicts in responsibility involves situations where our own personal interests are at odds with our obligations as a public official or our professional values. There may be combinations of conflicting roles and tensions between sources of authority, but more typically these occasions simply present us with an opportunity to use our public office for the sake of our private gain or to the private gain of our friends or relatives. They represent conflicts between the public role and self-interest, and between objective responsibility and the possibility of personal gain or advantage.

As we shall see in more detail later, here we are dealing with something broader than the legal definition of conflict of interest.

In this sense "interest" includes, as Michael Davis (1982, p. 23) suggests, "all those influences, loyalties, concerns, emotions, or the like" that can make competent judgment "less reliable than it might otherwise be." Conflicts of interest involve collisions between these various kinds of influences and the interests of the public we serve.

The ethical problem presented by these conflicts is that our fiduciary role as trustees of the public interest may be jeopardized by a loss of trust in our professional judgment. If some private personal interest is able to influence our reason and conduct, we may serve it rather than the interests of the citizenry, or at least we may be perceived as doing so. Our judgment may be impaired in this way or may appear to be; either will call into question our trustworthiness as representatives of the public interest.

Tussman (1960, p. 17) locates the roots of these conflicts in the Western "spirit of individualism." With the emergence of the individual as the locus of political and social rights and obligations comes a tendency to see him "chiefly as a complex of values, desires, drives, or interests" (p. 17). Given this perspective, it seems quite natural for individuals to pursue their own interests. Satisfying personal desires and enhancing one's own life are viewed as legitimate forms of conduct. Tussman points out that acknowledging the right to behave in this way is generally what we mean by the phrase "respect for the individual."

Nevertheless, as Tussman hastens to observe, we do seek to impose duties to serve the collective interest of the public on these legitimately self-seeking individuals. Certain individuals assume extensive duties as public agents on behalf of the citizenry, generally as employees (elected or appointed) of a public jurisdiction. However, the role of citizen is the most universal form of this collective obligation. Citizenship requires all self-interested individuals who are members of the polity to act, in their public role, on behalf of the public good.

These claims of the collectivity on the individual are acknowledged, but with reluctance and ambivalence. Our Western liberal heritage causes us to view any constraints on individual self-realization with suspicion and uneasiness. Nevertheless, the fact that we do ultimately support these public claims is "evidenced by the indignation we feel when a public trust is betrayed by self-interest. The public agent," asserts Tussman, "is expected to do his duty" (1960, p. 18).

In the problem of conflicts of interests, we are, at base, confronting this "inescapable tension between interest and duty, between the inclinations of the private life and the obligations of the public role" (Tussman, 1960, p. 18). This tension is inescapable, not only because individualism dominates in the Western world but also because it is inherent in the structure and dynamics of modern society. Modernization places this exalted individual into a network of complex interrelationships and interdependencies that constantly impose collective demands. Urban industrial society thus intensifies the tension that Tussman identifies, and postmodern conditions erode any clear normative foundations to which one might turn for help in finding resolution. It is not surprising, then, that people employed as public servants, particularly those with elected and administrative roles, experience frequent tension between public and private interests and quandaries over how to manage them.

Dorothy Emmet (1967) helps us focus on the particular problem for public administrators by noting the discrepancy between two dimensions of modern complex organizations. She contends that an organization must be viewed as both "a community with a common purpose" and "a field within which people hope to have a career" (p. 196). In our case, public organizations are not only collectivities established to serve some public interest, but also the arenas within which individuals attempt to realize their self-interests through the development of careers. If this is so, the pluralistic nature of modern society, and the assertiveness of this diversity instigated by postmodern conditions, suggests immediately that conflicts will emerge between individual interests and organizational interests.

Presumably the way this tension is resolved depends to a great extent on the relative values attributed to the private and public spheres of our lives. Richard Sennett (1974) has concluded that the trend over the past two hundred years has been toward devaluing the public sphere for the sake of cultivating the private. He argues that a narcissistic preoccupation with inner feelings as the basis for personal identity in modern society has led us to believe that the impersonal world of public affairs is of secondary importance. If he is correct, we should not be surprised to find a tendency to resolve the tension in favor of personal private interests.

Small (1976), in his survey of the problem of conflict of interest in American government, produced findings that support the conclusion that this tendency has been on the increase in modern society. He writes: "Increasingly, then, in the late Twentieth Century it becomes more and more difficult to separate the simplistic, completely personal interest from the public interest. Because these interests are overlapping and no longer separable, older norms of right and wrong, desirable or undesirable are inadequate" (p. 554). He concludes that it is "part of the human condition" to seek money and power from public sources for the sake of private gain.

If this kind of conduct can be attributed to the human condition, it may be because the public sphere of life has come to be no different from any other common property resource. If the affairs of government and the common resources of the citizenry are, as Sennett (1974) suggests, viewed as having lesser importance than private individual interests, then it seems quite likely that they will be exploited. Garrett Hardin's analysis (1977) of the "tragedy of the commons," in an article by that title, may help us to understand why this occurs.

Hardin asks us to imagine a pasture that is open to all the village herdsmen for grazing livestock. Each herdsman quite rationally seeks to maximize his gain; this is the logical consequence of individualism. In attempting to acquire the greatest benefit for himself, the herdsman considers, more or less consciously, what the utility would be of adding one more animal to his herd. Hardin notes that this utility has two components, one positive and one negative. The positive component is a function of adding one more animal; he receives all the proceeds from the sale of this additional animal. The negative component is a function of the overgrazing created by the additional animal. However, since the effects of this overgrazing are borne by all the herdsmen, the negative utility for the herdsman is only a fraction.

The result is that when these positive and negative partial utilities are added together, there is a clear net gain, and "the rational herdsman concludes that the only sensible course for him to

pursue is to add another animal to his herd. And another . . . "
(Hardin, 1977, p. 20). The problem, of course, is that every other
herdsman is drawing the same conclusion. Each one feels compelled to increase his herd without limit until the pasture is over-
grazed to the point of being useless for all. Hardin observes from
this scenario that "ruin is the destination toward which all men
rush, each pursuing his own best interest in a society that believes
in the freedom of the commons. Freedom in a commons brings
ruin to all" (p. 20).

It may be that the public sphere is a "commons" subject to this
kind of abuse. It may have become so secondary to the pursuit of
individual interests that we are constantly tempted to "overgraze"
it. In the short run, we seem to experience personal gain by resolving conflicts between private and public interest in favor of ourselves. However, the long-term result of that course of conduct by
millions of individual citizens and citizen–public servants, each
seeking to maximize personal gain, is the ruination of that commons we call government.

Conflict of interest therefore can be an insidiously difficult
problem, especially for public administrators. Citizens in public
administrative positions have special access to the governmental
commons that most ordinary citizens do not. This access presents
unusual opportunities, and therefore temptations, to exploit governmental resources for personal gain. Furthermore, administrative responsibilities often include the obligation of supervising,
coordinating, and monitoring the conduct of others who are confronted with similar opportunities and temptations. As fiduciaries
of the public interest, public administrators are responsible not
only for managing their own conflicts of interests, but to some
extent those of peers, subordinates, superiors, and private citizens
as well.

With this conceptual background in mind, let us turn to some
specific definitions and types of conflict of interest. An extensive
study conducted by the Association of the Bar of the City of New
York (1960) reflects the apparent tendency of those concerned
with the legality of conduct to opt for narrow definitions of conflict of interest. After identifying a continuum of situations, ranging from bribery at one end to policy conflicts at the other, this

report limits its concern to conflicts between officials' duties and their personal economic interests. Consequently, bribery, which involves overt payment to influence official action, is identified as the clearest instance of conflict of interest. At the other extreme, differences over public policy, which might be attributable to past or present affiliations, are ruled out of consideration as being too removed from economic interest. This definitional constraint is found also in Lieberman's approach. He identifies "the conflict between a Government employee's official responsibility and his private economic interests" as the generally accepted conflict of interest in public affairs (1973, p. 206).

The strict definitions in these legal approaches seem, reasonably enough, to grow out of a concern for the most effective legislative remedies. It seems likely that the contribution of the New York study to the passage of the Federal Conflict of Interest Statute of 1962 was due, in large part, to its narrow legal orientation. However, the bar committee report justified its limitation to economic interests on three grounds: "The simplest reason is that it is better to control whatever fraction of improper behavior is attributable to economic motives than to control none. The second reason is that regulatory schemes have to be administered. Restrictions on outside economic affiliations can be written with reasonable particularity and enforced with moderate predictability; no one has yet devised a method for sorting out acquaintances, friends, relations, and lovers for purposes of a rule of permitting official dealings with some and not others" (Association of the Bar of the City of New York, 1960, pp. 17–18). The final reason is that the bar committee conducting the study believed that the major concern of the public is with the economic corruption of government. Because, in its view, public confidence is a primary consideration in the conflict-of-interest problem, economic matters should be the center of attention.

Since the New York bar report, the debate has continued over broader and narrower definitions of conflict of interest. Some understand it quite broadly to involve role conflicts (Margolis, 1979). Others prefer to view it as a conflict between one kind of role—those with fiduciary responsibility for acting on behalf of someone else's interests—and a broad range of personal interests: material, psychological, and moral (Davis, 1982). Still others continue to argue for a restricted definition consistent with legal provisions. They focus on conflicts between the fiduciary role and personal material interests, usually financial (Luebke, 1986).

This strictly delimited scope may be quite appropriate for those whose chief concern is with the most socially manageable types of conflict of interest and who therefore need to focus on economic interests as the most treatable by legislation. However, an examination of the ethics of conflicting interests must necessarily proceed from a broader perspective. Our concern is with the principled systematic and rational exercise of administrative responsibility. Thus, we must take into account in our ethical reckoning the full range of human interests, which may not be controllable by law but nevertheless influences conduct. Economic interest is only one, however powerful, kind of interest. Other significant interests include affection, social status, power, social relatedness, predictability, personal well-being, the well-being of some others, and recognition.

Actions proscribed by law certainly fall within our purview, but our boundaries must be more inclusive. This is because the law may be understood as only a moral minimum established by society based on widely accepted standards of conduct. Ethical considerations go beyond these minimum standards to examine acts that may be acceptable under the law but may not measure up to certain ethical norms and principles. Just because an act is legal does not necessarily make it ethical. Using terms like *nigger, broad,* or *fag* may be legal, but uttering them may provoke the moral censure of society because they are understood as demeaning the dignity of other human beings. Granting some people greater access to administrative decision makers than others may not be illegal, but may well be judged unfair by the citizenry of a community.

Furthermore, in some situations, we may challenge the legitimacy of the law on ethical grounds as not meeting the minimal moral standards of a society. This may lead to civil disobedience and the generation of test cases, as occurred during the civil rights movement of the 1960s and the women's rights and environmental movements of the 1970s and 1980s. Reform movements of these kinds, if successful in achieving broad public support, are able to establish new and higher minimum standards for conduct, although they still do not preempt ethical considerations.

Thus, although much attention about conflicts of interest is focused on economic interest and legal remedies, it is important to remember that there are other important dimensions of this kind of conflict of responsibility. Ethics legislation tends to preempt ethical reflection, as Foster (1981) has noted. Once the moral judgment of the community has been crystallized in the form of law, we tend to narrow our consideration to the question of whether some course of action is legal. Legality becomes our fixation, and whether it is ethical tends to be forgotten or devalued. It is essential that we resist that tendency. Conflicts of interest are broader than economic ones and require ethical assessment as well as legal regulation.

Some analyses of conflict of interest do adopt a more general definition or use one similar to the New York bar, but construe "economic interests" in a broader fashion. For example, Beard and Horn (1975) use the New York bar definition but then identify five types of conduct, some of which exceed the boundaries of the bar study.

A report prepared by Kenneth Kernaghan (1975) for the Institute of Public Administration of Canada seems to offer a definition that is broad enough for our purposes: "Conflict of interest may be defined as a situation in which a public employee has a private or personal interest sufficient to influence or appear to influence the objective exercise of his official duties" (p. 13). Personal interest includes more than economic matters. Kernaghan then identifies seven situations that fall within this definition: influence peddling, financial transactions, outside employment, future employment, dealings with relatives, gifts and entertainment, and bribery. To complete the array of conflict of interest types, we should add an eighth situation borrowed from Beard and Horn: information peddling.

Bribery

This is the illegal acceptance of money or other valuable considerations in exchange for special favors from public servants having to do with their official duties. The critical condition here is that the bribe giver clearly intends to distort the objective, even-handed conduct of the official, and the receiver intends to willingly comply. Thus, the official, faced with personal interests, pecuniary or otherwise, in conflict with the laws, policies, and procedures for the conduct of his office, is induced to resolve it in favor of himself. Although bribery usually involves money, it may include other rewards, such as sexual favors, promises of favorable publicity, or offers of access to exclusive social circles.

Influence Peddling

This is when a public employee attempts to influence a governmental decision in favor of a third party in which the employee has an interest. Understood in typical legal terms, this might include such cases as policy decisions regulating a business in which the employee holds shares, developing a general plan affecting the value of land owned by the employee, or approving a federal grant to a local school district where his children attend school. This becomes an actual conflict-of-interest situation whenever the employee stands a high chance of significant gain.

Beyond the economic motivations for influence peddling we might include such interests as religious beliefs or racial ideologies. For example, a public administrator whose religion strongly opposed contraception or abortion might use his insider influence to restrict funding for family planning services or subsidized abortion clinics. A public administrator affiliated with a white supremacy organization might use her influence to derail equal employment opportunity legislation.

Information Peddling

Officials who are privy to information not available to the general public and use it to their own advantage, monetary or otherwise, are guilty of this. The key factors are the power of the information and privileged access to it. Actual conflict of interest is present when the information is highly confidential and the official in question is responsible for maintaining the confidence.

Suppose a city planner had information about proposed redevelopment plans for an area where a friend's home was located. He was not a member of the planning team for that area but had access to the changes being considered. As an employee of the city planning department, he was obliged to maintain confidentiality about the plan until it was publicly disclosed to the entire community. However, the friend had offered money in exchange for advance information. If the planner had accepted the money, that would have been information peddling.

Financial Transactions

These become conflicts when a public servant has direct or indirect financial interests that directly conflict with the responsible performance of the job. Actual conflict of interest is present to the extent that an official is in direct personal control over a decision that will produce significant personal gain. This differs from influence peddling in that the official in question effectively controls the outcome—for example, a planning director who could influence the location of a new airport near undeveloped land that he owned.

Gifts and Entertainment

Seeking or accepting gifts and hospitality creates a conflict if they influence a public employee's impartial discharge of his or her duties. This category simply amounts to a broadening of our understanding of bribery. It includes such things as discounts on purchases, theater tickets, sex, vacation trips, use of vehicles, lavish meals, recreational equipment, and liquor. Typically gifts of this kind are given with no specific favors requested, as would be the case with bribery, but they nevertheless are intended to create a generally positive predisposition toward the donor.

Outside Employment

Part-time employment, consulting, contractual retainers, and self-employment may cause a conflict of interest with official duties. Conflict situations include the use of public employment status to enhance a private employer (or oneself), the draining away of effort and energy required for official duties, and the use of government services and equipment in outside work.

Being employed outside does not necessarily create a conflict of interest; the type of employment and the magnitude of the commitment are both critical factors. A captain in the fire department might very well spend a few hours a week at home painting land-scapes and selling them without any conflict of interest. However, if he worked with a private consulting group as an expert in fire-fighting, with his official status prominently advertised, a definite conflict would exist. His private consulting activities would profit from his status as a captain in a fire department. Or if his painting became such an obsessive preoccupation that he neglected his official duties, a conflict would also exist.

Future Employment

If a public employee intends to seek employment in the future with a firm he or she now transacts official business with, the tendency may be to give favored treatment to this prospective employer in hopes of encouraging a job offer. Also, the government employee may present his inside contacts and knowledge of agency proce-dure as an attractive package for a firm that does regular business with that public organization. The widespread "in-and-out" or "revolving door" syndrome, particularly problematic in the defense industries, creates some of the most serious conflicts (Beard, 1978). As people move back and forth between public and private sector service, intertwined interests resulting from past work and future employment expectations can become extremely complex.

Dealings with Relatives

Situations in which a public administrator may be in a position to do favors for a relative can also create conflict. We might think of this form of conflict of interest, sometimes called nepotism, as a special class of influence peddling because the motivation is simi-lar to other such cases just discussed. Essentially it involves using influence to gain preferential treatment in hiring, promoting, awarding contracts, or other business practices in which a relative will benefit. The public administrator who engages in such prac-tices gains not directly but indirectly, by reinforcing family bonds and mutual support.

This kind of conflict of interest might well be rooted in noneconomic interests. A case similar to the information-peddling example was presented by a planner in an urban redevelopment agency, except in her case it was her aging parents' home that was affected. As a member of the planning group, she discovered at an early stage that their home was to be replaced with commercial development. It was not fear of financial loss that worried her, but the disturbance in continuity and stability of their lives. Their home, which they loved and from which they derived a great sense of security, would be bought by right of eminent domain and demolished if the plan were adopted. Her affection for her parents and concern for their well-being, deep and powerful human interests, were in conflict with her obligations as a public servant for objectivity and equal treatment of all residents. She felt strongly inclined to encourage her fellow planners in the department to change the plan to exempt her parents' home.

Maintaining the Public Trust

Each of these situational types represents a potential conflict of interest. Whether it becomes an actual conflict depends on the extent to which a public servant yields to the temptation. However, as the New York Bar Association report strongly emphasized, being in a potential conflict-of-interest situation is almost as serious as an actual conflict. Because maintaining the public trust is a crucial aspect of administrative responsibility, the appearance of conflict of interest may be sufficient to jeopardize faith in the integrity of government.

The implication of this risk from only the appearances of evil is well summarized by a report of the National Academy of Public Administration after Watergate. The academy observed that many of the officials involved did not understand that "their obligations to the public as a whole entail an additional and more rigorous set of standards and constraints associated with the concept of public trust. Many practices which are permissible, even normal, in the private sector are, or should be, forbidden in government" (Small, 1976, p. 561). As we face situations that are ethically problematic, we must consider possible public perceptions of our actions as well as the acts themselves. The reflective process of imagining alternatives, projecting the consequences of each, considering the justification for our conduct, and attempting to anticipate how we will feel about ourselves in retrospect is particularly demanding in these cases. It is also necessary to imagine whether objectively honorable behavior is likely to be perceived otherwise.

The mentality that public servants need to cultivate as a guide to this reflection is one that counterbalances the tendencies toward an overweening individualism inherent in Western culture. Weisband and Franck (1975, pp. 187–188) argue that what is required is a "higher consciousness of one's wider responsibility," which is "the apex of personal maturity" and essential "to the collective survival of an interdependent world." They refer to the work of Lawrence Kohlberg, which indicates that the highest stage of moral development "comes when life decisions and actions are rooted in an autonomous, principled judgment of right and wrong, in full consciousness of responsibility to the larger social community." This perspective is based on an assumption that the long-term interests of the governmental commons are our interests as well.

Conclusion

In this chapter, we have examined three types of conflict of responsibility, all of which involve problems of defining subjective or objective responsibility, or both. This typology is not intended to suggest that there are any inherent or fundamental differences in the way an administrator handles these situations. The reflective process outlined in Chapter Two is appropriately used as a guide to resolving quandaries arising from all these types of conflict.

Rather, the typology is presented to assist in the descriptive task discussed in Chapter Two. This entails identifying and understanding the key characteristics of the problems presented by each type of conflict. Thus the typology helps focus attention on the particular others, and our relationships with them, that must be managed if we are to maintain responsible conduct of our public office.

With conflicts of authority, we confront clashes between two different definitions of our objective responsibility presented by two inconsistent sources of authority. These are situations, such as in "The Major, the Captain, and Corporal Montague," where we face serious consequences for ourselves and the organization, but they are episodic in nature. They do not involve a need to redefine our role for all future situations. The task is to act responsibly in the specific instance, recognizing that it is not typical of the routine performance of our role.

To determine whether to respond to one and resist the other authority, or resist both, we need to clarify our own subjective responsibility to know where we stand in responding to the competing authorities. Thus, examining our professional values and ethical principles becomes the prominent consideration in the reflective process here.

In dealing with role conflicts, we face the need to examine and redefine our roles within the employing organization, as in the Rancor County sheriff's department case, or one role inside and another outside the department, as in the case of "Politics and Toilets." These are not instances of such intense conflict that we feel pushed into a crisis over our relationship with the organization and the work role, such as we will consider in Chapter Eight. However, they are sufficiently serious and with sufficient implications for routine performance to require role clarification and adjustment. These may involve conflicts of subjective responsibility with ongoing future consequences when the key authority (the boss) is supportive and not imposing a particular course of action, as in "Politics and Toilets." Or they may represent conflicts of subjective and objective responsibility in which the authority (the boss) is imposing an objective responsibility that conflicts with your subjective responsibility. However, in either case, we confront the need to review, clarify, and redefine our roles, not only for the specific situation but also for the future.

In conflicts of interest, we must deal with legal as well as ethical considerations. As this particular form of conflict of responsibility has received the major attention of ethics legislators, we need to be cognizant of any laws that apply to the situation at hand. However, that should not take the place of ethical reflection. Usually the law is an adequate guide to the considered ethical judgment of the political community in which we function; it may represent a moral minimum that is sufficient for resolving the immediate quandary. However, to prevent legal thinking from displacing ethical reflection, we must examine how our personal interests weigh in relation to the objective obligations we bear as public servants.

In thinking about possible personal gain from our public service roles, it is crucial that we avoid even appearances of conflict of interest. Public trust in our fiduciary judgment requires not only that we be free of conflicts but that we also appear to be free. The most typical ways of avoiding a conflict, or dealing with the existence of one, are withdrawing from handling a decision, disclosing assets and relationships, or divesting ourselves of them. Even if there is no legal requirement to take these actions, we may feel compelled to do so on ethical grounds.

Up to this point, we have dealt with public administrative ethics from the perspective of the individual practitioner confronted with ethical dilemmas of various types in the course of making administrative decisions. In the next three chapters, we shift to the perspective of the organizational setting. Chapter Six focuses on administrative ethics from the viewpoint of the manager and addresses the problem of maintaining responsible conduct within a public organization. The central question addressed is, "How do I as a manager keep the members of my organization from engaging in unethical conduct?"

Part Two

Ethics in the Organization

Maintaining Responsible Conduct in Public Organizations
Two Approaches

How can a manager of a public organization maintain the responsible conduct of the public's business by subordinates faced with the array of possible conflicts discussed in the previous chapter? That is a crucial question and must be answered by both individual managers and organizational policies. The reflective process outlined in Chapter Two provides a way of dealing with ethical conflicts concerning individual responsibility. Also, most of the material in Chapters Three and Four has been developed from an individual perspective. However, the organizational management and policy dimensions must not be neglected. While we are attempting to help individual public administrators cultivate an awareness of ethical dilemmas, develop ways of conceptualizing them, and practice ways of thinking about their resolution, we must consider also the larger organizational arena within which this reflection occurs. Designing and managing an organizational environment that is supportive of ethical conduct is a central ethical obligation of managers, one that becomes increasingly important with movement up the organizational hierarchy.

The idea of "managing" organizational ethics seems to have first appeared in an article by James Bowman in 1981 entitled, "Ethical Issues for the Public Manager." He suggested that establishing a code of ethics for an organization is an act of ethics management. Since Bowman's essay, a number of other authors have addressed the management of ethics in organizations (Berman and West, 1997; Berman, West, and Cava, 1994). Don Menzel's comprehensive review of approaches to the management of ethics in public organizations concludes that the literature on this subject "strongly suggests that managers should take a systemic and comprehensive approach toward building ethical organizations" (2001, p. 364).

Implied in the idea of managing the ethics of an organization is the existence of a plan or design. Earlier I indicated that a design approach to administrative ethics is the central theme of this book. Being able to manage to some extent the ethics of an organization's structure and culture requires one to think like a designer, which means looking carefully and systematically at the givens of a specific organization and understanding its ultimate constraints, perhaps rooted in law or mission or history. It also suggests the need to think creatively about how one can work with and around those constraints to find the leverage points for change, the opportunities presented by events—even crises—and those within the organization who function as role models and standard setters. We will come back to this with an illustrative application later. Suffice it to say at this point that designing an organizational environment that is both supportive of expected ethical conduct and preserves space for ethical autonomy is what an administrator ought to see as the goal.

Conflicts of responsibility that people experience within public organizations should not be resolved in an idiosyncratic fashion. If public administrators are to be responsive to the wishes of a democratic citizenry, their general course of conduct toward serving the public interest must be guided by established policies that should enforce and reinforce prescribed public service values. That is, they should support the basic principles of the particular polity involved and oppose the tendencies of individuals and organizations to become self-serving.

There must be limits to loyalty and conformity to particular organizational hierarchies, and these will be dealt with in Chapter Eight. However, it seems reasonable to expect someone who accepts employment in a public fiduciary role to act generally in accordance with the values of the citizenry, as expressed through a political system and direct citizen participation. Otherwise, democratic government would be subverted by an aggregation of individuals employed by the public but functioning only according to their personal individual values. In a democracy, the public has a right to expect some consistency and predictability in the actions of its employees. It is entitled to a public service that can be held accountable for carrying out the designated mission. It should be able to expect its administrative corps to conduct itself in accordance with the explicit and implicit role obligations of a position.

Internal and External Controls

There are two general approaches to maintaining responsible conduct within public organizations: internal and external controls. The typical American response to the discovery of breaches of ethical conduct is to adopt new legislation, make new rules, or issue new regulations. And perhaps the second common recourse is to rearrange the organizational structure or create new organizations to establish more careful monitoring. Both approaches are forms of external control—attempts to impose on the conduct of individual public servants constraints that originate from outside themselves.

For example, after Watergate, President Jimmy Carter urged, and Congress subsequently adopted, an ethics legislation package—the 1978 Ethics in Government Act. It set out new and more stringent rules about disclosure of income and employment practices following federal government service. It also established the first U.S. Office of Government Ethics to implement these new strictures. Similarly, President George H. W. Bush, after scandals during the Reagan administration, called for certain amendments to the 1978 act that extend and strengthen its controls. These were adopted by Congress as the Government Ethics Reform Act of 1989 and remain intact, with no major legislative changes since that time. The primary focus of these acts is the prevention of conflicts of interest in the executive branch of the federal government. The U.S. Office of Government Ethics is the primary enforcement agency in implementing the rules and regulations pursuant to the legislation. External controls of these kinds assume that individual judgment and professional standards cannot be counted on to maintain ethical conduct.

Still, we sometimes, although less often, witness a different response to ethics scandals: an attempt to cultivate and strengthen the professional values and standards of people in public service through training and professional socialization. For example, a treatment of professional values and ethical decision making is being included in an increasing number of criminal justice systems' preservice and in-service training programs. Police academies are including units on ethical standards and ethical problem solving, and command training programs are devoting blocks of time to the ethical dimensions of leadership. Professional associations related to public service are placing ethics discussions on the agendas of their national and local meetings. The annual conference of the American Society for Public Administration (ASPA) typically offers an array of panel discussions dealing with ethics in public service and frequently presents preconference workshops on administrative ethics. ASPA conducted its first national conference on government ethics in November 1989. In 1997, the Section on Ethics was organized by Don Menzel and James Bowman and established within ASPA. It has now become one of the largest and most active units within that national association, sponsoring a scholarly journal, *Public Integrity,* holding conferences, organizing resources available on its Web site, and engaging in ongoing discussion through its Internet listserv, ethtalk@aspaonline.org. (See http://www.aspaonline.org/ethicscommunity for further information.)

All of these efforts are attempts to develop internal controls through training, education, formal and informal exchange of ideas, and scholarly research as means to maintain ethical conduct in public organizations. These controls are internal in that they consist of values, beliefs, concepts, knowledge, and ethical standards cultivated within each public servant and are intended to encourage ethical conduct in the absence of rules and monitoring systems. They reflect to a greater or lesser extent the evolving consensus among others in the field, but take root inside each participating individual.

These two policy perspectives—internal and external controls—are often associated historically with Carl Friedrich and Herman Finer, but the fundamental viewpoints advanced during the 1930s in the debate between these men are very much alive today among both practitioners and scholars. Friedrich asserted the importance of internal controls; Finer insisted on the essential nature of external political and institutional controls. Subsequently advocates of the New Public Administration in the 1970s (see the later discussion in this chapter) tended to support an approach like Friedrich's, while others such as Victor Thompson opted for a position more like Finer's. The numerous people who focus on creating and administering compliance-based ethics regulations and ethics legislation in ethics agencies at all levels of government also reflect his perspective.

It should be clear at the outset that seldom is this argument, in its serious forms, developed dichotomously, as though a final triumph of one or two antithetical approaches were at stake. When pressed, most participants in this debate will acknowledge that it is not a matter of resorting exclusively to one or the other. Usually advocates will admit that the critical issue is one of emphasis. As we confront problems of behavior that are not consistent with the mandates of the citizenry, the question is usually whether we should pay more attention to passing laws, improving management controls, and tightening performance evaluation procedures or be more concerned with counseling, education, training, and the professional socialization process. This is a problem of designing and managing an environment conducive to consistent ethical conduct.

Nevertheless, in spite of such qualifications, differences in emphasis do tend to move to the forefront in the heat of debate and sometimes begin to sound absolute: those on one side seem ready to dismiss legislation, rules, sanctions, and hierarchies as devoid of merit; others seem to be proposing that administrators be dealt with as robots whose inner controls are useless or unreliable. Drawing battle lines in this sharp, unyielding fashion may be interesting as a scholarly exercise to force proponents to test the validity of definitions, concepts, and supporting evidence, but the realities of life in public organizations force us beyond dichotomies. The real issue is almost always how these two approaches can best be integrated into a design that will achieve the most responsible conduct within the given constraints of time, effort, and human nature. But first it may be helpful to delineate the two perspectives.

"Much Ado About Something"

The department of education of a populous state in the heartland of the nation has come under severe public criticism. For several years, stories have cropped up in the news from time to time suggesting that all is not well in the organization. A few months ago, the state chapter of the association of parents passed a resolution harshly criticizing the superintendent of instruction for his poor management of the department. After several members of the state board of education followed suit, he resigned. A new superintendent has just been hired, but Grassroots, the largest public interest advocacy group in the state, has issued a scathing report entitled "Much Ado About Something: Maladministration in the State Department of Education."

Grassroots charges that the agency has become "a playpen" for the middle- and upper-level administrators, to the neglect of the educational mission for which it was established and for which it is funded "with millions of taxpayers' dollars every year." The Grassroots investigation turned up numerous cases of administrators in the department engaged in questionable activities:

- Two unit supervisors have been receiving substantial profits from royalties generated by textbooks they had authored and then recommended for statewide adoption. In each case, coauthors not employed by the agency had taken the visible lead in proposing the adoption of the texts and appearing before the board.
- One of the personnel administrators is living with the president of a teachers' union local.
- The associate director for curriculum development is involved in extensive consulting for companies supplying educational materials and equipment.
- A new school is being constructed, with state assistance, adjacent to a proposed residential development in which the director of facilities planning holds a significant share. The new school will reduce the travel time for students who live in this development.
- Two administrators in the department have been actively subverting the new director's policies through speeches before

citizens' groups, conversations with state board members, and anonymously through leaks to the press.

- One area supervisor is a member of an aggressive fundamentalist sect who always opens student assemblies and teachers' meetings with prayer.
- There are twelve cases at various levels of appeal in which two administrators are alleged to have grossly manipulated the fair employment practices policy adopted by the department.

You have been retained as a management consultant by the new superintendent to assess the situation and make recommendations. In his briefing session with you, he indicates that though he wants you to look into the particular cases mentioned in the Grassroots report, his overriding concern is with raising the level of responsibility throughout the organization. He wants the department to become more accountable for its public mission. You accept the assignment and begin to think about your basic strategy.

With this case in mind, let us review the two major perspectives mentioned briefly at the beginning of this chapter. As the arguments for internal and external controls have not been spelled out more clearly and precisely than in the Friedrich-Finer debate, we will review their opposing viewpoints as they developed them some time ago.

External Controls

In 1936, in an article entitled "Better Government Personnel," Herman Finer argued that "though the codes of ethics, interior discipline, and all the arrangements to make these effective, offer the guarantees of inventiveness, agility and fruitful administration, nothing is more important in our own day than the fundamentality of political control, or political responsibility" (p. 583).

Finer was moved to this assertion by the suggestions of Carl J. Friedrich a year before, in "Responsible Government Service Under the American Constitution," that there is a "psychological factor which supplements 'objective' responsibility" (1935, p. 38). Against Friedrich's acknowledgment of subjective sources of responsibility, Finer insisted that only the set of legal and institutional controls that rest in the hands of the governed can be viewed as producing responsible conduct.

It should be noted parenthetically at this point that there was a degree of ambiguity about the status of codes of ethics in Finer's argument. For example, in the quotation from him just cited, "codes of ethics" is followed by "interior discipline," which might suggest that they were viewed similarly. However, a careful reading of his other works, such as "Administrative Responsibility in Democratic Government" ([1941] 1972), indicates that codes of ethics were likely considered a form of external control, whereas professional standards referred to the internalized values of the profession. Finer found both inadequate to maintain responsible conduct. He favored external controls, which were necessary expressions of political accountability. However, for the purposes of this book, the full array of internal and external controls will be considered. Codes of ethics here will be understood as forms of external control, as they represent values collectively imposed on individuals by organizations, professional associations, or political jurisdictions.

In 1941 Finer reasserted his general position by arguing the necessity of viewing responsibility "as an arrangement of correction and punishment even up to dismissal both of politicians and officials" ([1941] 1972, p. 327). Finer was, once again, responding to Friedrich in language that echoed the earlier philosophy of Max Weber. It reflected a belief that "the servants of the public are not to decide their own course," but rather "they are to be responsible to the elected representatives of the public, and these are to determine the course of action of the public servants to the most minute degree that is technically feasible" (p. 328).

In this same work Finer argued that this view of the administrative role in government rests on three doctrines of democratic government:

1. The mastership of the public requires that both politicians and public employees work for what the public wants, rather than their perception of what the public needs.
2. This mastership needs institutions with a centrally located elected organ.

3. Public mastership includes not only the ability to inform government of its wants, but also the power to exact obedience to orders.

From Finer's perspective, the responsible administrator must be subject to the external political controls implied by these doctrines. Government exercises a monopoly that can be held accountable to the public in no other fashion. Reliance on the administrator's conscience or subjective moral sense of responsibility will always result in the abuses of power we have come to expect from any monopoly. According to Finer, without "external punitive controls" employees of the public will inevitably resort to "nonfeasance," "malfeasance," or "overfeasance" (1941, p. 329).

Finer grants, in his 1941 piece, that education, sensitivity to public opinion, and the technical standards espoused by professional associations all have roles to play as "auxiliaries" to legal sanctions, but they are only that and nothing more. The basic problem with all these auxiliary approaches is that they rely for their effectiveness on informing the exercise of discretion by officials; they have no power to compel and control conduct. Reflecting on this fact, Finer observes: "My qualm is that the official is very likely to give himself the benefit of the doubt where the information he elicits admits of doubt, whereas when the legislative assembly asserts an opinion it also asserts a command" (p. 343). Thus, these internal controls may serve a supplemental function, but they should not receive primary attention.

Rather, our first concern, according to Finer, should be with improving legislative controls over public servants, along with the devices of legal responsibility. Beyond that, we should consider the more effective use of intradepartmental discipline through the hierarchical structure. We should pay more attention to such levers as career prospects, pay raises, promotions, recognition of distinction, and retirement pensions.

Haque (2004) argues that limiting the discretion of administrators was not the focus of the Friedrich-Finer debate. Rather, the focus was "when, how, and for what purposes should [discretion] be used?" (p. 704). This assertion is puzzling since immediately before stating this position, he quotes from Finer to the effect that "servants of the public are not to decide their own course . . ." (p. 704). In fact, the extent to which the discretion of the administrator should be curbed by external controls was precisely the central point of the differences between these two scholars. Finer did not trust public administrators to exercise discretion guided by internal controls; therefore, he sought to constrain discretion by establishing external ones. Friedrich understood the necessity for discretion and saw a set of internalized standards and sensitivities as the only effective guides to its exercise.

In arguing for the primacy of external legal and political sanctions to govern the actions of public administrators, Finer was reaffirming the traditional perspective of the administrative role that had its roots in Max Weber ("Politics as a Vocation," 1946). In Weber's eyes the administrator must be "conditioned to obedience towards these masters who claim to be the bearers of legitimate power" (p. 80). Administrative responsibility involves refraining from making substantive judgments about what the public should receive. Administrators deal only with instrumental judgments about how to deliver most efficiently what has been decided by the politicians. They are to carry out their duties "without scorn or bias" (p. 99) in an impartial fashion.

Weber (1946) insisted, "The honor of the civil servant is vested in his ability to execute conscientiously the order of the superior authorities, exactly as if the order agreed with his own conviction. This holds even if the order appears wrong to him and if, despite the civil servant's remonstrances, the authority insists on the order" (p. 99). This subservient conduct is maintained by organized political domination, with a monopoly on the use of force and control of material resources. As with Finer, control of administrative behavior is founded on concrete external sanctions such as the power to grant and withhold wages or to give and take away a position.

This traditional Weberian perspective, which is evident in Finer's approach, was also clearly discernible somewhat later in Victor Thompson's *Without Sympathy or Enthusiasm: The Problem of Administrative Compassion* (1975). Similar to Finer's emphasis on the "mastership" of the public is Thompson's argument that the public is the "owner" of public organizations. These organizations are "machinelike instruments" of an "external power"—the public. They are artificial systems of prescribed roles and rules. Bureaucrats, then, are to be viewed as "tools" of the organization who are under a contractual obligation to achieve the "owner's" goals.

The problem of maintaining responsible administrative conduct, Thompson admits, is that these "tools" are people and therefore have tendencies toward autonomy and goal formation. They have a strong propensity for developing their own unplanned, spontaneous "natural systems," which parallel the artificial organizational system and distort its functions. The inclination to make informal decisions about the goals and ends of the organization, which characterizes these natural systems, is tantamount to a "theft" of the public's property.

Public administrators, from Thompson's viewpoint, are to deal only in functional rationality—the rational application of means to prescribed ends—and to leave substantive rationality—the evaluation of ends themselves—to the politicians. Substantive rationality is one of three core values for a public administrator, as I addressed in earlier work (Cooper, 1991). How to control bureaucrats through suppressing their substantive rationality is viewed by many students of administration, according to Thompson, as the number one problem in sustaining a high level of administrative responsibility. Unquestionably Thompson's view of public organizations and the role of public administrators within them is highly dependent on the external controls represented by law, legislative oversight, and bureaucratic hierarchical structure. "Tools" must be manipulated and used within the "machinelike" ranks of an organization. Any other approach is too susceptible to unpredictable idiosyncratic behavior at variance with the wishes of the public. In a sense, Thompson's argument was the last significant restatement of that perspective in a consistent and arguably extreme form. It was evoked by the position being advanced in the mid-1970s by the New Public Administration that acknowledged the unavoidability of administrative discretion. Supporters of that movement maintained the necessity for public administrators to be committed to exercising discretion guided by a set of professional ethical principles, primarily that of social equity, and engagement with the citizenry—a very Friedrichian orientation.

"Much Ado About Something" and External Controls

Advocates of external controls would approach your management consulting job with the state department of education from the perspective generally typified by Weber, Finer, and Thompson. They would probably focus their attention on laws or organizational policies and the effectiveness of the hierarchy of the department.

They would want to know, for example, whether there are laws, codes of ethics, or departmental rules that regulate consulting activity and potential conflict-of-interest situations. Are the two unit supervisors violating any existing ethical codes or regulations in the handling of their texts? Is the personnel administrator guilty of any violation through her relationship with someone in a potentially adversarial role? Is the associate director for curriculum development breaking any rules or violating any laws? What about the director of facilities planning?

In the absence of rules and legislation, if you were a believer in external controls, you would likely want to propose that some be developed and adopted. You would recommend that these regulations be spelled out in detail, along with clear and significant sanctions. Also, you would want to give serious attention to the means for enforcing them effectively.

Beyond rules, professional codes of ethics, and regulations, you would probably want to examine the supervisory arrangements in the department. You would want to know how clear the lines of authority are, and you would look at the span of control at every level. Reporting procedures and systems of accountability would also receive your attention. You would likely want to know how supervisors monitor the activities of their subordinates. How are subordinates informed of improper, undesirable, or ineffective behavior? How is overall performance evaluated? Is good performance rewarded and poor performance punished? How? Are the problems with the "subversive" administrators and the "praying" area supervisor a result of structural and procedural deficiencies, or simply the irresponsibility of particular individuals?

The essential point here is that advocates of external controls tend to think about changing the organization and the regulations or the laws that govern its operation rather than turning to ways of changing the subjective states of the people within it. Responsible conduct is sought through establishing limits, requirements, boundaries, standards, and sanctions instead of persuasion, education, and sensitizing. Two typical forms of external control used by the general public, interest groups, and reformers within government are laws (so-called ethics legislation) and codes of ethics. I should note that the media or press can serve as a kind of external control; however, they are not instruments of the public. In other words, the media can exercise fiduciary control, but not with a public tool.

Ethics Legislation

It might be argued that coupling ethics and legislation is inappropriate—that once legislated, a matter is no longer a question of ethics but of law. If individuals can no longer freely apply their values to a given situation but are coerced by the sanctions of the state into certain types of conduct, any activity covered by law, as the argument goes, has been removed from the realm of ethics. People need not waste time reflecting on their obligations in these cases because personal discretion has been circumscribed. The law defines obligations.

This argument has merit, but only in a limited sense. It is true that the binding and punitive attributes of the law are intended to preempt the decision-making process of individuals to some degree. However, it is possible to view the legislative act as a collective ethical judgment, as a moral minimum established by the political community. The basis for proscribing certain forms of behavior by law is still ultimately an ethical one, although political and economic considerations may be involved also. The ordering of principles is as crucial to legislative decisions as it is to decisions of individuals. The collective nature of the decision process creates far more complexity in arriving at priorities, but the dynamics are essentially similar.

Furthermore, there is an element of ethical reflection and decision making in our decision to accept or reject the law as binding for our conduct. We regularly engage in acts of law breaking—jaywalking, violating the speed limit, disturbing the peace with our stereo systems late at night, cheating on our income tax, lying to avoid jury duty, parking illegally, committing perjury in court.

Ethics legislation does attempt to preempt the decision-making field for everyone within its jurisdiction, but we still engage in ethical assessments of the law as it applies to specific cases before us. These assessments vary considerably in seriousness, sophistication, and legitimacy, but they are our means for retaining some measure of ethical autonomy.

Legislation dealing with the ethical conduct of public officials first emerged in the United States in the post-Jacksonian era in the mid-nineteenth century. In 1829, with the inauguration of President Andrew Jackson, the "common men" of Jackson's campaign replaced what they viewed as the entrenched vested interests in the federal government (Small, 1976). In the absence of any concept of the public servant or a professional perspective on government employment, the jobs they claimed were regarded as "the legitimate rewards for service to the party"—the spoils of victory (Association of the Bar of the City of New York, 1960, p. 29). It is not surprising then that influence peddling, selling information, and the use of public funds for personal gain were commonplace. Consequently, the first conflict-of-interest laws were passed during the 1853–1864 period to deal with these abuses. Resorting to legislation as a means of dealing with ethical problems has a substantial history of more than 150 years in the United States.

According to the Association of the Bar of the City of New York (1960), there have been several other significant pieces of ethics legislation at the federal level during the century and a half since the first congressional responses to the spoils system. They are also primarily focused on the problems of conflict of interest and have dealt with postemployment conduct, outside compensation, and reporting financial interests. The Civil Post-Employment Statute of 1872 forbade employees of executive departments to serve as counsel, attorney, or agent during the two years following their federal employment in the prosecution of any claims pending in the department while they were in office. This was followed by legislation in 1919, 1944, and 1948 to extend the coverage to all agencies of the United States, as it had been determined during World War II that the army was not included under the 1862 Act. Also, a criminal penalty was established for violating the act's provisions.

The New York Bar (1960) further reports that in 1917, an outside compensation act was passed by Congress forbidding federal employees from receiving any "salary in connection with their services as such" (p. 55) from any nongovernmental source. Also, it prohibits anyone outside the federal government from making any contribution to or supplementing the salary of a government employee "for the services performed by the government" (p. 55).

The first major comprehensive review and appraisal of existing ethics legislation at the federal level was undertaken by the Association of the Bar of the City of New York in 1955. This five-year study, published in 1960, revealed the following:

> In the overwhelming majority of instances it appears that, where the statutes are recognized and considered at all, government appointees and their lawyers lean over backwards in an effort to comply. But the crude style of the ancient conflict of interest statutes is an inducement to artifice, and there will always be a minority ready to pursue every advantage. When compliance with the law becomes mainly a matter of form, the law is made to appear ludicrous, legal administration is undermined, the underlying policy of the law may be subverted, and the most conscientious bear the heaviest burden. And it is usually a sign that the law is out of touch with reality [p. 71].

The study concluded with a set of detailed policy recommendations for a more effective approach to conflict-of-interest legislation and a proposed Executive Conflict of Interest Act. One year later President Kennedy appointed the three-person Advisory Panel on Ethics and Conflict of Interest in Government. This panel's proposals were melded by the Congress with those of the New York Bar in a new ethics act (Public Law 87-849), which became effective on January 21, 1963 (Small, 1976).

President Lyndon Johnson issued Executive Order 11222, Presidential Order on Federal Ethics, in 1965; it prohibited government officials from holding "direct or indirect financial interests that conflict substantially with their responsibilities and duties as federal employees." It also attempted to control outside income in a more specific manner and required that financial statements be filed with the heads of agencies or other designated persons.

In spite of these efforts to close loopholes, smooth inconsistencies, and extend the coverage of federal ethics legislation, problems in effectiveness continued to exist. Common Cause issued a "Conflict of Interest Report" in 1976, an analysis of the findings of an investigation by the General Accounting Office. The report concluded that violations of the conflict-of-interest legislation in existence at that time were infrequently prosecuted, the financial reporting process was inadequate, and postemployment conduct was insufficiently regulated (Beard, 1978; Kneier, 1976).

A further attempt at rationalizing, specifying, and extending federal ethics legislation was undertaken by President Carter and Congress in 1978. On October 26, the president signed into law the Ethics in Government Act of 1978 (Public Law 95-521), which covers all three branches of the federal government. The act established more detailed financial disclosure provisions and postemployment regulations, with substantial penalties (a ten thousand dollar fine, two years in prison, or both for violating postemployment restrictions). It also had two major innovations: it created the Office of Government Ethics (OGE) located in the Office of Personnel Management, with responsibilities for implementing the provisions of the act and recommending changes in ethics legislation, rules, and policies; and it established mechanisms for appointing an independent counsel to investigate charges of criminal activity by high-ranking officials in the executive branch.

The Ethics in Government Act of 1978 was amended twice in 1979 (Public Law 96-19, 97-28) and again in 1982 (Public Law 97-409), 1983 (Public Law 98-150), and 1988 (Public Law 100-598). The 1988 amendments separated the OGE from the Office of Personnel Management, established it as an independent executive agency, and extended the director's responsibility for ensuring that each executive agency in the federal government develops systematic formal procedures for collecting and reviewing financial disclosure information. Appropriate authority, including the power to conduct investigations, was also granted to the director.

In 1989 additional legislation at the federal level was passed by Congress and signed into law by President George H. W. Bush as the Government Ethics Reform Act of 1989 (Public Law 101-194). Its provisions include a tightening of restrictions on representing private parties before government agencies in which one was previously employed, including specific references to federal personnel who had participated in foreign trade and treaty negotiations. Some of these provisions were extended to cover more people in the executive branch, including certain White House staff members, and members of the legislative branch. The act also included restrictions on gifts of seventy-five dollars or more to members of Congress. Furthermore, members of the Senate were specifically prohibited from accepting gifts "from any one source with a direct interest in legislation that aggregate over $100 in any one year and from any other source that aggregate over $300 in one year." House members and executive branch employees were prohibited from accepting honoraria; senators were specifically exempted from this provision. Since 1989 there have been numerous specific pieces of federal legislation that fall under the jurisdiction of the OGE. Beyond OGE, reforms of the Hatch Act were adopted in 1993 and are administered by the Office of Special Counsel. (For further information on these legislative acts, the OGE Web site is comprehensive and useful: http://www.usoge.gov/home.html.)

In addition to federal ethics legislation, most of the fifty states have been actively involved in adopting similar legislation. Although these are too numerous and diverse to summarize and analyze here, it is clear that conflict-of-interest restrictions, financial disclosure requirements, and postemployment prohibitions are the common concerns there as well. Many states also have established ethics boards and commissions to administer these laws. The reports prepared each year by the Council on Governmental Ethics Laws provide updates of legislative and judicial action on ethics laws state by state (see http://www.cogel.org/ for more information).

It is interesting to note that a movement toward establishing international ethics standards for public management has been gaining momentum over the past five to ten years. Indeed, I have identified this phenomenon as one of the four "Big Questions" in the field of administrative ethics (Cooper, 2004a). In another article, my coauthor and I discussed specific international efforts to establish public service ethics that transcend single nations and the values that undergird such efforts (Yoder and Cooper, 2005). It is a burgeoning and important area that merits further study.

Codes of Ethics

Codes of professional ethics are the other major form of external control. They usually lack the specific concrete sanctions of legislation and are much broader in the types of conduct covered.

Codes vary considerably in their sanctioning power and mechanism for enforcement. The Center for the Study of Ethics in the Professions has an online database with more than eight hundred codes of ethics being used by professional associations of all kinds (www.iit.edu/departments/csep/PublicWWW/codes/index.html). This rich source of information about codes of ethics includes both older and newer documents for a number of associations to make possible the study of how codes for a particular organization have changed over time.

Many codes carry only the authority of professional peer esteem and have no formal means for enforcing their prescriptions. For example, the Law Enforcement Code of Ethics of the International Association of Chiefs of Police (King, 1976) is a nine-hundred-word statement that acknowledges the highest obligations of police officers to the law and the public. This statement is accompanied by a somewhat longer Canons of Police Ethics, including eleven articles of a more specific nature: primary responsibility of the job, duty to be familiar with the law and with responsibilities of self and other public officials, use of proper means to gain proper ends, limitations of authority, cooperation with other public officials, conduct toward the public, private conduct, arresting and dealing with violators of the law, handling of gifts and favors, presentation of evidence, and attitude toward the profession. The code has been adopted by many major police associations and agencies in the nation, but the level of seriousness with which it is taken is unclear. There is no means for requiring departments to adopt this particular code or to enforce it.

The American Public Works Association has replaced its code of ethics with a very brief "Standards of Professional Conduct" document that expresses support for the public trust, the public interest, sustainability, public health and safety, personal integrity, legality, and respect for the environment (http://www.apwa.net/documents/organization/standardsofconduct.PDF). There is no formal enforcement machinery; however, the document does provide a link to the Online Ethics Center for Engineering and Science (http://www.onlineethics.org), where a help line and a rich array of other resources are available. Those who are employed in public works may tend to look more to this kind of ethics resource, the American Society of Civil Engineers, and the licensing procedures for the civil engineering profession for the definition of their professional obligations. Loss of membership in the American Public Works Association would not effectively bar anyone from professional employment. Adherence to the "Standards of Professional Conduct" is purely voluntary, with no apparent strong incentives to do so.

In the wake of the Watergate scandals, George Graham prepared a document entitled "Ethical Guidelines for Public Administrators: Observations on Rules of the Game" (1974) for the National Academy of Public Administration; it bears similarities to a code but is not purported to be one. The guidelines deal largely with the concept of administrative due process in decision making within a public organization. The responsibility of a public administrator "to be informed, to be fair, to be rational, and to be reasonable" is stressed (p. 91). No authority is claimed for the provisions of the document "except to the extent that they may reflect a consensus, or at least preponderant opinion" (p. 90).

The Code of Ethics for Government Service was passed as a joint resolution of the Eighty-Fifth Congress during its second session in 1958 (House Concurrent Resolution 175) for all government employees and office holders. It does not have the binding force of law and is not administered as an oath of office. This code is lofty in its language but quite general in its prescriptions, hortatory in style, and brief. The use of this statement is determined by each department of the federal government.

Two professional associations that have taken a more aggressive approach to codes of ethics are the National Educational Association (NEA) and the International City/County Management Association (ICMA). The NEA code for teachers in public schools (1975) is of medium length, about twelve hundred words. It is organized around a preamble laying out the democratic context of public education and two fundamental principles concerning commitment to the student and commitment to the profession. Adherence to the code is a condition of membership, and a committee on professional ethics holds the power to "censure, suspend, or expel any member for violation of the code subject to review by the Executive Committee." Members may appeal the decision of the ethics committee within sixty days.

The ICMA's is perhaps the most elaborate and operational of the public sector codes of ethics (www.icma.org). Its twelve tenets and accompanying guidelines provide considerable detail in both interpreting and enforcing the code. Members may be suspended, censured, or expelled from the association if found to be in violation of the code. Explicit rules of procedure for handling such cases and informing the membership of their disposition are spelled out. The ICMA also notes detailed procedures for enforcing its code of ethics. If an ethics violation of a member is alleged, an investigative committee is appointed for fact finding, review, and assigning sanctions, including private censure, public censure, expulsion, and/or being barred from membership (see the member benefits section at www.icma.org).

ASPA adopted a code of ethics in 1984 and a set of guidelines for its implementation in 1985. That code began with a preamble statement that set out the general responsibilities of ASPA members for striving to serve the public in a professional manner according to principles meant to guide administrators—"not merely preventing wrong," but "in pursuing right through timely and energetic execution of responsibilities" (American Society for Public Administration, 1985). It then proceeded to outline these principles in twelve brief articles, ranging from commitment to certain personal attributes such as honesty, fortitude, and integrity to obligation to improve the legal and constitutional arrangements that "define the relationships among public agencies, employees, clients, and all citizens." The implementation guidelines discuss the more specific meaning and implications of each article for administrative conduct.

ASPA reformatted the code of ethics in 1994 and converted it into a much more succinct and comprehensible document (American Society for Public Administration, 1994). It can now be presented on one page instead of the previous three and a half (www.aspanet.org). The current version is organized around five main obligations of ASPA members: (1) serve the public interest, (2) respect the Constitution and the law, (3) demonstrate personal integrity, (4) promote ethical organizations, and (5) strive for professional excellence. Under each of these, four to eight brief statements are listed to provide some behavioral specificity. The result is a statement that lacks literary grace and inspirational power but is probably more useful to practitioners. That conclusion seems to be supported by the Bowman and Williams (1997) study of 750 public managers who are ASPA members, which is a replication of a similar study conducted by Bowman in 1989 (Bowman, 1990).

Bowman and Williams found that although in 1989 only 58 percent of respondents claimed familiarity with the code, in 1996 79 percent professed knowledge of its provisions. Furthermore, the degree of familiarity in 1996 was substantially greater than in the previous study. Bowman and Williams conclude that "ASPA's code now enjoys widespread support and use among the participants in the study" (p. 525). Some of this increased awareness and consequent use may be attributed to the code being printed frequently on the back cover of *Public Administration Review*. However, it is also reasonable to believe that revision of the code has contributed to this change.

Although proposals for establishing enforcement mechanisms have been made from time to time, none has been adopted by ASPA. The major reasons seem to be a lack of consensus about the functions and purposes of a professional code, a belief that ASPA's membership is so diverse that enforcement would be difficult at best, and an assumption that ASPA's sanctioning power is extremely weak because it has no ability to impose penalties and exercises no control over whether a violator continues in public service.

Interestingly, very few studies have been done on the effectiveness of codes of conduct. Much of this research has been done by researchers in business. The studies that have been done conclude that codes of conduct are effective only on a small scale and do not promote higher levels of ethical behavior in organizations. For example, in a study of a thousand financial administrators in colleges and universities, Rezaee, Elmore, and Szendi (2001) conclude that codes of conduct are "low-road" approaches that do not enhance ethical behavior or generate trust on a large scale. In another study of Australian businesses, Farrell, Cobbin, and Farrell (2002) concluded that there was no association between codes of ethics and consistent ethical behavior. Indeed, the topic of effectiveness of codes of ethics is a gap in the administrative and business ethics research.

One thing is certain: the development of external controls such as ethics legislation and professional codes of ethics has not arrived at perfection. They present a very mixed bag of results. In spite of more than a hundred years of passing ethics laws at the federal level, scandals still occur; from time to time, men and women in government service continue to violate the trust with which they are endowed. However, on the whole, public service has probably been improved through the establishment of these boundaries for conduct. There are pros and cons to be acknowledged for both ethics legislation and professional codes. We will review them briefly.

Pros and Cons of Ethics Legislation

In the case of ethics legislation, the "pros" include the following. The administration of the public's business must be rooted ultimately in law. Discretion exercised by administrators is necessarily broad in modern government, but it must be generally consistent with the wishes of the citizenry. Judgment exercised in the day-to-day conduct of an agency's affairs requires flexibility and latitude to effectively address specific concrete situations. However, the range of possible decision options should be constrained by the will of the people as expressed by the legislative boundaries established by elected officials. Ethics legislation provides these broad constraints within which the ethical conflicts and dilemmas that public administrators face are to be resolved—formal statements of the moral minimum for a political community.

Ethics laws also provide sanctions for public servants caught stepping beyond the limits established by the citizenry. Fines, prison sentences, and administrative penalties for misconduct are ways of establishing the sovereign right of the people to require that their will be done. Legal sanctions confront the whims, greed, and self-assertion of an irresponsible public administrator with a reminder that she or he is employed on the public's behalf and that this obligation may not be taken lightly.

Finally, although ethics laws are negative in nature—oriented toward catching crooks by establishing a moral minimum for conduct rather than fostering the highest idealism—they do provide a means for setting negative examples. On those rare occasions when a wayward public servant is publicly dismissed and brought to the bar of justice, a vivid object lesson is provided about what those employed by government must not do. Although inadequate as a way of cultivating the most responsible public service, these examples may discourage a drift toward seriously irresponsible conduct. In other words, laws provide a minimum standard of conduct, but they do not move us toward exemplary behavior or inspire us to elevate our behavior.

When we consider the cons of ethics laws, three points emerge. First, they are seriously lacking in specific reference to particular situations; they address general conditions. Fritz Morstein Marx once observed that "even though administrative responsibility gains its direction from legislative decisions, neither the statute nor the budget can attempt to outline specifically the path of administrative action. The law never addresses itself to the concrete case" (1940, p. 247). Consequently, the interpretation of the law for particular situations is inherently indeterminate and problematic to some degree, depending on the extensiveness of the precedents established by previous cases and the knowledge of the interpreter. Well-intentioned public administrators may simply misunderstand the law. Also, people inclined to report apparently illegal conduct by government employees may very well feel uncertain about the applicability of the law in a particular instance. As tools for accomplishing Finer's goal of determining the course of action of public servants "to the most minute degree that is technically feasible" ([1941] 1972, p. 328), they are blunt instruments indeed.

Second, ethics legislation has generally been difficult to enforce. Loopholes in the ethics law, the difficulty in acquiring hard evidence, and the reluctance to report fellow employees suspected of misconduct have resulted in irregular and infrequent prosecution. Also, the inadequacy of government-wide enforcement machinery has left these laws without the necessary tools for effective implementation. The lack of consistent and effective enforcement of ethics laws can only contribute to the disrespect for law in general and encourage the flouting of these in particular.

Third, a serious attempt to enforce ethics legislation may erode the morale of government employees. When legislation becomes so detailed and restrictive, it can breed resentment among public administrators because discretion is threatened. The machinery required for more effective administration of these laws may be so enormous and pervasive that an oppressive atmosphere of suspicion and "big brotherism" might result. Creativity and legitimate risk taking might be diminished even further in bureaucratic organizations already burdened with infighting, self-protection, and fear.

At the federal level, the Office of Government Ethics, established by the Ethics in Government Act of 1978, has nearly three decades of history behind it. As it has grown in resources and authority, it has played an increasingly active role in heightening the awareness of ethical considerations in public service. However, it is not clear whether this has created morale problems for the majority of public administrators and other public servants who obey the law faithfully.

Pros and Cons of Codes of Ethics

When we turn to codes of ethics, we can identify the following pros. Codes of ethics can go much further than legislation in projecting ideals, norms, and obligations for particular professional groups. Ethics laws generally focus on conflict of interest and tend to be negative in their prescriptions. They rule out certain types of conduct, but they do not prescribe, in a positive fashion, the highest expectations for performance. Codes can do this. They can present the loftiest values of a profession in a hortatory fashion that would be inappropriate for legislation. Codes can establish an ethical status to which members of a profession may aspire—the moral optimum rather than the moral minimum established by ethics legislation (Chandler, 1983).

Codes can also be tailored better to the typical situations of a profession. Whereas law tends to be universalistic, or at least more inclusive, codes can be more particular in their audience. The NEA code of ethics can address the obligations of teachers to their students, the law enforcement code can deal with proper conduct in arresting suspects, and the code of the ICMA can refer to relationships with the citizens of a municipality.

A code of ethics can provide a mechanism for clarifying and internalizing the values of a professional group. If a code of ethics is not prepared by a few in isolation from the majority, it can be a means of socializing members into the profession. Durkheim (1957) correctly warned against codes that are prepared and imposed by a few rather than evolving through the active participation of many. He suggested that this participatory, ongoing process of defining, refining, and revising a code of ethics is one important way individuals resolve their inherent antagonism with any group. Discussing the code, applying it to concrete problems, and proposing changes in its prescriptions can bind individual interests to group interests. In the case of public administration, it may also offer a way of binding the group's interests to those of the public, toward the enhancement of the political community. To ensure that this occurs, public involvement in the formation of the code is essential.

A review of empirical research on ethical decision making by Ford and Richardson (1994) indicates that when codes of ethics are adopted by employing organizations, they "will positively increase an individual's ethical beliefs and decision behavior" (p. 216). This is especially true when the codes are backed up with positive and negative sanctions for conduct. Such codes may be more effective than those of professional associations because they are viewed as "surrogate indications of top management's commitment to ethical behavior" (p. 216).

Codes of ethics have shortcomings as well. They are often so vague, abstract, and lofty that they are difficult to apply in specific situations where ethical guidance is needed. For example, consider the following language: "my fundamental duty is to serve mankind," "I will keep my private life unsullied as an example to all," and "honest in thought and deed in both my personal and official life." It is far from clear what specific behavior is expected in particular instances. The words are noble but subject to widely differing interpretations. When a set of more specific canons accompanies such codes, some of their lack of specificity is provided. All too often, however, professional codes of ethics fail to heed the admonition of the U.S. Senate Subcommittee of the Committee on Labor and Public Welfare: "The broad moral code, to which members of a society owe allegiance, is not enough. Its principles must also be applied to the professional activities in anticipation of the issues and dilemmas which arise, so that professional obligations can be seen clearly and understood, free from the tensions and temptations which beset a busy professional life" (1951, p. 35). Professional groups are sometimes reluctant to take this step toward concretion and practicality for fear of potential division and conflict in the ranks.

In many cases, the code of a professional group carries no means of gaining compliance. Either literally or figuratively, they take the form of elegant plaques that are hung on the office walls and thereafter ignored. They may be quoted on ceremonial occasions, but are never taken seriously enough to use in assessing the conduct of individual members. As a form of external control they are generally weak because they seldom have operational enforcement structures and procedures. With respect to public administration, they do not provide the public with "the power to exact obedience to orders" (Finer, [1941] 1972, p. 329).

Even when codes of ethics have enforcement mechanisms and even when they are used, they may still be meaningless. Because most professional associations in the public sector are not the gatekeepers for their professions, censure or expulsion may have little effect. They do not license practitioners in their fields, so a wayward member's career is not likely to be significantly affected by the actions of a professional association.

As well, codes of ethics can stifle discretion and inhibit an administrator's ability to do his or her job. Blitz (2005) argues that responsibility in administration "rarely means being directly accountable to an extraconstitutional order or to a professional code of practices and principles" (p. 40). In fact, suppressing the intuition and instincts of a public administrator may be damaging to his or her efforts to serve the public. Blitz continues, "The responsibility we need from the public servant is that he actually does his own job, as effectively as he can. Sometimes this means that he exercises a freedom that seems too unregulated or even seeks to expand his responsibilities beyond what his job appears to require" (p. 40). If an administrator fears the imposition of sanctions based on an external code, the best intentions of a code of ethics may be self-defeating.

Internal Controls

Herman Finer's assertions in 1936 and 1941 about the primacy of external controls were responses to the views of Carl J. Friedrich. In *Problems of the American Public Service,* published in 1935 by the Commission of Inquiry on Public Service Personnel, Friedrich had suggested that responsibility has a "psychological factor" as well as an objective external accountability dimension (p. 38). He began by identifying a kind of responsibility exemplified by the medieval church as it "sought to make governments responsible to God": it was not responsibility in terms of accountability to some person or body, but a "moral or religious" (p. 30) responsibility, an idealized political responsibility. It was a feeling, a sense, of responsibility to a transcendent ideal.

Five years later in "Public Policy and the Nature of Administrative Responsibility" ([1940] 1972), Friedrich carried this notion further. From an argument that politics and administration are not neatly separated, Friedrich concluded that political accountability is inadequate to ensure responsible administrative conduct. As public administrators in modern society are regularly involved in making policy and as the complexity of contemporary governmental activities prevents them from submitting all their actions to elected officials for review, accountability of administrators to politicians must at best be partial. Administrators and politicians are not even able to communicate sufficiently to maintain accountability through agreement on policy.

Given this unavoidable limited responsibility to elected officials, Friedrich (1935) asked, "But are there any possible arrangements under which the exercise of such discretionary power can be made more responsible?" His general answer was that before considering additional institutional safeguards, we should "elucidate a bit more the actual psychic conditions which might predispose any agent toward responsible conduct" (p. 320). Upon examining those conditions, Friedrich concluded that administrative responsibility amounts to responsiveness to two dominant factors: technical knowledge and popular sentiment. "Responsiveness" for Friedrich connoted an inner attitude or disposition to act, even though the two dominant factors refer to sources outside the individual. It is an internalization of "technical knowledge" and a positive sensitivity toward "popular sentiment" that is crucial.

Friedrich viewed technical knowledge as a standard for which public administrators can be held accountable, but only by "fellow-technicians who are capable of judging his policy in terms of the scientific knowledge bearing upon it" (1935, pp. 321–322). As he viewed modern government, Friedrich argued that administrators are increasingly involved in specialized, highly technical decisions that neither politicians nor the public can effectively monitor and control. However, the administrators' colleagues in a particular field of expertise can scrutinize and evaluate their work.

Friedrich (1940) acknowledged that John M. Gaus had developed a similar view several years earlier in "The Responsibility of Public Administrators" (1936). Gaus predicted that in the system of government emerging in the mid-1930s in the United States, "one important kind of responsibility will be that which the individual civil servant recognizes as due to the standards and ideals of his profession. This is his 'inner check'" (p. 40). Both men sought to avoid becoming ensnared in what they perceived to be a "literary struggle" or "argument over words" over whether this new kind of responsibility was "subjective" or "objective" (p. 40). Friedrich (1936) suggested that it might be best to eschew such language altogether and instead talk about "technical" or "functional" responsibility on the one hand and "political" responsibility on the other.

At about the same time, Fritz Morstein Marx began to develop a line of thought similar to Friedrich's. Marx had also begun to move away from the notion that administrators have no role in policymaking. In *Public Management in the New Democracy* (1940, p. 237), he recognized that statutes must be transformed into "a mass of detailed orders" and that although they "must bear a close relationship to the letter of the law," nevertheless, "their formulation is a creative act, separate from the making of the law itself." Marx concluded, therefore, that external political controls are an inadequate source of responsibility. He argued that legislative control is necessary, but added: "Judicial redress, official liability, and the whole gamut of disciplinary measures are poor substitutes for a sense of duty. No formal device for accountability can give us a clue as to the components of answerable conduct. One cannot commandeer responsibility. One can only cultivate it, safeguard its roots, stimulate its growth, and provide it with favorable climatic conditions" (p. 248).

Returning to Friedrich's argument, the other "dominant factor" in maintaining a responsible exercise of administrative discretion is public sentiment. In a democratic society the public will freely communicate with the government "in the form of inquiries, criticisms, and suggestions" ([1940] 1972, p. 325). Furthermore, the magnitude of legislative work has become so great that citizens will become "more and more accustomed to turn directly to the administrator" (p. 325). Administrators will be required by the public to be responsive to their preferences and demands. Moreover, the administrator will increasingly need to be attuned to changing societal trends: "Instead of administering according to precedent, the responsible administrator today works according to anticipation" (p. 324). The public relations task of public administrative organizations involves attempting to identify probable resistance by the citizenry to new policies and adapting them to public preferences.

These two factors in administrative responsibility have external dimensions: the public and the professional community with its technical standards. However, they are referred to here as internal controls because the source of their power to shape behavior is ultimately not a matter of external regulations and procedures manipulated by someone else in the form of commands and directives, but a set of internalized attitudes, values, and beliefs. Administrators are not responsive to the professional opinions of colleagues unless they have incorporated the norms and standards of that profession into their value and belief system. Considerable latitude of discretion remains in the application of those professional values. Similarly, responsiveness to public opinion is directly related to the extent to which they have internalized a set of values that attribute high status to the views of citizens.

Having argued for the existence and value of these internal controls, Friedrich acknowledged the continuing importance of the traditional political responsibility of public administrators. In "Public Policy and the Nature of Administrative Responsibility," he acknowledged that "a double standard" is necessary for responsible public policy. Administrative responsibility is never perfectly achieved, and "institutional safeguards designed to make public policy thus truly responsible represent approximations, and not very near approximations at that" ([1940] 1972, p. 322). Consequently, political controls must be supplemented with the influences of technical standards and popular opinion.

The New Public Administration

Friedrich's insistence on these internal sources of responsibility, alongside political controls, was given renewed impetus by the so-called New Public Administration movement (Marini, 1971), which had its first organized manifestation at the Minnowbrook Conference in 1968. Although this movement of the late 1960s exhibited considerable diversity in its effort to redefine the field of public administration, it has generally proceeded with the same basic assumptions expressed by Carl Friedrich thirty years earlier. In attempting to define the nature of administrative responsibility, both began with the observation that the separation of politics and administration is untenable. Public administrators are inescapably involved in policymaking, a function previously restricted, in theory, to the province of politics.

From this assumption about the political nature of public administration, adherents of the New Public Administration defined responsible administrators as those committed to certain values that guided their conduct. They are not simply neutral instruments of the elected officials, but bring to the policymaking and administrative task a commitment to change. According to Frederickson (1971), the change should be directed toward social equity. However, not only are administrators to view themselves as change agents in specific policy issues, but furthermore, argues Frederickson, they are obligated "to find organizational and political forms which exhibit a capacity for continued flexibility or routinized change" (p. 312). This is tantamount to the fundamental alteration of organizational machinery and processes.

Although organizational change is the fundamental strategy of the New Public Administration, it cannot be separated functionally or philosophically from social equity and good management; all three are inextricably bound together. Good management, insists Frederickson, implies change away from "entrenched, non-responsible bureaucracies that become greater public problems than the social situations they were originally designed to improve" (p. 312). It also involves using the most effective scientific tools of management, such as modern budgeting and accounting techniques, computer science, policy analysis techniques, and organizational development methods, to achieve greater social equity. In a similar fashion, social equity cannot be considered apart from fundamental change in public organizations and policies and the use of the best techniques of management.

An important further implication of this philosophy of administrative responsibility is that the administrator must be client oriented. Although this terminology of the New Public Administration, which refers to the people as clients rather than citizens, smacks of professional elitism, it does suggest that the public and its problems, rather than the institutions of government, are the focus of concern. Organizations must be reformed to serve the public, not just to become stronger or more efficient but in terms that benefit the citizen-client. Involvement of citizens in the policy process and major attention to the public impact of policies are manifestations of this concern.

Eugene Dvorin and Robert Simmons (1972, p. vii) provided one example of the New Public Administration's character in a "small volume dealing with big issues" entitled *From Amoral to Humane Bureaucracy*. They argue for "courage," "commitment to humane values," and "integrity" as the most important qualities of the public administrator (p. 48). Without this fundamental commitment to value, "no external check or combination of obstacles is capable of channeling bureaucratic power in the modern state toward humane ends" (p. 46). With "radical humanism" as their basic value orientation, administrators must operate with a "situational ethic" if human dignity is to be preserved for the public. Bureaucratic power must be guided toward achieving human dignity not by the constraint of institutional controls but by an inner moral sensitivity. Bureaucracy "can never in the long run be restrained by external means only" (p. 63).

Michael Harmon (1971) may have carried the argument for internal controls to the most extreme position. Harmon was critical of both Friedrich and Finer for sharing the same premise about human nature. He maintains that both believe checks of some kind are necessary to prevent administrators from selfish and capricious behavior, and thus both hold negative views of human inclinations. Harmon turned to Abraham Maslow for a more positive appraisal of human potential. He tells us that Maslow "has predicted that the choices of self-actualizing people are more likely to meet the test of 'responsible' behavior than those of less healthy people" (1971, p. 178). It follows, then, that administrators should be encouraged to seek self-actualization. They should seek to develop their own values, assert them openly, and encourage others to do likewise. Harmon acknowledged that there is no guarantee of responsible behavior in this approach, but argued in response that "it is also clear that the opposite assumption—that public administrators will act irresponsibly unless otherwise checked—is similarly devoid of empirical support" (p. 178).

Although he insists he is not proposing that narrow self-interest become the governing ethic of public administrators, Harmon's commitment to self-actualization would make it difficult for him to identify misconduct. If an existentialist posture is to be adopted for the public administrative role, there are neither universal nor independent normative grounds for evaluating the behavior of anyone occupying it. Thus, administrative ethics would be a rather pointless concern.

In the perspectives of these advocates of the New Public Administration are significant parallels with Carl Friedrich's positions:

- All recognize that administrators are inevitably involved in politics and policymaking.
- All acknowledge the necessity for some form of political control over the bureaucracy.
- All acknowledge the inadequacy of external political controls alone to ensure administrative responsibility and the necessity of internal controls.
- All except Harmon acknowledge the importance of other points of reference that enhance responsible conduct through the internal values they engender: public management techniques, professional standards, and democratic government.

It is interesting to note that the importance of internal controls seems to have found a permanent place in the basic assumptions of public administration during the almost four decades since the emergence of the New Public Administration. The dominant themes of the Minnowbrook II Conference in 1988, commemorating the twentieth anniversary of the original New Public Administration meeting, suggest that values and ethics are now viewed as central to the field. This session was attended by most of the original participants, some representatives of their age cohort who were not at the first conference, and a group of younger scholars reflecting the 1980s. At Minnowbrook II the significance of social equity for administrative practice was no longer seriously questioned, and the client orientation of many at the 1968 conference had grown into a broad commitment to the cluster of values associated with democratic political theory. Concern for civic virtue and the responsibilities of citizenship in a democracy typified this perspective (Mayer, 1989; Guy, 1989; Porter, 1989).

The American Society for Public Administration

The ASPA, in addition to adopting a code of ethics, a form of external control, has also attempted to encourage the development of internal controls within its members. The initial means for accomplishing this was the publication of a booklet entitled *Applying Professional Standards and Ethics in the Eighties: A Workbook Study Guide for Public Administrators* (Mertins and Hennigan, 1982). One of the first major tasks the ASPA Professional Standards and Ethics Committee placed on its agenda, soon after being established in 1976, was to develop a guide to ethical reflection that practicing public administrators might use. The consensus at the time was that raising probing questions that might stimulate ASPA members to become more self-conscious about their own professional values and ethical perspectives was more important than writing a code of ethics. The idea was to provide a publication that individuals and groups could use. One might read through it alone for self-assessment and personal professional development, or it might be discussed by groups of administrators in ASPA chapter meetings, in educational and training settings, or among members of a public organization.

The workbook that resulted provided brief background statements on such topics as "Relationship to Law," "Responsibility and Accountability," "Citizenship and Responsibility," "Conflicts of Interest," and "Whistle-Blowing." These statements are followed by a list of self-diagnostic questions that public administrators ought to be able to answer for themselves, for colleagues, and for the public. The underlying assumption was that this kind of self-reflection and discussion will contribute to the cultivation of internal controls in the form of professional values and ethical standards.

"Much Ado" and Internal Controls

Proponents of the primacy of internal controls would approach your management consulting job with the state department of education with concern for the development of public service values and sensitivity to the public. They would probably recommend developing ethics training courses at both the point of entry into the organization and in-service programs for those already employed. These courses would deal with the distinctions between private and public interest and the importance of avoiding even the appearance of conflicts of interest. They might well examine the process of ethical reflection and analyze the cardinal ethical principles inherent in American public service, such as equality, freedom, beneficence, respect for individuals, popular sovereignty, and justice.

Pros and Cons of Internal Controls

Let us consider briefly the pros and cons of greater reliance on internal controls as means to enhance administrative responsibility. First, we look at the advantages. Values that are internalized by an administrator are always present in the decision situation. Even when a supervisor is absent, lax in discipline, or corrupt, the administrator's internal controls still operate. Even when the legislative mandate provides no guidelines for conduct, an administrator can call on those inner guides. External institutional controls are not as immediately experienced in decision making as are one's own values. Many of the problems you encountered as a consultant for the department of education could have been prevented if the administrators involved had been deeply ingrained with a set of professional values. Lacking these, you are left with catching crooks and punishing bad guys after the fact.

Internal controls are likely to create a more responsive and creative bureaucracy. Even when uniform external controls work, they prevent administrators from addressing the unique dimensions of concrete situations. They encourage the faceless bureaucrat syndrome: the public servant who is unwilling to respond to the particular needs of citizens for fear of violating the rules and being reprimanded. Cultivating a set of internal value controls provides a sense of self-confidence in exercising judgments, a feeling of structured autonomy in dealing with unanticipated circumstances. Administrators can take risks and depart from the book because they are not acting capriciously but are governed by a consistent value system.

Problems—the cons—also need to be acknowledged with internal controls. In a pluralistic society, it is difficult to achieve agreement about which values public administrators should adopt. One of the most common criticisms of an emphasis on the inner check is that values are relative in modern society. Whose values will become the norm for the bureaucracy? Will it be Catholic values? Protestant values? Scientific values? Economic values? Who will decide? Will all administrators operate with the same professional values?

Internal controls are not completely reliable. If an individual administrator applies her own values to a decision situation, we cannot be certain that she will not do so in a manner that is self-serving. As values are by nature private and hidden from view, there is no possibility for public review of the values that govern a decision. We cannot determine easily whether a public administrator is employing agreed-on professional values or personal values.

There is a possibility of conflict among competing values. For example, if Friedrich's deference to public opinion and technical standards is viewed as a significant internal control, is it not likely that these two will be at odds from time to time? Imagine an environmental administrator whose technical standards tell him that air quality will suffer seriously if a new steel mill is constructed, but who is faced with a public that desperately needs the job opportunities. What or who will guide a public administrator through such conflicts?

Assumptions About Human Nature

Behind the debate over internal versus external controls stand some conscious and unconscious assumptions about what human beings are like in essence. Some of these assumptions lead to an attitude of trusting people to behave in a socially constructive fashion; others evoke suspicions that people, left to their own devices, will act only in self-interest.

When you think back to your consulting job with the department of education, your experience probably tells you that the people who have been overindulging their self-interests may have behaved quite differently at other times. They may have expended considerable effort in their assigned work; perhaps they do so even now while involved in questionable practices. If you were simply to proceed as though people at the state board of education were totally self-centered and needed to be controlled entirely by external means, you would be ignoring their potential for self-control and self-discipline. However, if you assume with equal simplicity that they are all likely to be cooperative and socially oriented if only allowed to work unimpeded by rules, regulations, and supervision, you would be flying in the face of your own experience and the evidence before you.

The critical task is to design a balance between internal and external control, as well as congruence between them. That is, there must be enough control from outside the individual to discourage those inclinations toward indulgence of self-interest, but enough internal control to encourage the most socially constructive, idealistic, altruistic, and creative impulses to flourish. This balance of controls is essential for the fully responsible conduct of a public administrator.

However, it is also necessary that the internal and external controls reinforce each other; they must support the same kind of behavior. They must not give conflicting signals. All too often in organizations, we set up policies, performance standards, regulations, and supervisory processes that are at odds with the publicly espoused values with which public servants are to function.

In the next chapter, we will begin to map out a synthesis of internal and external controls; we will attempt to integrate ethics and values with laws, rules, codes, and bureaucratic organization. This is the design approach to administrative ethics.

Chapter Seven

Integrating Ethics with Organizational Norms and Structures

This chapter continues the examination of the problem of maintaining responsible conduct from the perspective of the manager. In the managerial role, we sometimes feel perplexed about our inability to achieve the desired results from changes in rules, policies, training programs, laws, and organizational arrangements. In spite of our efforts, people in public organizations still do not conduct themselves consistently with the goals we have in mind. They do not always enthusiastically direct their energies and skills toward implementing new policies and abiding by added rules; at other times they clearly behave unethically, even illegally.

Although we tend to think of unethical activities and willfully inadequate work performance as two separate problems, both are forms of irresponsible conduct. Both represent a diverting of the public's resources from the fulfillment of its preferences and demands. Using a public organization's information and access to key people for personal gain, on the one hand, and simply bending the direction of policies and programs away from their mandated objectives, on the other, are both failures to serve the citizenry. They are two faces of irresponsibility.

If a deficiency in basic abilities to undertake the job is not the underlying impediment, both forms of conduct must be the result of insufficient congruence between internal and external controls. A public administrator may behave irresponsibly because his subjective responsibility and the objective responsibility of the position are not well linked. A conflict among internal and external controls reflects faulty design and is conducive to conduct we might consider unethical and also to conduct we might view as inadequate effort toward accomplishing the organization's designated goals.

Conflicts Among Internal and External Controls

Let us look at several examples to illuminate these dynamics.

Sexual Orientation in Law Enforcement

The Fair City Police Department conducted a recruitment campaign to hire an experienced police officer on a lateral-entry basis. The department received fifteen applications from officers in other departments throughout the state. All were put through the usual selection process involving written examinations, interviews, medical checks, psychological evaluations, and background investigations. At the conclusion of this process, the top candidate was a patrolman named Adam with five years of experience in another department in the county. He had scored substantially higher than his competitors, his previous performance appraisals were strongly positive, and his current supervisors praised his work.

However, just before Adam was sent a written offer of employment, a hitch developed: one of the senior officers in the unit where Adam was to work approached the personnel officer and expressed a "gut feeling" that Adam was gay. This senior officer had participated in the interview process. Although he did not express concern at the time, he subsequently began to feel that something about Adam's mannerisms seemed "suspicious."

The personnel officer agreed that Adam seemed ever so slightly "effeminate," then revised his opinion—"No, not really effeminate, just not as masculine as most cops." The personnel officer reminded the senior officer that the city had an equal employment opportunity ordinance that prohibited discrimination on the basis of sexual orientation. The senior officer chuckled and reminded the personnel officer that the police department had a well-established tradition, which had never been challenged, of not hiring gays. The personnel officer agreed and admitted that hiring a gay man would create serious problems within the department. Most of the officers would refuse to work with Adam if he were gay, or even if they thought he was, not to mention the harassment to which they would subject him. They would see Adam's presence among them as somehow eroding the status of their profession and likely to evoke the ridicule of other police departments in the region. Inevitably, they would hound him out of the department eventually.

Both officers agreed that this could be a costly hire in a multitude of ways and that it required special handling. They decided that their own recourse was to check further on Adam's background and conduct some surveillance to determine whether their suspicions were well founded. Within a week, they had information that confirmed their initial intuitions. They decided to "adjust" his scores so that he would not be the number one candidate. They were convinced that this was for the good of the department, the city, and even Adam.

What we see in this case is the impotence of an external control like a city antidiscrimination ordinance to produce responsible conduct when there is conflict with a powerful internal control like the norms of the police subculture. The deeply internalized and long-standing macho values of a male-dominated, action-oriented occupation like law enforcement represent an enormous barrier to the effective functioning of external controls like laws and even departmental regulations. Unless we can devise training and organizational development strategies that reshape these values and beliefs, as well as personnel selection procedures that result in hiring people with values more consistent with the law, the law is likely to be flouted.

Natural Death

A more complex example of conflict among internal and external controls concerns a piece of legislation passed by the legislature of a large western state. An active, well-financed interest group called Die Free was deeply and passionately concerned that an increasing number of terminally ill patients were being kept alive artificially by the sheer power of modern medical technology, many in an unconscious vegetative state or in great pain. Its spokespersons maintained that this was an affront to human dignity and a violation of the human right to control one's own life, including its termination. Keeping people alive who have no hope of recovery, they insisted, deprived them of their freedom and privacy with no benefit for themselves or society. They also argued that it created heavy financial and emotional burdens for the families of the patients. Consequently, they asserted, people should be given the opportunity to anticipate such a situation for themselves and decide in advance how it should be handled.

Die Free was successful ultimately in pushing through the state legislature, and getting the governor to sign, a bill providing for "natural death." This meant that anyone age twenty-one or older could sign a declaration stipulating that in the event that he or she was found to be terminally ill by two physicians at any future date, no efforts were to be made to "artificially prolong the moment of my death" and "that I be permitted to die naturally."

According to the statute, physicians were its key implementers. Doctors were to inform their patients of this new right and offer them the opportunity to sign a declaration and file it with them. The directive would be in effect for five years and then would expire unless renewed.

One year after this statute went into effect, a survey of physicians throughout the state revealed that no evidence could be found that even one declaration had been signed. Shocked that apparently physicians had not done their duty under the law, the leadership of Die Free convened a conference of leading physicians, medical educators, legislators, policy analysts, attorneys, and ethicists to try to discover the root of the problem.

It did not take long to figure out why the new act had had no effect: there was a conflict between significant internal and external controls. If we examine the controls operating in this case, we discover two external controls—the natural death act and the courts—and one internal control—the ethical norms of physicians. One external control, the natural death act, was in conflict with the other external control, the courts. It also ran counter to the internal control represented by the ethical norms of physicians. The conflict lay in the fact that the new act was attempting to get physicians to do something that was inconsistent with the values and norms they had internalized through medical training and practice and would expose them to malpractice litigation in the courts.

Doctors are trained to save and prolong life, not to terminate it, or even to allow it to be terminated if they can effectively intervene. The ancient Hippocratic Oath, although not officially an operative external control over the conduct of physicians today, still reflects a two-thousand-year-old tradition of medical ethics. Central to this tradition is the physician's obligation to avoid providing assistance in the termination of life.

Furthermore, physicians are trained and socialized to protect the doctor-patient relationship from anything that might violate the bond of trust. The idea of suggesting to their patients that they consider signing a termination of life declaration and filing it with them was seen as antithetical to this trust relationship. Doctors feared that patients might not understand their motives and might view such advice with suspicion.

In addition to these long-standing and widely held norms of practice, the risk of being sued for malpractice provided a potent external control in further conflict with the new act. Although there were provisions in the act to exempt physicians from such litigation, those present at the conference expressed fear that they were not adequate. The attorneys agreed that this concern was well founded. They indicated that criminal charges and civil suits would likely be filed by survivors against physicians who participated in any way in the declaration and natural death process.

As the conference deliberation unfolded, it became clear that the new act alone was not a sufficiently powerful external control to overcome the resistance of the very potent controls, one internal and one external, arrayed against its provisions. Its language was imprecise, its protection from litigation was insufficient, and it placed the wrong person, the physician, too squarely in the role of implementer with no attention to reeducation.

Congruence with Policy Objectives

In cases such as these two, ethical components of decision making are left unshaped by public policy. The lack of potent external controls with clear sanctions, coupled with internal and external controls that are not congruent with the intent of the new policies, leave other external controls, personal values, the norms of an organizational subculture, or a professional tradition dominant in the decision-making process rather than those intended by the public's representatives. Unless those values can be reoriented and made more congruent with those of the policy objectives, there is not likely to be consistently responsible conduct. The wishes of the citizenry, as expressed in the public policy, may not be fulfilled by their servants.

The Components of Responsible Conduct

Ethical conduct cannot be effectively shaped and maintained in isolation. The reflective process discussed in the earlier chapters of this book requires a supportive environment if it is to result in responsible conduct. As Figure 7.1 indicates, the internal controls represented by individual attributes must be generally consistent with organizational structure, organizational culture, and societal expectations. These are the key elements for designing an environment supportive of ethical conduct.

Figure 7.1. Components of Responsible Conduct

Individual Attributes
Ethical decision-making skill
Mental attitude
Virtues
Professional values

Organizational Culture
Exemplars
Norms for conduct
Symbols

Responsible
Conduct

Organizational Structure
Clear accountability
Collaborative arrangements
Dissent channels
Participation procedures

Societal Expectations
Public participation
Laws and policies

Individual Attributes

These include our skills in making ethical decisions; our virtues, understood as character traits or inner moral qualities; and our professional values. Most attention from scholars and practitioners concerned with administrative ethics during the first two decades of administrative ethics as a field of study (1970–1990) was devoted to these individual attributes. It is still a major concern, but has been complemented by research on the other three areas of Figure 7.1. Within this general category, the greatest effort has been directed toward the development of ethical decision-making skills.

In developing these skills, the typical approach has involved the use of case studies along the lines suggested in Chapter Two of this book. Ethics workshops of this kind have focused on learning to apply decision models to case studies. In these sessions, administrators typically are taught a series of steps that will help develop a clear understanding of the ethical problem they are facing and then how to work toward its resolution in the form of a decision for action. They learn to use these models by applying them to cases either written by the participants or prepared by the trainer.

Case studies have also been used to cultivate an internalized professional ethic, as suggested also in Chapter Two. The assumption here has been that only when ethical standards embodied in codes of ethics are discussed in connection with actual life situations from the experiences of working public administrators do they achieve relevance as guides for conduct. In in-service training sessions and university classes, this often takes the form of analyzing case studies of administrators confronting ethical dilemmas and attempting to relate them to a written code of ethics or significant ethical principles. In this way administrators can develop a sense of what abstract ethical principles or general provisions in a code of ethics mean in terms of their own professional conduct. (Codes of ethics are not listed as a separate component in this chapter because they are relatively weak forms of external control that seem to have their most significant effects on conduct when used not as a form of control but as an educational tool for inculcating professional values.)

Although most work in administrative ethics during the past three decades has been directed toward cultivating applied knowledge of professional ethics and developing ethical decision-making skills, other individual attributes have come to prominence more recently. Virtue, or character traits that incline us toward ethical conduct, emerged in the literature of administrative ethics in the 1980s as an increasingly important personal attribute. (For an overview of the literature on virtue as related to administrative ethics, see Hart, 2001.)

Just because we have internalized a rational understanding of professional ethics and acquired some ethical decision-making skills does not necessarily mean that we will act accordingly. It is also essential that we be predisposed to carry out what we understand to be ethical conduct—that we have a set of attitudes and a commitment of will to behave ethically. For example, knowing the course of action that best upholds social justice must be supported by a personal inclination to behave justly, and understanding the truthful alternative for conduct must be supported by a predisposition to tell the truth, if these ethical principles are ultimately to be upheld in an organization.

Although interest in virtue as an essential individual element in administrative ethics has broadened and intensified in recent years, Stephen Bailey in 1965 highlighted the importance of certain inner qualities that might be understood as virtues. He identified three essential "mental attitudes" and three "moral qualities" that are desirable for "all public servants in every branch and at every level of government" (p. 313). He attributed these concepts to Paul Appleby's fragmentary but suggestive treatment of the personal morality of the individual public employee. According to Bailey, the necessary mental attitudes are the following:

1. A recognition of the moral ambiguity of all people and all public policies. This means that the dual tendencies within all human beings toward self-interest on the one hand and altruism on the other must be acknowledged by those in public service.
2. A recognition of the contextual forces that condition moral priorities in the public service. Generally consistent with the approach to the ethical process outlined in Chapter Two of this book is the notion that values must be reordered as the ethical problem and its context change.

3. A recognition of the paradoxes of procedures. This attitude acknowledges both the need for standardized procedures and the threat they represent. Order, predictability, efficiency, and equality of treatment all require some kind of established procedure in conducting the public's business. (Still, procedures have a way of becoming ends in themselves.)

Along with these three attitudes, ethical administrators need a set of what Bailey calls "moral qualities." He identifies three:

1. Optimism. This quality should not suggest a kind of Pollyannic euphoria, but rather a tendency to assume that it is possible to achieve positive ends.
2. Courage. The essential meaning of this quality is suggested by the phrase "without fear or favor." The willingness to resist the illegitimate pressures of politicians, the influence of powerful interest groups, and the intimidation of experts and favor-seeking members of the public requires considerable internal strength.
3. Fairness tempered with charity. Bailey describes this as perhaps the most essential moral quality for public servants. It must be viewed as "the principle above principle." This quality represents the ability to balance courageous commitment to equal standardized treatment of all, with a sensitivity to significant individual difference.

Two seminal works—Alasdair MacIntyre's *After Virtue* (1984) and Edmund L. Pincoffs's *Quandaries and Virtues* (1986)—have stimulated interest in the relevance of virtue for administrative ethics. MacIntyre's work has attracted the interest of public administration scholars because of the way he defines virtue in relationship to complex forms of human activity, which he terms "practices." Practices are organized around certain "internal goods" that cannot be achieved except through the practice. For example, medical practice is organized around certain human goods that have to do with the well-being of the body, which presumably cannot be accomplished otherwise. The practice of architecture is oriented to aesthetic goods in the form of physical structures that are assumed to be unobtainable through other means.

A virtue, then, in this context is "an acquired human quality the possession and exercise of which tends to enable us to achieve those goods which are internal to practices and the lack of which effectively prevents us from achieving any such goods" (MacIntyre, 1984, p. 191). This formulation of the meaning of virtue provides a potentially useful way of understanding the relevance of character traits to various human goods, which are sought through an array of practices. These virtues are predispositions to behave in a way that encourages the pursuit of the internal goods of a practice and protects them from external goods, such as money, fame, power, and organizational aggrandizement, that constantly threaten to displace the internal goods and become the dominant concern of the practice. This general perspective has offered a way of understanding how virtues relate to the practice of public administration, in which goods like justice, freedom, and equality are being pursued within public organizations that may tend to forsake these values for external goods like turf expansion, larger budgets, and political support. (See Cooper, 1987, for one application of this perspective to public administration.)

Pincoffs's book has caused many who have been addressing the development of public administrative ethics to pause and take stock of their basic assumptions and the focus of their efforts. He acknowledges appreciation for the recent explosion of interest in professional ethics, but decries what he views as a misguided preoccupation with ethical theory and its application. He attacks the idea that ethical judgment simply implies skill in using an ethical theory to solve a problem. Pincoffs views this approach as reductive and simplistic. From his perspective, moral judgment is more crucially linked to moral character—to virtue—than to the application of theories. He maintains that "the primary business of ethics ought to be with qualities of character, with the virtues and the vices" (p. 5). This assertion that virtue should be our central concern is a challenge to reorient the emphases and directions of much of the work that has been done in public administration ethics during the past twenty years.

Perhaps the earliest recognition of the importance of virtue specifically for public administrative ethics during these years came from David K. Hart. In 1984 he described the "honorable bureaucrat"—one who bears the same obligation as the citizenry to uphold civic virtue, but beyond that to seek honor. In 1985 with George Frederickson, he focused on the specific virtue of benevolence as central to the ethical public administrator in a democratic society. In 1989, in the collection of papers published from the Minnowbrook II conference, he set forth his concept of civic humanism, rooting his argument in founding thought.

Although it seems increasingly clear that virtues are necessary personal attributes if ethical conduct is to be maintained, two things are not so clear yet: how to identify and select virtuous people for the public service and how to cultivate virtue in those already employed. These problems are among the frontier agenda items for public administrative ethics.

One approach to these problems is the use of role models or exemplars of virtuous practice. In the research for *Exemplary Public Administrators: Character and Leadership in Government* (Cooper and Wright, 1992), members of the field, both practitioners and scholars, were asked to identify persons who exemplify virtue in the practice of public administration. Having selected a cross section of eleven such persons so identified, biographical character studies were then developed for each. The assumption behind this project was that presenting exemplary public administrators to current members of the field would have the effect of creating role models who would inspire emulation. Reading about the moral struggles and victories of persons such as George Marshall, C. Everett Koop, Harvey Wiley, Austin Tobin, George Hartzog, Beverlee Myers, William Ruckelshaus, Elsa Porter, Elmer Staats, Marie Ragghianti, and Paul Appleby might evoke virtuous impulses in the readers.

Analysis of these eleven studies in virtue revealed the bases for their status as powerful role models for public administrators. All of them had engaged in "moral processes" throughout their careers (Hart, 1992; Cooper, 1992b). These involved routine "moral work," as well as planned "moral projects." Moral work is just doing the right thing in the routine course of daily work such as telling the truth, treating others fairly, and eschewing racial prejudice. Moral projects include special efforts to recruit underrepresented minorities and women, undertaking ethics training for the staff, and seeking to root out corruption.

Furthermore, examination of these eleven professional lives revealed that it was these ongoing moral processes that laid the foundation for handling "moral episodes" that include both "moral confrontations" and "moral crises." Moral confrontations are when superiors, peers, elected officials, or others must be addressed in clear and direct terms about their unethical conduct. Moral crises are those intense and highly risky situations such as whistle-blowing, taking a public stand on a controversial issue, or opposing the long-standing practices of one's organization. It was the character developed during years of moral work and moral projects that made it possible for these eleven exemplary public administrators to survive moral confrontations and moral crises with integrity.

Another kind of individual attribute that has been recognized as significant is the professional value system of the public administrator. As Rokeach (1970) suggests, values are beliefs about conduct and goals; they are more cognitive than character traits, which are predispositioned to act in a certain way. These have more to do with ideas about what is desirable or undesirable.

John Rohr's work is an excellent example of a treatment of values that a public administrator ought to internalize and reflect on. He suggests (1989) that a course in administrative ethics based on "the values of the American people" be adopted in public service education. In his earlier work (1976), Rohr suggested that these "regime values" are to be found in the "writings and speeches of outstanding statesmen, in major Supreme Court opinions, in scholarly interpretations of American history and even in the rhetoric of standard Fourth of July oratory" (p. 401). In his later treatment of regime values, Rohr (1989) narrows the focus to the central values found in the U.S. Constitution—freedom, equality, and property—and their interpretations by the Supreme Court.

To those who would question prescribing the values of a particular regime, Rohr responds that this approach presupposes that we have previously decided whether the regime in question is "fundamentally just." If we enter the public service of a regime, this more basic issue should be resolved first. However, it should also be clear that Rohr is not proposing lockstep indoctrination of bureaucrats, but a thoughtful study of the very complex field of values associated with the history and institutions of the United States. He further argues, "The purpose of 'regime values' is not to make all bureaucrats march in lockstep. There is no one 'authoritative' interpretation of the American experience that all bureaucrats must adopt. What is important is that they accept the moral obligation to put themselves in touch with the values of the American people. Just how those values are interpreted is a decision only the bureaucrat himself can make" (Rohr, 1998, p. 28).

Taking this general approach but extending it beyond Rohr's specific focus on the U.S. Constitution, we might note these regime values associated with the American tradition: the beneficial aspects of a pluralism of interests, the creative possibilities in conflict, the sovereignty of the public, the rights of the minority, the importance of citizen participation in government, the societal values of freedom of expression, and the centrality of justice in the relationship between the people and their government. These are but a few exemplary values that might emerge as important in such a broadened study (Cooper, 1991).

A body of research that may provide a link among ethical decision making as a rational exercise, virtue as character traits that support ethical conduct, and professional values that provide the substance of both decisions and conduct is associated with the work of Lawrence Kohlberg. His path-breaking research on cognitive moral development will be discussed further in Chapter Eight, but at this point it should be noted that one of the findings of those who have continued working in the Kohlbergian tradition is an ever strengthening connection between principled thinking and ethical conduct. While that link is only partially understood, it appears that ability to reason, chastened by a focus on ethical principles, may contribute to the cultivation of character. People who engage in principled reasoning, consistent with the decision-making model presented in Chapter Two, appear to cultivate the character necessary to act on principle.

These inner qualities provide continual guidance for the exercise of administrative discretion. Laws and internal organizational policies can never be specific enough to cover all the situations and contingencies encountered by an administrator. Neither can public participation reach into the detail of day-to-day administrative conduct. Nor can supervision monitor more than the broader boundaries of activity. The gaps that remain are significant and extensive. Only a deeply internalized set of individual attributes can maintain congruence with the organization's goals and, beyond that, consistency with the obligations of citizenship in a democracy. These attributes also are essential for the effective functioning of hierarchical organizations. Bailey has observed that although Appleby emphasized the "series of political and organizational devices for promoting ethical choices" (1965, p. 313) that he found in the American governmental system, he also assumed certain inner qualities of a public administrator as essential. He concludes that these internal factors are necessary for the functioning of organizations according to Appleby's ideal.

Organizational Structure

Another important set of factors in maintaining ethical conduct in public organizations is associated with the structure of organizations. All too often the focus of concern seems to be the individual administrator and ways of making him or her more ethical without also addressing the nature of the organization. Kathryn Denhardt has rightly maintained that "there has been too little emphasis placed on understanding the important dimensions of practicing administrative ethics in an organizational setting" (1988, p. viii). However, she further asserts the importance of dealing with individuals and organizational structure simultaneously: "A failure to direct reform efforts toward the individual at the same time as one develops reform for the organization can result in a situation in which the new or reformed arrangements serve as substitutes for the individual moral conscience, rather than as a method of encouraging ethical decision-making" (p. 133). (See also Burke, 1986, on the importance of organization structure.) The key to responsible conduct seems to be neglecting neither the individual nor the organizational structure. Van Wart and Denhardt (2001) argue this well and add that lessons in structure may be learned from the private sector. They write, "Recognizing the importance of the organizational culture context has been essential for any successes that private sector organizations have had in developing quality products and services, and in creating the truly values-based organization. For these successes to be repeated in public sector environments, especially insofar as planned cultural change orients public organizations toward the operationalization of democratic values, organizational culture must be an important consideration" (p. 258).

Others have addressed the topic as well. Wittmer (2004) identifies the organizational variables important to ethical decision making, among them, the reward-punishment structure. Wittmer calls an organization's sanctions for unethical behavior and the rewards for ethical behavior "one of the most obvious factors that influences ethical decision-making" (p. 61). In contrast, Baucus and Beck-Dudley (2005) note that an organization that depends on the reward and punishment system to enhance ethical behavior is wrong-headed because the system fosters "low levels of moral reasoning and unethical behavior" (p. 368). Lynch, Lynch, and Cruise (2002) agree, saying that by employing an organizational design for ethics based on sanctions means "we unbalance our organizations and we lessen their productivity due to the unnecessary extra work required of red tape, which even dampens group creativity and initiative" (p. 367). Other researchers have begun to acknowledge the limitations of focusing solely on the individual and the importance of other factors of organizational structure, including performance evaluation and the "systems of partitioning and assigning decision-making rights and responsibilities to workers" (James, 2000, p. 45), "values-based communication" (Schnebel and Bienert, 2004, p. 209), and leadership strategies (Grojean, Resick, Dickson, and Smith, 2004). Indeed, how organizations can be designed to support ethical conduct is one of four big questions of administrative ethics, as I have identified elsewhere (Cooper, 2004).

One suspects that beneath the tendency to focus on individual administrators lies our American individualistic orientation with its roots in the liberal tradition. From this perspective, the fundamental reality is the individual moral agent who must be set right or constrained before social collectivities such as organizations, communities, and nations can function ethically. The coequal reality of organizations as shapers of character, values, and identity has not been fully assimilated into our worldviews. However, the recent works of Yankelovich and Bellah, among others, reflect a growing recognition of the inescapable links between individual and social reality (Yankelovich, 1981; Bellah and others, 1985, 1991; Berger and Luckman, 1966; Berger and Neuhouse, 1977; Selznick, 1992).

Within the field of public administration, we are very conscious of, even preoccupied with, the power of organization. However, it is essential that we firmly link that understanding with our treatment of administrative ethics. The organizational structure is an important part of the work environment within which individuals function, and it exercises significant influence on their ethical conduct. The problem in focusing exclusively on the attributes of individual administrators is that we may hire virtuous people and do an effective job of training them to understand what is required by professional ethics and to reason their way to a justifiable decision, but they may work within an organizational structure that discourages, or even blocks, acting ethically.

One such example is illustrative of many reported in case studies for ethics training workshops. It involved a young police officer still on probation, thus very vulnerable to dismissal. This officer noticed that his chief often arrived at crime scenes with some of his command staff and took items such as televisions, computers, and jewelry and loaded them into the trunk of his car. A check of the evidence locker at the station house revealed that none of these items had been logged in as evidence and were not to be found in the locker. The obvious conclusion was that the chief and his staff were stealing from crime scenes, as departmental regulations required that anything removed from the site of a crime be reported in the log. But what does a young officer on probation do with such information?

This officer began to systematically note items removed from crime scenes that never showed up in the evidence log. After several months of observing and recording these events, the officer went to his chief and asked for an explanation. The chief dismissed his concerns, informing the officer that this was not his responsibility and telling him to forget about it. In this case, the chief used the authority granted him by his position in the organization's structure to cover up his own illegal conduct. The person in the position bearing the greatest responsibility for ethical conduct in the department was not only stealing from citizens, but telling a subordinate to ignore these crimes.

Given the chief's response, the officer was presented with an intense ethical dilemma fraught with great risk: forget about these incidents and allow corrupt conduct to continue by the highest authority in the department, or take the matter outside the department and risk losing his job. We will come back to this story later, but suffice it to say at this point, that all too often the structural authority of organizations is used to suppress ethical conduct.

One of the problems identified by some scholars is the tendency of organizations to diffuse individual responsibility. As Dennis Thompson has observed: "In public life, especially organizations, the problem of identifying the moral agents, of finding the persons who are morally responsible for a decision or policy, becomes at least as difficult as the problem of assessing the morality of the decision or policy" (1985, p. 559). He terms this perspective, which views the organization as a whole, as the proper focus of moral judgment, "the ethic of structure" in contrast to an ethic of individual responsibility. Similarly, Robert Jackall, on the basis of one hundred interviews with managers in the private sector, concludes that bureaucratic organizations are "moral mazes" that separate "substance from appearances, action from responsibility, and language from meaning." Bureaucracy "erodes internal and even external standards of morality, not only in matters of individual success and failure but also in issues that managers face in their daily work" (1983, p. 130).

These characterizations of bureaucracy are somewhat at odds with the normative bureaucratic theory of Paul Appleby summarized in Chapter Four. There is obviously a discrepancy between the "is" and the "ought" in this case. However, the solution is not to conclude that organizations must necessarily be deleterious to responsibility. What is needed to counter the erosion of individual responsibility and minimize the inhibiting influence of organization structure is generally suggested by what Elliott Jaques (1976, p. 2) refers to as "requisite organization."

Contrary to those who have viewed hierarchical organizations as inherently stifling and insensitive to the dynamics of human behavior, Jaques argues that they can "become agents of human feeling, pluralism and community" (p. 2). On the basis of extensive empirical research on bureaucracies in both the public and the private sectors, he maintains that they are "dependent institutions" that "per se are neither centralizing nor localizing powers, neither humanizing nor dehumanizing" (p. 2). In any particular case they may be either, but ideally should be requisite in the sense of encouraging human collaboration.

Jaques begins with the assumption that it is normal for human beings to engage in collaborative interaction. The human species has survived through its ability to establish reciprocal relations among its members, which includes communication, trust, confidence, and love. These qualities are requisite for the maintenance of human existence. Without them, families, communities, the production of goods and services, social activities, artistic enterprises, and political systems would be impossible. To the extent that they are absent, organizations do not function effectively in achieving their goals.

Jaques terms "antirequisite" the organizations that discourage or impede confidence, trust, and collaboration. These organizations "arouse suspicion, envy, hostile rivalry, and anxiety, and put brakes on social relationships, regardless of how much individual goodwill there might be" (p. 6). This type of "alienating," or "paranoiagenic," organization not only creates a destructive work environment, but also weakens social bonds and increases anxiety throughout a society. It undermines responsible membership in both the organization and society as a whole. Covert behavior replaces open and honest communication; cooperation gives way to a competitive struggle for personal advantage. No one can trust the system to provide means for ensuring security, opportunity, and well-being. When this occurs, personal energy and other resources are diverted from the organization's mission, and its effectiveness is diminished accordingly. (This perspective is generally supported by Roderic Gorney in *The Human Agenda,* 1972.)

Jaques argues that the solution is not to jettison hierarchical organizations but to manage them differently. If we are to avoid covert conflict, we must clarify the limits of authority and the lines of accountability as precisely as possible. Members of the organization must know who can make various kinds of decisions, and there must be a means of holding those individuals strictly accountable for their conduct. The formal and informal organizations must be brought into congruence by reducing the need for political maneuvering, which is at odds with the formal decision-making structures, or even the possibility of engaging in such activities.

The key attributes of a requisite hierarchical organization are those of a "constitutional bureaucracy." In such an organization, authority is strictly defined at all levels, and policy is established through participation by strictly accountable elected representatives of employee groups. Also, strata within the organization are justified on the basis of the organization's function. Constitutional bureaucracies permit consultation, negotiation, and the recognition of diverse interests as part of their normal operation rather than only when crises occur. Conflict is surfaced and systematically resolved as a function of the organization's structure and constitution instead of being suppressed or ignored.

Basic to this entire approach is a recognition that real power is held by people at the various levels of an organization and not only by those at the top of the bureaucratic pyramid. Those with client interaction roles can distort or obstruct the organization's mission by the way services are delivered to the public. Also, information can be transformed as it is communicated up the chain of command. Secretaries control work flows and play critical roles in an organization's communication system. Budget analysis and accounting personnel hold the power to interpret and channel expenditures. Every category of employee holds and wields some portion of the organization's power. That power will be exercised overtly or covertly; it will be directed by political machination behind the scenes or by generally understood explicit constitutional rules. Therefore, it can be held accountable only if it is recognized, identified, sanctioned, and bounded.

Actual power in the hands of individual employees must be transformed in this way into legitimized and controlled authority to exercise that power and then made accountable to a manager. Furthermore, all individuals must be specifically accountable for their exercise of authority to a superior at the next highest level. When manager-subordinate relationships span more than one level, they tend to become confused and ineffective.

This entire system of individual authority and accountability should be rooted ultimately in constitutional arrangements for the organization, which include elected representation of all employee groups in the organizational policy process and decision-making rules to govern that process. It is also essential that authority be linked to accountability. The role of elected representatives to the organization's legislative council must be defined as involving the authority to make specific commitments for their constituents that are legally binding in nature—hence, the necessity for strict accountability of representatives to their electorate. Otherwise, representatives may not feel responsible to support the general interests of their constituent groups in the legislative process. This may lead, in turn, to a flouting of collective decisions and the resurgence of informal organizational networks.

Although in government the constitution of an organization may be imposed in part by law, thus constraining the range of discretion of its members, the concepts Jaques articulated may be adapted to these special circumstances. Although the legal mandates with which an agency must comply generally specify the public goals to be addressed, there is typically a considerable amount of latitude as to how the work is to be accomplished. Public organizations might still function as constitutional bureaucracies within these discretionary limits.

Requisite organizations contribute to administrative responsibility in several ways. First, objective responsibility is enhanced at every level through clear and direct specifications of accountability. The organization's expectations for performance are channeled directly to the employee through the one-stratum manager-subordinate relationship. Conduct is also reviewed through this proximate relationship. Thus, behavior and feedback are linked in a fashion that reduces both confusion in the communication of wishes and a delay in evaluative response. If there is a lack of clarity about either, the subordinate knows whom to go to for consultation; the person directly above him is authorized to speak for a specific area of the organization's mission and to review the work of her subordinates. There are no obfuscating chains of coordinators who have no precise authority and therefore cannot actually hold others accountable.

Second, subjective responsibility is enhanced at every level through the constitutional nature of the organization. Members of the organization are motivated to feel responsible for its effectiveness through representation and participation in the policy-making process. Orders are not simply handed down from some oppressive oligarchy at the top of the organization; rather, they flow from an elected council in which the interests of all constituent groups are acknowledged. Within the limits of the organization's legal mandates, the citizenship of all employees is affirmed; all are members of the public whose needs the organization has been established to serve; all carry responsibility for the fulfillment of its mission. Consequently, working within the organization under the supervision of a manager is not as likely to be experienced as subjection to an alien force. The orders received from above find their legitimacy not only in public law but more proximately in the collective decision-making process of a constitutional bureaucracy.

Finally, heightening both objective and subjective responsibility throughout an organization focuses effort toward achieving its goals. Much of the irresponsible draining off of time and energy into organizational infighting among various competing units can be surfaced and dealt with overtly through the constitutional structure. Similarly, individuals cannot as easily distort the organization for the sake of personal goals. Responsibility for the legislatively mandated goals of the organization is reinforced by both the constitutional process and the arrangement of one-stratum strict accountability with commensurate authority from top to bottom. Objective and subjective responsibility are brought into greater congruence by the integrative effects of these two mechanisms.

The point here is not to prescribe Jaques's constitutional bureaucracy as a panacea. The importance of Jaques's work for this discussion of organizational structure and ethical conduct is that it suggests the kind of thinking that is needed to protect the ethical autonomy of individuals while providing for accountability for their conduct. It requires that we adopt a design approach that addresses ethics at the organizational scale and asks what the dimensions are of an organization's structure that encourage or discourage ethical conduct.

Organizational Culture

The third set of factors in maintaining ethical conduct in public organizations concerns the culture of organizations. During the 1980s, the research methods of anthropology began to be applied to the study of organizations so that it is now possible to understand better the peculiar culture of organizations, similar to our understanding of the culture of larger societies. Scholars such as

Edgar Schein in *Organizational Culture and Leadership* (1985) and Ralph Kilmann in *Beyond the Quick Fix* (1984) have focused our attention on an informal set of rituals, myths, values, and norms that exist alongside the formal structure of an organization. These organizational cultures exercise powerful influence over the conduct of employees apart from, and sometimes in opposition to, the formal rules, regulations, procedures, and role authority of the managers.

The problem presented by organizational culture is noted by Grosenick and Gibson (2001) when they suggest that it is "a ubiquitous presence that can stymie the attempts of individuals to refocus their decisions, or leaders to remake their organizations" (p. 243). Organizational cultures may subvert the best efforts of organizational leaders with respect to the first two sets of factors just discussed. We may do a relatively effective job of selecting and training ethical individuals, and the organizational structure may have clear accountability, collaborative arrangements, open dissent channels, and supportive administrative leadership, but the informal culture may powerfully discourage ethical conduct, or even encourage unethical conduct.

This problem is encountered regularly with police organizations where the culture generally includes a code of silence—an informal norm among police officers that strongly discourages reporting unethical conduct of a fellow officer. Police administrators face serious problems in dealing with misconduct because rank-and-file officers will not often report accurately, if at all, what they have observed their fellow officers doing.

For example, when the young officer reported his chief's illegal activities to the district attorney and the chief was prosecuted in court, this officer was shunned by the other officers in the department and subjected to constant verbal and physical abuse. This officer, who was attempting to uphold the law and the ethics of law enforcement, was the target of death threats against himself and his family and had to have an armed guard at his home for two years. In this case, the organization's culture reinforced the corrupt norms exhibited by its structure.

Lawrence Sherman (1987) describes the potency of the police subculture in a treatment of how officers learn the ethics of their profession. Even in police academies, Sherman asserts, the culture "begins to convey folklore that shows the impossibility of doing things 'by the book' and the frequent necessity of 'bending the rules.'" He explains that "the central method of moral instruction" is the "war story." Sherman concludes from his observation of police training that "the war stories not only introduce police work as it is experienced by police officers—rather than as an abstract ideal—they also introduce the ethics of police work as something different from what the public, or at least the law and the press, might expect." This kind of cultural formation of ethical norms continues throughout the socialization process of an officer's career.

A shocking example of this is the case of prisoner abuse at Baghdad's Abu Ghraib prison. I have written elsewhere (Cooper, 2004) that Abu Ghraib, an Iraqi prison that coalition forces used for detainees, became an "organization run amok" due to several factors. First, military superiors were not consistent in their management of operations at the prison. As well, managers failed to establish an organizational structure and control within the prison that would allow easy oversight. Furthermore, the rules and procedures used for interrogation at Abu Ghraib had migrated from the procedures used at Guantanamo Bay in Cuba; no rules and procedures were designed specifically for the task and culture of the Iraqi detention center. Finally, military personnel were assigned duties for which they were not trained, and their instructions were ambiguous at best. While some have wondered if the abuses at Abu Ghraib were the results of only a few rogue military personnel, Pfiffner (2005) has argued that the "torture was the result of public policies and not merely the arbitrary actions of a few sadistic and ill-trained guards" (p. 1). "Rather," he continued, "the politics that led to torture developed through a series of legal memos, policy changes, and operational decisions that took place over several years" (pp. 1–2). Pfiffner also argues that the torture administered by low-level prison personnel was not only due to a lack of leadership traced up the chain of command to the commander-in-chief, but also a result of the prison culture and guards who were not trained to distinguish between those being held by mistake and hostile detainees.

Nevertheless, the existence of organizational culture offers opportunities for encouraging ethical conduct if it is managed effectively. Schein (1985) has argued that the most powerful influence on the culture of an organization is the conduct of its leaders. In fact, he maintains that "the unique and essential function of leadership is the manipulation of culture" (p. 317). What leaders pay attention to, how they react to critical incidents and organizational crises, the deliberate role modeling they provide, their criteria for allocating rewards and status, and their criteria for recruitment, selection, promotion, retirement, and excommunication are the primary shapers of an organization's culture, including its ethical norms. The implication of these observations is that those who lead hold potentially powerful leverage for developing a culture that is supportive of ethical conduct. Of course, the contrary is also true: leaders may espouse high ethical standards, but by their actions encourage the opposite.

Oriented mainly to the private sector, but useful for public administrators as well, are the findings of Kilmann (1984) and Peters and Waterman (1982). Kilmann eschews the tendency toward quick fixes in books on organizational development and management and identifies instead five tracks along which organizational change must be directed. One of these is organizational culture, which he engages through a group process intended to identify gaps in the culture between what is desired and what is actually done. Peters and Waterman offer numerous examples of how the culture of an organization can be constructive or destructive.

Wittmer narrows the focus to ethical climate as one element of an organization's culture. He defines it as "the shared perceptions of the ethical aspects of an organization's culture" (1996, p. 560). From his perspective, it is not the whole of an organization's culture that affects ethical conduct, but only those factors constituting these shared perceptions.

Wittmer's focus on ethical climate is adopted also by Ford and Richardson (1994) in their review of empirical research on ethical decision making. They conclude that the studies they examined support the proposition that "the more ethical the climate and culture of an organization is, the more ethical an individual's ethical beliefs and decision behavior will be. The strength of this influence may be moderated by the structure and design of some organizations" (1994, p. 217). In this conclusion, we find support for the need to link consideration of organizational structure and culture in an approach that focuses on the design of the organizational whole.

As for public sector examples of cultural intervention, the Los Angeles County Sheriff's Department conducted an extensive ongoing effort to positively shape its own organizational culture beginning in 1984 (Preimsberger and Block, 1986). This program involved twenty-four street deputies as facilitators of "Career Integrity" workshops with their fellow officers throughout the department. Of the total seventy-seven hundred members (regular and reserve), four thousand to five thousand went through at least one round of training before the program was terminated due to budget cuts a decade ago.

The name of these workshops suggests the way the culture of the department was engaged from the outset. Instead of calling the program "ethics training," the leadership of the department has presented it as "survival training"—career survival training. Comparisons are drawn between the relatively small number of deputies who are injured or lose their lives in tactical situations, and the much larger number whose careers are "killed" or "wounded" because of ethical misconduct. Thus, the ethics workshops were designed to preserve career integrity just as tactical training is designed to protect the integrity of life and limb. This way of engaging the culture of the department has been effective in heightening interest in the program and avoiding resistance to ethics training.

The workshop sessions were partially structured and partially open and freewheeling. The objective was not to train deputies in ethical decision making or to teach them a code of ethics. Rather it was to provide opportunities to examine with their peers what the prevailing norms are, the implications of operating with those norms, and alternative norms that might be more desirable. This was done in part through war stories of the negative sort—cases dealing with misconduct that had dire consequences for the deputies involved. The code of ethics, the department manual, and appropriate ethics laws were introduced when relevant as a way of reshaping the norms of the culture. Members of the department participated in these sessions with their own peers, including the command ranks, and there was exchange of information among levels.

Unfortunately, this approach to intervening in organizational culture to encourage norms more supportive of ethical conduct was curtailed in the mid-1990s because of resource constraints, but it was so successful that it was approved in July 1988 by the Commission on Peace Officer Standards and Training of the State of California for in-service training throughout the state (Peace Officer Standards and Training Commission, 1988). Although it no longer functions within its original setting, it created a model that police managers from all over California are being trained to implement.

Another intervention approach is one I have been developing for a number of years using a questionnaire entitled "Ethical Norms of Organization Culture" (Cooper, n.d.). This instrument is designed to assess the gaps in an organization's ethical norms at various levels in the hierarchy. For instance, it can be used to identify and roughly gauge the differences in norms between the top-level executives and those at the line service delivery level or between executives and middle managers. The assumption is that organizational culture is not homogeneous, but consists of various subcultures that may reflect rank or function.

The instrument provides a list of forty-two statements about specific kinds of conduct (such as lying on reports to get the job done or following orders even when told to do something clearly unethical). Respondents rate each of these items on a six-point scale according to how acceptable they think this conduct is perceived to be by others similar to themselves (for example, all middle managers or all social workers) in the organization. Then the forty-two items are repeated again, but this time respondents rate each item according to how acceptable they think it is perceived to be by some other group, such as top management or their own subordinates. The two sets of responses can be compared to identify significant gaps in the ethical norms of the culture. These items can then be considered for various kinds of interventions to close the gap: training, staff meetings, policy changes, organizational structure changes, or creation of new positive and negative sanctions.

This "Ethical Norms of Organization Culture" instrument has been used effectively in ethics training, organizational development, and the creation of values statements. It has not been published but suggests the kinds of techniques that one might create and employ.

The keys to dealing with problems of a resistant or ethically subversive organizational culture seem to be twofold. First, organizational leaders need to realize and constantly remember that they are the most significant ethical role models within the organization's culture. Consistent with the positions of Schein, Kilmann, and Peters and Waterman, empirical research for several decades (Baumhart, 1961; Brenner and Mollandar, 1977), including work by Warren Schmidt and Barry Posner (1983, 1986), indicates clearly that employees take their moral cues from the leaders of the organization. Ford and Richardson's review of 103 empirical studies on ethical decision making concludes that an "individual's ethical beliefs and decision-making behavior will increasingly become congruent with top management's beliefs as defined through their words and actions as rewards provided for compliance congruency are increased" (1994, p. 216).

This means that the conduct of the leaders, not just their words, is crucial. Chester Barnard (1952) maintains that responsible executive leadership requires that leaders act according to the values they espouse and that they do so consistently. Leadership of that kind creates positive organizational norms, builds trust in the leadership, and induces similar conduct in subordinates. At the other extreme, leaders such as the chief who stole from crime scenes are powerful negative examples sure to corrupt the ethics of their subordinates.

Therefore, if you verbally encourage ethical conduct but make exceptions for yourself, your subordinates will pay attention to the moral exceptions rather than your nice words, and the culture of the organization will be shaped accordingly. If you overlook the ethical transgressions of certain members of the organization just because they get the job done, your subordinates will understand that you do not really value ethical conduct.

If you say you support being ethical but do not devote time and resources to ethics training, your subordinates will read that as devaluing ethical conduct. The allocation of time, money, and personnel for training in administrative ethics can be an indicator of the importance you as a leader attach to ethical conduct. The members of an organization learn to "read" its values and ethical standards not only through the conduct of its upper echelons but also through its budget. When the boss sets aside four full working days for ethics training for all the administrative personnel from middle management up, expresses his expectation that everyone will spend time preparing in advance, and indicates his desire to follow up with a working group and annual refresher courses, then ethics may be perceived as something that the organization values. If the boss also prepares and participates directly in the training, the significance is intensified. But if the person at the top herds everyone into a room for a one-hour lecture or a videotaped presentation on ethics, that action is quickly interpreted as perfunctory, not to be taken seriously. It is clear to all that lip-service is being paid.

Visible significant rewards for ethical conduct may be another method for leaders to engage and shape the culture of their organizations. One difficulty with direct rewards to individuals is the impossibility of measuring systematically how ethically people are conducting themselves under routine conditions. Ethical considerations in day-to-day decision making may be invisible to an observer because they are generally subtle and undramatic. Consequently, the most effective approach may be to reserve rewards for those less frequent, more dramatic, identifiable instances of ethical courage within the organization—for example, when employees take action to rectify corrupt organizational activities at some risk to their own careers, face up to safety or quality problems rather than ignore them or cover them up, or move forthrightly to deal with discriminatory practices. One recent proposal involved giving up to four twenty-five thousand dollar annual cash awards from a fund raised by a philanthropic foundation to encourage ethical conduct in the public service. Promotions, commendations, and salary increases are alternative rewards.

Although some may consider these kinds of rewards distasteful because we all ought to pursue the good and the right for their own sake, we need to realize that more is going on in this process than just paying people to be good. Such action provides dual role modeling; both the executive giving the rewards and those receiving them are providing models of ethical organizational conduct. The recipients exemplify the appropriateness of ethical fortitude in a particular organization; the executive's conduct encourages others to act in this way. This is also one of the ways that organizational culture is shaped. The activities we publicly reward reveal the values of the organization and reaffirm and confirm them for its members. Of course, this entire process is fragile; one instance of an employee experiencing retribution from a resentful boss for engaging in courageous ethical conduct will obliterate ten instances of rewards and drive the real moral heroes into whistle-blowing outside the organization.

In order to deal with both organizational culture and structure, the design approach to administrative ethics suggests that Gabris (1991) is correct in calling for organizational development techniques as means of achieving and maintaining ethical conduct. This involves examining both structure and culture to develop a systemic relationship in which culture and structure work together to cultivate, reward, and maintain public service values.

Societal Expectations

The final set of components has to do with what a society expects of its public servants. These components are the most difficult to deal with and some are the least susceptible to manipulation by organization leaders. The point here is that a society projects in many ways what it expects from people who work in government: the relative level of remuneration for public servants, the body of law that regulates official conduct, public opinion of public administrators, and their public image as revealed in popular culture, including books, plays, political cartoons, and movies. To some extent, a society gets from its career government employees the level of ethical conduct it expects. Here we examine two expressions of societal expectations.

First, let us look at public participation. Carl Friedrich (1935) was correct in identifying public sentiment as a dominant factor in administrative responsibility. He rightly predicted that the legislative task would become so enormous and complex that citizens would increasingly turn to the administrator to affect the workings of government. Friedrich saw that administrators, faced with this direct interaction with members of the public, would have to begin anticipating their preferences, demands, and resistances. Administrators would need to be more and more aware of the social trends relevant to their duties.

However, Friedrich did not anticipate the developments of the late 1960s and early 1970s in the United States. During those years, segments of the public began to feel inadequately represented by their elected legislative representatives, especially at the federal level, and began to insist on greater participation in shaping the goals, objectives, and policies of government. African Americans, Latinos, students, and women demanded more direct opportunities to express their preferences and needs. Legislators tended to respond to these demands by inserting requirements for public participation into legislation providing public goods and services. As I have argued elsewhere, in effect this amounted to passing along to public administrators the responsibility for responding to direct public expressions of need, preference, and demand (Cooper, 1979).

Although Friedrich believed that the public in a democracy would freely communicate with its government, he did not foresee the legislative mandates that are now included in many important pieces of legislation, and he apparently did not anticipate the proactive role that would be required of administrators. Given the diversity of publics in modern society and the increasing complexity of public programs, it is not sufficient for administrators to passively await the voices of the citizenry. Administrative initiative is often required by law, but more important it is essential if useful information is to be generated from the public and if participation costs for citizens are not to be prohibitive.

Opportunities for participation must be carefully planned and systematically structured, using a variety of techniques to elicit the views of the public. The unstructured expression of public sentiment seldom gives direction to administrators. Instead, it tends to reinforce the notion among some administrators that the public does not know what it wants, and it heightens the frustration of citizens who attempt to have their opinions heard by government.

In achieving and maintaining administrative responsibility, public participation serves two major purposes. First, it maintains an awareness of the public in the minds of public administrators. Although all appointed and elected public officials are obligated to serve the public interest, it is easy to lose sight of the human reality. The demands of functioning within large bureaucratic organizations can cause administrators to become isolated from the public whose interests they are to serve. Negotiating turf and resources with other agencies or with other units of their own organization can obscure the difficult task of taking into account the complex and conflicting views of the citizenry. Also, the development of professional expertise within an organization can give rise to assumptions that "we know what is best for the public" in spite of their contrary preferences.

Regularly confronting live human beings who expect things from government is a healthy reminder of our service obligation and the sovereignty of the people in a democracy. It is a potentially constructive counterbalance for the tendency of any organization and its members to become self-serving and omniscient. Engaging the public directly may be anxiety producing, frustrating, time-consuming, and at times embarrassing, but for administrators it serves a purpose similar to one of the benefits of election campaigning for elected officials: it maintains the people of a government as a primary point of reference; it is an enactment of the accountability of the administrator.

Public participation also can assist in clarifying and specifying the intent of laws and policies. When diverse public preferences and demands are aggregated in the policymaking process, much detail is, of necessity, either never considered or lost. The scale for which laws are written generally does not permit the inclusion of specific implementation promises and alternatives. Translating broad legal mandates into specific programs, regulations, and standards has become largely a matter of administrative discretion.

This exercise of discretion by administrators must be informed by particular publics in particular places if laws and policies are to be congruent with the will of those publics. To serve effectively the public will of a pluralistic society, after diverse perspectives have been aggregated into law at a large scale, they must be disaggregated again in the implementation process. Of course, we might well go further and agree with public choice theorists such as Ostrom (1974) that the scale of governance itself needs to be reduced to the boundaries of these pluralistic preferences and demands, thus avoiding the need to aggregate them in the first place. However, whenever that has not been done, as is the case generally in the United States, administrators carry a heavy responsibility for refocusing and reparticularizing governmental activities in the implementation process.

Well-designed public participation efforts are an essential means toward that end. They can provide feedback from the environment that makes possible an open and adaptive governmental system. If the full range of citizen participation techniques is used appropriately, it can generate information about values and attitudes as well as the local conditions to which a policy should be fitted.

However, the responsibility lies with public administrators to develop their knowledge of participation methods beyond the all-too-common practice of holding a public hearing or appointing a citizens' advisory board. Survey research, iterative techniques such as Delphi, structured group interaction, charettes, and workshops are only a few of the citizen participation methods that have been underused by public agencies. Acquaintance with these participation tools, and either the skills to employ them or access to people with those skills, are essential for responsible public administration. Rosener (1977) has developed a type-function matrix that should be helpful. Also, Arthur D. Little has published a catalogue of techniques, *Effective Citizen Participation in Transportation Planning* (1976), that provides a good survey of the available options.

My argument for a normative ethic for public administration in the United States is grounded in this kind of thinking about the importance of the citizenship role and seeing the administrator as a professional fiduciary citizen who must have regular contact with the citizenry. The historical and theoretical framework for this normative approach to administrative ethics is to be found in *An Ethic of Citizenship for Public Administration* (Cooper, 1991).

Second, let us turn to laws and policies. Although it is necessary to particularize and adapt the activities of government to specific publics, this needs to be undertaken within a broad framework of laws and public policies that represent more general and continuous expression of public will. Cohesion, order, stability, and predictability are maintained in a society as conflicting interests confront each other and resolution is sought through the policy process. This is especially important for a large-scale heterogeneous society like the United States. The centrifugal forces of pluralism must be offset, to some extent, by the centripetal influences of laws and policies. The task in such a society is to arrive at a calculus of these opposing tendencies that maintains the necessary degree of cohesion and order with the greatest opportunity for the expression of diversity.

In administrative responsibility, laws and policies serve two significant functions. First, they provide external constraints on the conduct of the administrator that identify the broadest boundaries of administrative discretion. This is at the opposite purpose from that served by citizen participation. Here we are not concerned about informing the specific decisions of administrators, but rather with establishing the limits of their professional activities.

Through the legislative process, the people of a jurisdiction, through their elected representatives and usually with input from administrators, determine the general courses of action and major goals they consider desirable. Then they hold administrators accountable for working within that framework. Conduct that clearly falls outside these established boundaries is deemed irresponsible, and formal sanctions may be applied. Although strict enforcement of the laws within which public administrators carry out their duties may be irregular and infrequent, the occasional identification of flagrant violators serves as a reminder that public servants are ultimately governed by law and have a responsibility to be aware of its prescriptions.

In turn, public organizations further define the boundaries of administrative effort and activity through the establishment of policies pursuant to the law. Typically these policies provide standards, procedures, and regulations for implementing the legislative intent.

Second, laws and policies link administrative responsibility to the legislative, executive, and judicial offices of government. The discussion in Chapter Three concerning the fallacy of the politics-administration dichotomy notwithstanding, the constitutional authority of elected officials ultimately must be maintained. It is not the political versus nonpolitical attributes of the two roles that is crucial, but the final authority of constitutionally ordained officials to speak for the citizenry. Popular sovereignty is subverted if executive, legislative, and judicial officers do not have the formal power to override administrative judgments, even if they are cloaked in experience, expertise, concerns for efficiency, and warnings about risks for an agency's survival.

The law, and policies pursuant to the law, are both symbolic and actual connecting links between the administrative branch and the constitutional officers of the citizenry. Although bureaucratic power has grown significantly during the past half-century, it is always finally dependent on legislative mandate and interpretation.

The very fact that administrators seek to engage and manipulate the legislative process is a reminder that at least the boundaries of bureaucratic power are defined ultimately in that arena.

The Key Relationships

These four major components must be taken into account and managed to some degree if responsible administration is to be achieved. They need to be brought together in a design approach that seeks to create an environment in which all the components work together to reinforce each other.

In developing such a design, the most fundamental relationships in a democratic polity are those between societal expectations and each of the other three components. In this way, the democratic values and processes are supported, and the primacy of the citizenry is recognized. Individual attributes of public administrators must be supportive of responsiveness to a democratic public through commitment to citizen participation and respect for law, organizational structure must provide channels for public access, and organizational culture must be built on norms that incline members of public organizations to obey the law and engage the public in the governance process.

"Much Ado About Something"—Revisited

Let us return to the department of education that has hired you as a management consultant to design an organizational setting more conducive to ethical conduct (see Chapter Six). If we approach the problems of this organization using the four components just outlined, we will be opting for neither Finer's external controls nor Friedrich's internal controls, but rather seeking to optimize the implicit connections among them.

For example, the requisite characteristics of the department might be improved by establishing an internal policymaking body composed of elected representatives of all significant groups within the organization based on strict accountability to their constituents. Several public members elected from relevant interest groups might also be included. This policy council might be asked to begin work on three major efforts: developing an operational code of ethics, identifying all key decision points at which public input should be solicited, and initiating training programs in values and ethics for various levels of employees from the top of the department to the bottom.

The code of ethics might be drafted by a subcommittee after representatives have had an opportunity to discuss the issues with their constituents. The first draft could include both an attempt to outline the ideas of the members of the department and a summary of existing legislation applying to the conduct of public employees. After refinement in the policy council and further comments from the organizational constituents, some form of broad public input might be sought out before the code is finally adopted. This might involve public hearings, survey research (maybe a Delphi exercise), or meetings with key interest groups such as parent associations, public interest organizations, professional associations, and unions.

In defining the appropriate points for public participation, each organizational constituent group might be asked to review its functions with this concern in mind. Each group might attempt to identify areas of administrative discretion where there are likely to be multiple preferences and demands from the citizenry. Grassroots, the organization that prepared the allegations against the department, along with the state chapter of the association of parents, could be invited to participate in this review process. The goals for this effort might be a citizen participation plan for the department and the development of expertise in conducting public participation.

The ethical norms of the department might be assessed using something like the "Ethical Norms of Organizational Culture" instrument to provide the basis for designing appropriate training interventions. Training programs in values and ethics might be designed differently for the various levels of the department, but all of them would probably include some conceptual material on the values of the American democratic heritage, as well as skill-building exercises in the ethical process using actual cases experienced by the participants. Public representatives might be invited to participate in these sessions as a means of heightening awareness of public expectations. The policy council and the top echelons of management should probably receive the most extensive training because they are role models and most crucial in the maintenance of accountability. Developing the code of ethics would be, in essence, the beginning of the training process for everyone.

In addition to these three projects, the departmental management might work with you on an assessment of the organizational structure to determine the points at which strict accountability is attenuated by multiple layers without clear accountability for performance at each level or by confusing cross-relationships among units. A reorganization plan might be prepared for presentation to the policy council.

This, of course, is a very brief hypothetical discussion and may be impracticable in various ways. There might, for example, be statutory requirements concerning departmental structures that would keep the reorganization from being as consistent or thorough as desired, or that would require approval by an elected body. However, these proposals will suffice to indicate general courses of action.

Conclusion

An optimal design for responsible public administration is one in which all four components of responsible administration support ethical conduct. It is an environment in which each of these elements is fine-tuned to maximize the reinforcing effects of each on the other in a balanced fashion. Within such a network of interacting forces, a public administrator will not only be motivated to engage in systematic ethical reflections but will be in a better position to consider alternative courses of action, imagine the consequences of each, and anticipate self-approval or disapproval.

Let us honestly acknowledge, however, that what has been presented here is an ideal type. It suggests how one might approach the task as a problem for which a complex set of responses must be carefully designed. It is offered as a model that may be used for diagnostic purposes in assessing the conditions within an organization. Seldom can we control these four components sufficiently to even approximate a fine-tuning of the relationships among them. Nevertheless, it is essential that we identify the deficiencies of public organizations and address them as much as we are able.

Lamenting the ethics of public administrators and deploring irresponsible conduct when it occurs are theoretical gestures not likely to improve the operations of government. Systematic and complex analysis of these problems, and a willingness to devote time and effort to their resolution, are more likely to bear fruit. Occasional tinkering with ethics laws, promulgating codes of ethics, or sporadic training programs in ethical conduct will not produce responsible public administration. We must undertake a multifaceted, systemic approach directed toward developing the four components of responsible administration into an integrated design. Nothing less will do.

In the next chapter we deal with the opposite perspective: the individual public administrator confronting superiors who are attempting to discourage ethical conduct. The key question there will be, "How do I maintain ethical autonomy in a corrupt organization with unethical superiors?"

Chapter Eight

Safeguarding Ethical Autonomy in Organizations
Dealing with Unethical Superiors and Organizations

As we discussed briefly in Chapter Four, administrative responsibility in its objective form has two major organizational dimensions: responsibility to superiors and responsibility for subordinates. The maintenance of responsible conduct was approached in the previous chapter from the latter perspective: management concerned with maintaining responsible conduct in public organizations and management exercising its responsibility for holding subordinates accountable. Most fundamentally, this calls for techniques for bounding and directing the discretion of subordinates.

As noted in Chapter Four, principal-agent theory, drawing largely from economics, might be adopted as a perspective for understanding this managerial task. The manager, viewed as the principal, needing to ensure performance by subordinates, viewed as his or her agents, fits this relationship in a general and abstract way. However, this theory seriously oversimplifies the principal-agent relationships in public organizations. The most fundamental inadequacy is its focus on efficiency to the exclusion of ethical considerations. Also, the multiplicity of principals to which any public agent must be accountable, and any kind of priority among them, is not addressed. Public agents are accountable to organizational superiors, elected officials, the judiciary, and the citizenry, all of whom may be viewed as principals. The assumption here is that the citizenry are the ultimate principal to which public agents are accountable and whose good they are obligated to serve.

Management by organizational superiors of the four components outlined in Chapter Six is essential. This is necessary in the routine course of work to prevent or discourage the irresponsible exercise of discretion through the pursuit of private interests and to encourage a consistent effort to serve the public interest.

The validity of this perspective rests, of course, on an assumption that organizational goals are congruent with the expectations and interests of the citizenry—that the manager is acting responsibly as a fiduciary principal of the people. However, that is not always the case; organizations and their managers sometimes deviate from their public mandate and become self-serving. When that occurs, individual administrators may find it necessary to define the limits of their responsibility to the organization in order to maintain their ultimate responsibility to the citizenry. This responsibility is expressed fundamentally through the U.S. Constitution and specifically through legislation. It ultimately rests on a set of regime values that transcend specific legislation (Rohr, 1989; Cooper, 1991). These are partially expressed in the Constitution, the Declaration of Independence, and other founding documents such as the Federalist Papers and the Antifederalist papers (Storing, 1981). On the basis of this basic obligation to the citizenry and their shared regime values, it may even become necessary to resist or oppose the organization and its leaders in order to keep faith with the public. This chapter addresses these sensitive and complex situations.

Responsibility to Superiors

Discerning the limits of our objective responsibility to our superiors is most often experienced as a problem of loyalty. Typically it is a matter of conflict between our formal obligation to those with a higher level of responsibility and authority within the organization, on the one hand, and our fiduciary relationship to the public, on the other. Objectively, public administrators are accountable to both their superiors and the citizenry—proximately and routinely to the former, but ultimately and more importantly to the latter. It is not surprising, then, that situations emerge in which these dual obligations come into conflict, thus giving rise to conflicts in administrators' subjective responsibility.

Cases of Conflicting Loyalties

Conflicting feelings of loyalty require assessing the limits of accountability to superiors. Our ultimate obligation to the public may call for actions that breach our loyalty to the organizational hierarchy—in other words, whistle-blowing. Several cases from recent history may serve to illustrate situations of this type.

A commitment to ethical conduct can be lonely and costly. The tragic story of A. Ernest Fitzgerald is widely known and often cited as the classic example of the price a public servant must be willing to pay for maintaining responsible conduct (Nader, Perkas, and Blackwell, 1972). As deputy for management systems in the Office of the Assistant Secretary for Financial Management in the Defense Department during the late 1960s, Fitzgerald was responsible for cost control. For almost three years, he reported to his superiors cost overruns of 100 percent and more in the development of the Lockheed C-5A cargo plane. In spite of his outstanding professional record and recognized expertise in cost analysis, Fitzgerald's efforts were at first ignored and then blocked. Feeling that he had no recourse within his department, Fitzgerald testified to Senator William Proxmire's Joint Economic Subcommittee in November 1968 that the C-5A project had experienced a $2 billion cost overrun and that the U.S. Air Force had known about it for two years.

The harassment, scheming, social ostracism, and dismissal by air force officials that followed Fitzgerald's congressional testimony is a record of shame for American public administration. Fitzgerald, rehired in a less prestigious position after prolonged and expensive litigation, is a living witness to the risks and hazards one faces at the limits of administrative loyalty. He arrived at those limits and decided to cross them for the sake of higher loyalties. He has been one of the more conspicuous public servants to make that decision in recent years, but by no means the only one. In Fitzgerald's own words, "The only thing that makes me unique at all is that I have not gone away quietly, whereas most of the others have" (Nader, Perkas, and Blackwell, 1972, p. 40).

No doubt there have been many who have gone away quietly, leaving us unaware of the crisis they faced. However, there have been other public servants who have openly breached their loyalty to organizational superiors and have gone public. In a report on whistle-blowing prepared for the Committee on Governmental Affairs of the U.S. Senate, Senator Patrick J. Leahy (1978) of Vermont indicates that his office was able to identify seventy federal employees who spoke out about corruption, waste, and unethical conduct in government and suffered serious retaliation. After seven months of reviewing these cases and interviewing the key parties, Senator Leahy's staff compiled a detailed report on fifteen who represent typical examples. This report vividly portrays the plight of the honest civil servant who attempts to maintain ethical practices in government.

One of the most astonishing cases concerned John Coplin, a U.S. Department of Agriculture (USDA) meat grading supervisor. After nine years of distinguished service at USDA, Coplin was appointed supervisor of the Philadelphia office, where he discovered widespread, large-scale corruption. Several wholesale meat-packing houses were falsely upgrading the quality of their meat from "good" to "choice," which would command a higher price from retailers. This routine practice was being overlooked by USDA inspectors in exchange for the opportunity to purchase meat for five cents a pound. Coplin's assistant supervisor was even running a meat shuttle service between these packing houses and the national headquarters of the USDA Meat Grading Service in Washington, D.C.

When Coplin became aware of this situation, he ordered his assistant to stop the delivery service and moved to reestablish legitimate meat-grading standards. Almost immediately his relationship with officials at national headquarters began to deteriorate. Coplin was soon transferred to Chicago, where he discovered similar irregularities and, working with the FBI, fired or forced the resignation of over 70 percent of the meat graders in that region for corrupt activities.

Although Coplin's meritorious service has been widely recognized, the upper echelons of his department have not been among his admirers. Coplin was not fired, but he set a record for the longest tenure in the Meat Grading Service without a promotion—over twenty-six years at the time of Senator Leahy's investigation. Beyond this passive opposition to his insistence on ethical practices, Coplin experienced a common form of active harassment: his unit was kept permanently short-staffed. The Leahy report indicated that "he has had 20–25 different assistant supervisors over the last twenty-five years. By the time he finished training one to the degree that he or she can be of real assistance, transfer orders come in and the process starts again" (p. 161). The report concludes that Coplin "has spent more time showing new assistants the ropes than having them help him run a smooth operation" (Leahy, 1978, p. 161).

Consequences for Whistle-Blowing

Refusing to be bound by loyalty to the administrative hierarchy when unethical or illegal activity appears to be condoned is clearly risky. Public administrators who ultimately choose to uphold their obligations as citizens in the face of organizational corruption and irresponsible conduct may seriously jeopardize their livelihood, career, reputation, and personal resources. They will, in all probability, become the object of informal harassment, such as reassignment to obscure, uninteresting, menial duties; being overloaded with extraordinary amounts of work and unexpected demands; exclusion from the organizational grapevine of informal communication; and frequent transfers of staff members. "Disloyal" civil servants may also become the object of formal techniques for applying pressure and making their lives generally miserable, such as suspension without pay, unsatisfactory job performance ratings, letters of reprimand, letters of admonition, or termination.

Interestingly, the federal government does not have an accurate count of the number of instances of whistle-blowing with severe consequences. In testimony before the House Committee on the Judiciary, J. Christopher Mihm (2001) argued that "because data are not readily available, there is no clear picture of the number of complaints of workplace discrimination and reprisal for whistle-blowing at agencies or governmentwide" (p. 1). Still, Mihm testified that the number of cases of reported discrimination and whistle-blower reprisal grew nearly 40 percent during the 1990s. One reason for the lack of data on whistle-blower complaints may be that no single statute has been enacted for the sole purpose of protecting whistle-blowers. As Kohn (2001) argues, there are "over thirty separate federal statutes or constitutional provisions governing various types of whistle-blowing, and each state has developed its own common law or statutory approach to whistle-blower protection" (p. 1).

Still, the idea of reprisal and retaliation for whistle-blowing is a key concept. According to Alford (2001), "In theory, anyone who speaks out in the name of the public good in an organization is a whistle-blower. In practice, the whistle-blower is defined by the retaliation he or she receives" (p. 18). Usually, he continues, the person blowing the whistle is not "fired outright. The organization's goal is to disconnect the act of whistle-blowing from the act of retaliation, which is why so much legislation to protect the whistleblower is particularly irrelevant. The usual practice is to demoralize and humiliate the whistle-blower, putting him or her under so much psychological stress that it becomes difficult to do a good job" (pp. 31–32).

The case of Roger Boisjoly is one of the most dramatic and poignant instances of whistle-blower retribution in recent years. Boisjoly was an engineer on the *Challenger* space shuttle in 1986 when very low temperatures prior to launch raised questions about the safety of proceeding with the flight. Boisjoly was consulted along with several colleagues, all of whom argued strenuously against launching on that day. After persisting in their opposition throughout the night, the management of Morton Thiokol decided to override the engineers and go ahead with the launch. Shortly after leaving the launch pad at the Kennedy Space Flight Center, the *Challenger* exploded, killing the entire crew.

Boisjoly was terminated shortly after the disaster for his testimony at a public hearing on February 25, 1986, even though he had been correct in his opposition. He was harassed and suffered enormous emotional and physical strain. He was ultimately diagnosed with posttraumatic stress disorder and unable to work for two years. However, in spite of this painful and costly ordeal, Boisjoly (1993) maintains that his kind of resistance to management is sometimes necessary and the only thing to do: "If good, caring and knowledgeable people observe wrongdoing and simply turn away to protect their own self interests without attempting to correct the wrongdoing, they become part of the problem. These same people also become a part of the overall 'unethical cancer' that ruins once productive organizations and dooms them to internal self destruction in the long term" (p. 67).

In spite of the suffering he experienced at the hands of malevolent authority, Boisjoly (1993) remained optimistic about what subordinates in a misguided hierarchy can accomplish: "The continuous lesson learned from these personal experiences, is that the good guys can win. But even if we lose a battle, we can have an influence on the outcome of the war, if enough employees stand up for what they know in their hearts is right" (p. 61).

In these instances, the external controls of the organization, which are experienced most directly, consistently, and with the most immediate consequences, are directed against responsible conduct. Hierarchical authority and power are set in conflict with the internal controls of ethical administrators whose commitment is to the well-being of the public, and also to other external controls such as laws and codes of ethics. These cases seem to demonstrate, as discussed in Chapter Seven, that it is extremely difficult to maintain responsible conduct only by cultivating the right individual attributes, intervening in the culture, or passing ethics legislation. Often public interest values, norms, and laws are present and operative but are overwhelmed by the force of contrary organizational pressures. Some extraordinary public administrators, such as those described here, do resist intimidation, but at unreasonable personal costs. Jos, Tompkins, and Hays (1989), in a study of 161 whistle-blowers, found that 62 percent lost their jobs, 11 percent had their salaries reduced, and 18 percent experienced harassment or transfers. Over half indicated that their actions embroiled them in controversy for more than two years, costing them an average of $28,166 of their own funds to defend themselves.

The young probationary police officer who reported his chief to the district attorney for illegal activities (see Chapter Seven) paid an enormous cost—not in dollars but in stress, fear, and anxiety for himself and his family for two years.

Nevertheless, Judith Truelson (2001), after years of studying whistle-blowing and the retribution whistle-blowers experience, has observed that "whistleblowers have become indispensable agents of accountability by exposing huge cost overruns at the Pentagon, numerous environmental hazards, and many other instances of government malfeasance" (p. 407). She notes that "since 1986, amendments to the False Claims Act have returned $1.8 billion to the U.S. Treasury that would have been lost to fraud but for the actions of individual whistleblowers" (p. 407). Truelson reviews the whistleblower protection policies that have been implemented and organizations that have been established to provide support for those compelled to blow the whistle, and concludes ultimately that hope rests in changing organizational cultures. Public organizations need to cultivate a sense of obligation to the public that would preclude whistle-blowing by motivating public administrators to hold each other accountable routinely for serving the public good.

Although consequences for whistle-blowing remain a threat, some researchers have argued that the number of whistle-blowers has increased. Johnson (2003) cites several reasons for the increases in people willing to come forward to report unlawful or unethical conduct, including laws that encourage and protect whistleblowers. Perhaps most interesting is Johnson's argument that the public's perception of whistle-blowers is perhaps becoming more positive. Part of the reason for that improved public image and for the public's being more receptive to whistle-blowing, argues Johnson, is that "whistle-blowers increasingly are raising health and safety issues that people personally care about" (p. 16). She calls the *Challenger* disaster a "milestone event for whistle-blowing" (p. 17) because of the media coverage and the corresponding public outcry and concern. If Johnson is correct about whistle-blowers enjoying a more positive public image, then perhaps public servants who are struggling with the threat of consequences for whistle-blowing may be enticed to illuminate wrongdoings.

Sources of Organizational Pressure: The Team Play Ethic

Where do they come from, these organizational pressures on those who expose corruption, waste, and abuses of power?

Political Pressure

Sometimes, such as during President Richard Nixon's second term of office, partisan political interests give rise to systematic and ruthless efforts to intimidate outspoken members of the bureaucracy. The notorious "Malek Manual" (*Federal Personnel Manual*, 1972), with its explicit prescriptions for harassing and removing, by devious means, certain "uncooperative" members of the U.S. Civil Service, epitomizes the unscrupulous use of political power to exact obedience and compliance.

At the local level, city managers and municipal department heads often report experiencing pressure from members of the city council to shape their recommendations and actions in ways that serve the political interests of the elected officials. City managers are particularly vulnerable as it typically takes only a majority vote of the council to terminate their employment.

Alford (2001) thinks that political pressure is often at the heart of an individual's willingness—or lack thereof—to report unethical behavior in his or her organization. He argues that "organizations are the enemy of individual morality" (p. 35). He fears that an individual's willingness to speak out on behalf of others is muted by undemocratic organizations. He writes that large, bureaucratic organizations "are the political world that matters most to people's lives, that part of politics that controls your career, your paycheck, your health insurance, your mortgage, your retirement, and your family's economic security" (p. 35).

The Team Play Ethic

However, more often the pressure to conform comes from within bureaucratic organizations. The Leahy report (1978, p. 12) identifies the underlying problem as the team play ethic: "The needs of any particular federal agency are best met if its employees remain 'team players'" (p. 12). The needs in this case are for total loyalty to the organization and to ensure that "the agency will continue to run smoothly and prosper" (p. 12). Consequently, any employee who attempts to exercise ethical autonomy by placing loyalty to the greater public good above the orderly operation of his or her agency is viewed as a serious threat that must be dealt with severely. As Caiden and Truelson (1988, p. 120) conclude: "The weight of organizational loyalty and conformity" is used "to intimidate and destroy the credibility of whistle-blowers and probably their spirit too." One learns very quickly, Leahy's report found, that "the key to success in the bureaucracy is to be quiet, to do competent work, and to move slowly up the hierarchy" (pp. 11–12).

Organizational needs for stability, order, and respectable image are allowed to supersede the kind of obligation embodied in statements of public service principles, such as the lofty phrases of the Code of Ethics for Government Services (U.S. House of Representatives and U.S. Senate, 1958):

- Put loyalty to the highest moral principles and to country above loyalty to persons, party, or Government department. Uphold the Constitution, laws, and legal regulations of the United States and all governments therein and never be a party to their evasion.

- Expose corruption wherever discovered.

- Uphold these principles, ever conscious that public office is a public trust.

Public servants who take these admonitions seriously and act accordingly soon discover that those above them in the bureaucracy do not necessarily do the same. The team ethic is often the dominant guide for conduct, not an ethic of responsibility to the public.

What are the roots of this team ethic? We turn to an examination of four reasons for its existence.

The Nature of Public Organizations

The Leahy investigation locates the source of the problem in the unique nature of public organizations. From this perspective, it is the lack of the profit motive and the incentives it creates that give rise to the "don't rock the boat" attitude that prevails in the bureaucracy. Survival in business and industry, goes the argument, requires that mismanagement, waste, inefficiency, and corruption be rooted out. The fundamental incentive to maintain and increase profits is said to overcome the defensive and self-protective tendencies of organizational hierarchies in the private sector. In the absence of a concern for profitability, public organizations become preoccupied with appearances; looking good is viewed as the way to survive. "Impression management" in relation to elected officials, the media, and the public assumes primary importance.

No doubt there is truth in this line of analysis. For example, on January 13, 1997, the Internal Revenue Service (IRS) released a report instigated by congressional pressure admitting that the agency had pressured its employees to pursue excessively aggressive, and even illegal, actions in collecting delinquent taxes and seizing property. In attempting to demonstrate productivity, quotas and statistics had been used to evaluate individual personnel and IRS district offices, a practice specifically prohibited by federal law (Vartabedian, 1998).

Long before the recent controversy over inappropriate procedures by the IRS, A. W. Carney, a former tax auditor for that agency, offered support for this point of view. He noted that the IRS operates with a quota system for auditing income tax returns; a certain number of cases are to be closed each week. Carney argued that the agency had become preoccupied with meeting or exceeding the quota, to the exclusion of the quality and effectiveness of the audits. He attributed this phenomenon to a concern for presenting an impression of good performance to the House and Senate appropriations committees. Carney, quoted in the *Los Angeles Times* ("Appearance of Success Is Key to Tax Audit System," 1979), concluded that ineffectiveness and inefficiency were allowed to continue because "both Congress and the IRS have been primarily concerned with the appearance of success, rather than with success itself."

However, the situation seems to be more complex than the Leahy report suggests. Weisband and Franck, in *Resignation in Protest* (1975), present an analysis that is somewhat at odds with the point of view presented there. In a comparative study of resignation behavior among American and British public officials, these two researchers discovered that there is a significant difference in willingness to resign over some ethical issue and publicly protest the wrongdoing. High government officials in the United States who resign for such reasons are much less likely to offer a public explanation for leaving their positions. Typically they give reasons of health, financial exigency, or family pressures rather than divulge the real causes for resignation. In Great Britain, the more typical behavior is to prepare a written statement arguing one's case, give it to one's superiors, and then release it to the press, thereby setting the stage for a public debate of the issues.

Of the 389 resignations by American high-level federal officials between 1900 and 1970, 355 (91.3 percent) departed without any form of public protest. Only 34 (8.7 percent) protested in some fashion. In contrast, of the 78 British instances of resignation studied, 42 (53.5 percent) made some public declaration of protest against a government policy. The protest rate of British resigners is more than six times that of Americans.

Furthermore, when the career consequences in each case are compared, it is clear that public protest is far more damaging to Americans than to their British counterparts. In the United States, only 1 person (3 percent) among the 34 protesting resigners was subsequently reappointed to an equivalent or higher post, whereas 73 (20.6 percent) of those who resigned quietly returned to government later in a position as high as, or higher than, the one they left. Only 4 of the 34 (11.8 percent) protesters were subsequently readmitted to either full-time or part-time prestigious posts, but 127 of the 355 (35.8 percent) who left quietly were given positions. In the British government, 19 of the 42 (45.2 percent) who resigned in protest later returned to equivalent or higher posts, but only 15 of the 36 (41.7 percent) who left quietly were returned later to similar or better positions. From these statistics, Weisband and Franck conclude, in the case of the British, that "those who resigned in public protest did marginally better—but in any event no worse—than their more complaisant colleagues" (p. 97). This stands in stark contrast to the American situation, where resignation with public protest is tantamount to closing the door to further service.

Why are those who call attention to corrupt practices, gross inefficiency, and abuses of power and then resign in protest so consistently harassed and banished from government in the United States? Clearly the answer cannot be so simple as the one provided by the Leahy committee. It is not just a difference between public organizations and those in the private sector, as that committee's study suggests. If it were only a matter of government organizations not being required to turn a profit and therefore becoming preoccupied with image management, why is this not true of Great Britain? Furthermore, the Senate committee report assumes a significantly stronger concern for rooting out corruption, mismanagement, and inefficiency in business and industry than seems justified.

Private Sector Norms

Both Weisband and Franck (1975) and the Leahy committee (1978) conclude that a team player ethic is dominant in the United States, but they disagree about its source. The Senate committee identifies this ethic with an absence of private sector incentives and demands, but the authors of *Resignation in Protest* argue the opposite—that the team ethic has its origins in business, industry, and the legal profession and is carried into government by officials from these areas of the private sector. They maintain that the ethical standards of law and big business have come to permeate the upper echelons of government, where the norms for the entire system are established. According to their research, 289 (76.9 percent) of the 389 American resigners were either big-business executives or attorneys, or both, before entering government. They conclude that the boardroom ethic of corporate loyalty and the tendency of attorneys to view their government employer as a client both militate against speaking out about an organization's dirty linen. Thus, the Leahy committee laments the lack of private sector influence in government while Weisband and Franck lay the blame on its presence.

Anti-Tattling

In addition to the operative values of business and the legal profession, Weisband and Franck identify two sources of the team player ethic: the more pervasive anti-tattling conditioning that most Americans experience from a very early age, together with the bureaucratic code of subservience to the hierarchy. In the former case, Jean Piaget's studies of child development are cited as evidence for a socialization process that discourages tattlers. Moral maturity is equated with maintaining peer group solidarity against adult authority; the tattler who ingratiates himself with authority figures is viewed as not only immature but also deserving of ostracism from the group. Although this rejection of dependence on adult authority may be a healthy requirement for reciprocal peer group relations among children, these authors argue that it tends to be maintained inappropriately into adulthood.

Sometimes popular culture reveals our ambivalence about tattling in vivid and powerful ways. For example, two movies, *A Few Good Men* and *Scent of a Woman*, provide conflicting perspectives on whether one should inform authorities about observed misconduct. In *A Few Good Men*, the setting is the U.S. Marine Corps; the story involves an incident in which hazing has resulted in a trainee's death. The attorneys assigned to the case by the U.S. Judge Advocate General's Office run head-on into a wall of resistance to their inquiries. The code of silence, similar to that often found in police departments, is adhered to firmly and enforced by the commanding officer. The argument by the commander is that honor requires that members of the corps not inform on a fellow member. He upholds loyalty to the corps as a higher value than subordination to legal authority. In this film, resistance to informing is clearly presented as quite the opposite: a lack of true honor in upholding the laws and regulations and a failure of honesty, courage, and forthrightness in identifying the wrongdoers. The message is unequivocally that one should inform authority when a party to information about serious misdeeds.

In *Scent of a Woman*, a young man at a private school is held up as an example of honor for refusing to divulge information about who among his fellow students vandalized the headmaster's car. This motion picture unmistakably represents the young student's silence as morally courageous, an act of honor, and an example of strong character. Conduct deemed admirable in this film is presented as despicable in *A Few Good Men*. Movies of this kind make for interesting discussion in a classroom or training session about responsibility in situations about which there is so much ambivalence in our society.

Bureaucratic Norms

The final source of the team ethic discussed by Weisband and Franck is the bureaucratic code of subservience to the organizational hierarchy. As public employees move up the career ladder, the norm of deference to those higher up tends to be internalized and reinforced through the bureaucratic socialization process.

However, what begins as an appropriate civil service ethic of acknowledging legally constituted authority can become so ingrained and dominant that some who rise through the ranks over a period of years to a position of considerable responsibility have difficulty acting against the illegal, improper, or abusive exercise of authority from above. In effect, these are cases in which the agent has become too conformed to the most proximate organizational principal and has lost a sense of accountability and obligation to higher principals such as elected officials, the courts, and the citizenry.

The Agentic Shift

Although the civil servant's tendency to be overly deferential to superiors may be intensified through the socialization process, there is evidence that this may be a far more pervasive problem in our society. Stanley Milgram's research (1974) indicates that a large percentage of the American population may be inclined to obey authority, even when doing so involves actions that are apparently dangerous to others. Milgram conducted a series of experiments designed to test Americans' willingness to obey authority, with a broad range of occupations included in each experiment.

The basic design of these investigations involved naive subjects who believed they were participating in experiments on the effectiveness of punishment in the learning process. These subjects, in the role of "teacher," were instructed to read a list of paired words to a "learner" whose task was to memorize them. Whenever the learner answered incorrectly, the teacher was instructed to administer a progressively intense electrical shock. After each wrong answer, the teacher pushed the next in a series of switches, which were labeled from 15 to 450 volts in strength, with verbal designations ranging from "Slight Shock" to "Danger—Severe Shock." The learner, who was in fact an actor hired to participate in the project, was not actually receiving the shock. Concealed behind a screen, he would play tapes with groans of discomfort, followed by loud protests against continuing the procedure, expressions of fear about a possible heart attack, and agonizing screams as the electrical shock reached high voltage levels, and finally complete silence.

The fact that 62 percent of the subjects were willing to administer the most intense level of shock—450 volts—under instruction from the experimenter was surprising to those conducting the study and to a panel of thirty-nine psychiatrists asked to predict the behavior of those involved in this kind of experiment. After hearing a lecture on the experiment, all thirty-nine expected disobedience before the halfway point on the shock scale, 195 volts. Yet almost two-thirds of those ordinary Americans were willing to follow orders obediently, even in the face of unmistakable evidence that another innocent human being was suffering severe pain and terror. A surprising number were even willing to force the learner's hand onto an electrode.

Why were so many so obedient under these circumstances? Milgram identified a number of factors in accounting for this surprising behavior, but the primary dynamic is rooted in the nature of hierarchical structures. He refers to it as the "agentic shift" (1974, p. 132). Individual behavior is limited and controlled, according to Milgram, by internal inhibitors that we sometimes refer to as conscience. However, when individuals are brought together in a hierarchical relationship, their actions must be coordinated; external sources of control must be created. Internal inhibitors, then, must yield to some extent to this external source of control: "The inhibitory mechanisms which are vital when the individual element functions by itself become secondary to the need to cede control to the coordinating component" (p. 129). Internal changes that suppress local control for the sake of system coherence must take place. In other words, conscience is diminished when a person enters a hierarchical structure.

Thus, in the organizational society, there are two functional modes: the autonomous, self-directed mode and the systemic or organizational mode. The transition from autonomous to organizational functioning is the agentic shift. It involves an alteration of attitude; we shift from acting out our own purposes to an attitude of acting as an agent who executes the wishes of another person. When an individual views himself in this agentic state, "profound alterations occur in his behavior and his internal functioning" (Milgram, 1974, p. 133). He renders himself open to control by those in authority. Milgram observes that the individual has a degree of freedom to choose whether he defines himself as being in an agentic state, but once he does so, "the individual no longer views himself as responsible for his own actions but defines himself as an instrument for carrying out the wishes of others" (p. 134). The extent to which any given individual is willing to make the agentic shift depends largely on socialization through experiences of obedience to authority in family life and organizational participation from the earliest years. In modern society, this process is intensified by the way individuals are taught to obey impersonal authorities based on "abstract rank, indicated by an insignia, uniform, or title" (p. 137).

Milgram's conclusion is particularly relevant to the concerns of this book: "The most far reaching consequence of the agentic shift is that a man feels responsible to the authority directing him but feels no responsibility for the content of the actions that the authority prescribes" (1974, pp. 145–146). An alteration in personal subjective responsibility occurs, which brings it into congruence with the objective responsibility defined and projected by someone in authority. "Morality," Milgram explains, "does not disappear, but acquires a radically different focus: the subordinate person feels shame or pride depending on how adequately he has performed the actions called for by the authority" (p. 146). The definition of a moral act becomes reduced to obedience to authority. Responsibility for the consequences of our actions is thus destroyed; we believe that the authority chose the act, not us; the person in authority is perceived to be responsible.

This displacement of personal responsibility is clearly evident in the legal defense presented for Colonel General Alfred Jodl at the Nuremberg trials of Nazi war criminals in 1945 (French, 1972). His counsel, Dr. Exner, argued:

> Whether or not to wage a war is a political question and is the politician's concern. The question of how to wage war is the only question concerning the Armed Forces. . . . But if he [the military officer] plans and carries out the plan of a possible war, that is, in case the political leadership decides on war, he does nothing but his evident duty. . . . One would object that it is not his affair, not an affair of his conscience to examine the admissibility of the war, but that this is the duty of the responsible state authorities [French, 1972, pp. 197–198].

The separation of politics from administration, the strict maintenance of monocratic hierarchical relationships of authority and responsibility, and a firm distinction between substantive and instrumental reasoning combine to exculpate the agent.

Adolf Eichmann, the Nazi S.S. architect of Hitler's "final solution" of the "Jewish problem," epitomized this shift in attitude and behavior. Feeling no sense of personal responsibility for the extermination of millions of Jews, Eichmann freely admitted his deeds when he was captured by Israeli commandos in Argentina, again under interrogation in Israel, and once again during his trial (Arendt, 1963; Harel, 1975). He repeatedly insisted that he was only carrying out the orders of his superiors and therefore was guilty only of "aiding and abetting" in these acts. In an attempt to deflect culpability from himself, Eichmann argued that he did not personally carry out those heinous acts of murder and torture, nor did he act out of any personal feelings of hatred for Jews in his organizational and administrative duties (Arendt, 1963).

In her study of Eichmann, Hannah Arendt concluded that he represented "a new type of criminal" who "commits his crimes under circumstances that make it well-nigh impossible for him to know or feel that he is doing wrong" (1963, p. 253). Viewing himself only as an instrument of a large hierarchical organization, Eichmann was devoid of any sense of a motivation of his own, save that of efficiently carrying out the will of others. Initiative did not lie within himself, but with the Nazi High Command. Arendt notes that his very language evidenced a total absorption of the self into a bureaucratic role. Eichmann seemed incapable of speaking anything but "officialese"; his vocabulary consisted of learned "clichés" and "stock phrases which obscured the stark realities of the death camps and the ovens. The longer one listened to him," says Arendt, "the more obvious it became that his inability to speak was closely connected with an inability to think, namely, to think from the standpoint of someone else" (p. 44).

If Arendt's analysis is correct, the agentic shift was almost total in Eichmann; self-deception was nearly complete. Reflective thought issuing from a multifaceted mentality capable of imagining alternatives and viewing one role in the complex perspective of many others had been all but smothered. The surrender to an instrumental role that appeared to obviate personal choice precluded the ability to empathize and to freely respond empathetically. Although certified as normal by half a dozen psychiatrists, Eichmann had apparently managed to so thoroughly become the "agent" that the connection between his conduct and its consequences for others was severed. Only the link between conduct and the will of superiors remained.

This diminution of personal responsibility for the consequences of one's action or inaction in the agentic state ought to be of major concern in a consideration of administrative ethics. If we worry that so few public servants speak out against destructive authority, if loyalty to superiors tends to override individual conscience and obligations to the citizenry, then Milgram's findings should cause us to inquire further into means of modifying the extent to which individuals in public service make the agentic shift. This is the dark side of principal-agent theory not well accounted for in that literature (Bowie and Freeman, 1992).

Another example from the experimental psychology literature is the prison simulation conducted by Phillip Zimbardo in 1971 at Stanford University (Zimbardo, 1992). Students were recruited to play roles typical of correctional institutions. With stark realism, the students were "arrested," handcuffed, and taken to headquarters by the Palo Alto Police Department. After being fingerprinted and photographed, they were taken to a basement on the Stanford campus that had been set up as a simulated prison environment with cells and offices. By drawing lots, some participants became prison guards and others became prisoners. Prisoners were subjected to delousing, required to don uniforms, and then placed in a locked cell by the prison guards, who were also dressed in appropriate uniforms.

The experiment was to run for two weeks but had to be terminated after only six days. The very real psychological and physical brutality had reached a level that prevented the continuation of the simulation. As in the case of Milgram's studies, the context of the simulated prison carried its own force and momentum. The participants were captured by their mutually antagonistic roles. All of the simulated trappings of the prison environment, such as uniforms, hierarchical authoritarian relationships, the imposition of rules, unequal power, and locked cells, displaced the humane impulses brought into that setting by the subjects. Removed from that situation, the student participants were stunned by their own conduct as they watched themselves on videotape.

Organizational Remedies

If fear of reprisal were the only impediment to individual ethical action, schemes to protect legitimate whistle-blowers would appear to be the most productive approach. The U.S. Office of Special Counsel (OSC) under the Merit Systems Protection Board (MSPB), set up to confidentially receive and investigate complaints of improper and illegal activities, seems a reasonable way to provide some degree of protection from hierarchical vindictiveness ("Proposed Civil Service Changes . . . ," 1978). Mechanisms such as the Fraud Task Force of the U.S. General Accounting Office (GAO), with a hotline for anyone aware of corrupt activities within the federal government, also offer hope for confidential handling of these matters.

It is clear that organizational strategies of this kind cannot provide total confidentiality, nor can they assure public servants that whistle-blowing will no longer be a hazardous enterprise. However, they do offer greater security in speaking out than previously existed; the risk level is reduced to some extent. The initial responses of federal employees seem to bear this out. During its first year, the OSC reportedly received 1,925 complaints with sufficient basis for opening a case. Whistle-blowers constituted 5 percent of the total, or 96 cases; an additional 27 percent, or 520 cases, dealt with complaints of reprisals (*First Annual Report to the Congress* . . ., 1979). This is an astonishing outpouring of grievances and concerns to a new and untried agency with no track record in protecting the anonymity of the complainant, which suggests that the will to maintain ethical conduct is strongly present among some in the public service. Given only promises of confidentiality, they will come forward with information.

The GAO Fraud Task Force experienced an even larger response, perhaps owing to its longer history and established credibility. According to Lawrence Sullivan, a member of the task force, during its first seven months of operation in 1979, over six thousand calls were received; after screening, approximately four thousand appeared substantive. At a meeting of the ASPA Professional

Standards and Ethics Committee on August 30, 1979, Sullivan indicated that although these complaints came both from outside and within the federal government, 28 percent of the callers were federal employees, blowing the whistle on illegal conduct. Apparently not all public servants make the agentic shift so totally as to impair their ability to act independently and exercise personal responsibility on occasion.

Unfortunately, the mechanisms provided by the OSC do not seem to have been very effective in protecting whistle-blowers from retaliation by their superiors. Caiden and Truelson (1988, p. 122), evaluating these reforms ten years after their establishment, conclude: "In practice, the new legislation has been weakly enforced. Congress, federal employee representatives, and the General Accounting Office (GAO) have all been critical of the Special Counsel for failing to provide adequate protection to whistle-blowers, of the MSPB's exacting standards of proof of reprisal action, and of the failure of the Special Counsel to convince the MSPB to take the necessary disciplinary action against victimizers."

Support for this pessimistic assessment comes from a report prepared by the MSPB (1984), which compared data from random samples of federal employees in 1980 (13,078 employees) and 1983 (7,563 employees) concerning whistle-blowing in the federal government. In both years, approximately 70 percent of those who reported direct knowledge of an illegal or wasteful activity said they did not report it to anyone. In 1980, 20 percent gave fear of reprisal as one reason for taking no action; by 1983 this number had risen to 37 percent. Thus, the number of fearful employees had almost doubled under the protection of the new mechanisms. (The most frequently cited reason, given by 53 percent in each year, was belief that reporting the misconduct would not bring about any change for the better.)

Similarly, Jos, Tompkins, and Hays (1989, p. 554), in their study of whistle-blowers, 55 percent of whom were from the federal government, found the OSC and the MSPB were rated among the least helpful. On a seven-point helpfulness scale (7 being most helpful), the OSC received an average rating of 1.4 and the MSPB of 1.9.

However, these authors do acknowledge that certain flaws built into the original structure and mission of the OSC may have been remedied by a whistle-blower protection act signed into law on April 10, 1989. This act "makes the OSC an independent agency, specifies that its mandate includes protecting whistle-blowers, and gives the OSC the authority to issue a 45-day stay prohibiting an agency from demoting or firing a worker who has filed a complaint" (Jos, Tompkins, and Hays, 1989, p. 558). It also revises the previous burden of proof by making it necessary for a whistle-blower only to show that his whistle-blowing was a contributing factor in his termination or harassment instead of a significant or predominant factor.

Although there has been no systematic longitudinal study of the OSC since these 1989 changes, the 1997 annual report from that agency to Congress does offer some signs of progress. Whistle-blower charges submitted to the agency increased by 93 percent from 1993 (177) to 1996 (252), apparently indicating a growing trust in the agency (U.S. Office of Special Counsel, 1997). Indicative of the broader results of OSC beyond whistle-blowing, which is only one of the responsibilities it bears for ethical conduct in the federal government, "During fiscal years 1992–96, OSC has negotiated over 600 favorable actions on behalf of federal employees who have brought prohibited personnel practice and Hatch Act complaints to the agency. This includes the 87 favorable actions obtained in FY 1996. By comparison, in the prior 11 years (Fiscal Years 1981–1991), OSC obtained approximately 250 favorable actions. In other words, OSC has obtained almost 2.5 times more favorable actions in less than one-half the time" (U.S. Office of Special Counsel, 1997, executive summary).

Beyond these specific devices for easing the burden of whistle-blowers, the American Society for Public Administration (1979) adopted a statement, entitled "Whistle-Blowing: A Time to Listen . . . A Time to Hear," which calls for a more comprehensive organizational approach to the problem. This position paper encourages those in government to obviate the need for whistle-blowing by addressing the underlying problems. ASPA emphasizes the importance of establishing and enforcing policies that articulate the ethical standards of public service, regularly communicating these expectations to employees, creating procedures for conducting "dissent channels to permit contrary or alternative views on policy issues to be reviewed at a higher level" (p. 3), and encouraging managers to focus on the substance and merits of an employee's allegations rather than being preoccupied with "the assumed motivations of dissenters or whistle-blowers" (p. 4).

These organizational approaches are necessary to make it possible for public servants to properly define the limits of administrative loyalty and respond responsibly. The organizational components of responsible conduct discussed in Chapter Seven, along with these measures specifically oriented toward whistle-blowing, are sufficient to suggest the outlines of the organizational requirements.

Individual Responsibility

However, these strategies, though important, are not in themselves sufficient. The more difficult long-run task for those concerned about ethical conduct in public administration involves buttressing ethical autonomy and individual responsibility among those who already possess these attributes in some measure, and extending them to others who may tend to function largely as agents with little clarity about the boundaries of loyalty to an organizational hierarchy. This effort must begin with the reassertion of individual responsibility for one's actions.

The Nuremberg Principle

The Nuremberg Charter, which established the principles and procedures for the trials of the Nazi war criminals following World War II, included these key articles in Section II:

> Article 7. The official position of defendants, whether as Heads of State or responsible officials in Government Departments, shall not be considered as freeing them from responsibility or mitigating punishment.

> Article 8. The fact that the Defendant acted pursuant to an order of his Government or of a superior shall not free him from responsibility, but may be considered in mitigation of punishment if the Tribunal determines that justice so requires [Jackson, 1947, p. 23].

Against the defense offered by Jodl, Eichmann, and others, these articles maintained from the outset that individuals are ultimately responsible for their deeds and must be held accountable before the bar of justice. Neither an official role nor obedience to authority may be used to excuse conduct.

In his opening statement before the Nuremberg Tribunal, Robert H. Jackson, chief of counsel for the United States, argued that the doctrine of individual responsibility for crimes in the international arena had a long history in matters of piracy and brigandage. He insisted, "Only sanctions which reach individuals can peacefully and effectively be enforced" (1947, p. 88). Jackson further maintained: "Crimes always are committed only by persons. While it is quite proper to employ the fiction of responsibility of a state or corporation for the purpose of imposing a collective liability, it is quite intolerable to let such a legalism become the basis of personal immunity" (pp. 88–89).

Jackson continued to advance this principle in his closing address before the tribunal by arguing that all those who sought refuge in the collective responsibility of the Nazi regime in fact individually supported that government and never directly challenged its policies: "Nowhere do we find an instance where any one of the defendants stood up against the rest and said: 'This thing is wrong and I will not go along with it'" (1947, pp. 88–89).

Although Hitler's Germany, with its mailed-fist totalitarianism, its bizarre pageantry, and its horrifying slaughter of human life, may seem far removed from the mundane ethical problems of contemporary public administrators, these Nuremberg principles are nevertheless relevant and worthy of attention. Under these principles, men were indicted and found guilty as "individually responsible for their own acts and for all acts committed by any persons in the execution of such plan or conspiracy" (Jackson, 1946, p. 115). They remind us that although we act as agents for others, we must never view ourselves as only instruments in their hands; although we accept roles that obligate us to act in ways that are not precisely congruent with the choices we would make if acting alone, we are not free to abandon conscience as we consider how to enact those roles and struggle to discern where the boundaries of loyalty lie. We are finally responsible for saying yes or no to superiors, peers, and collectivities in which we participate.

The Final Safeguard

Individual responsibility, insofar as it can be inculcated, is a necessary counterbalance to the agentic shift that bureaucratic organizations tend to require. Wakefield (1976) argues that both a feeling of being responsible as an individual and objectively being held accountable by the law and the citizenry for our deeds are the ultimate buttresses of public service ethics. Organizational arrangements, designs, and devices are desirable and necessary for the day-to-day routine maintenance of responsibility. However, when organizational goals are seriously diverted from their legal mandate and the public interest is displaced by private interests, the final safeguards against corruption and subversion of democratic government are a commitment to responsible conduct on the part of individual citizens employed by government and a public that can exact accountability from them.

This means that although we might not commit misdeeds directly and overtly ourselves, awareness of such conduct by subordinates, peers, or superiors imposes responsibility for rectification, as far as possible. In the judgment of the District Court of Jerusalem against Adolf Eichmann, the judges concluded that with complex crimes involving many people "on various levels and in various modes of activity—the planners, the organizers, and those executing the deeds, according to their various ranks . . . the extent to which any one of the many criminals was close to or remote from the actual killer of the victim means nothing, so far as the measure of his responsibility is concerned. On the contrary, in general the degree of responsibility increases as we draw further away from the man who uses the fatal instrument with his own hands" (Arendt, 1963, p. 225). If the impropriety of an act is recognized, distance from its specific overt commission quite likely provides greater perspective for moral judgment and also often implies broader administrative contributions that make that act, and others like it, possible.

Reflecting on the problem of individual versus collective responsibility for the massacre at My Lai during the Vietnam War, Stanley Bates (1972) maintains that although we are often implicated and constrained by our relationships and bonds to others, finally we are morally, if not legally, responsible for what we do or fail to do as individuals. A naive individualism that does not acknowledge the effects of socialization and the power of group identification is to be eschewed; we are not isolated entities free from the encumbrances of association with wrongdoers. Nevertheless, according to Bates, each of us is responsible for the particular things we do, as well as the things we omit. We may not have personally engaged in an act, but may have made it possible for someone else to do so. We may not have been directly involved, but may not have done anything to prevent the act. We may not have been able to prevent the act, but may have done nothing to expose the actors, or attempted to mitigate the damage incurred to individual victims or society.

From this perspective a public administrator is individually responsible for avoiding direct or indirect participation in unethical actions, for attempting to prevent such actions by others, for exposing to public view those things that could not be prevented, and for at least attempting to diminish the destructive impacts of wrongdoing. Responsibility in these forms may from time to time confront us with the necessity of defining the limits of loyalty to superiors and clarifying the boundaries of organizational obligation. Dealing with these situations requires a willingness to bracket the claims of the organization we work for or participate in. Maintaining individual responsibility may even ultimately call for resistance to organizational demands and pressures.

The internal source for such resistance is character, or virtue, discussed in the previous chapter. It is the virtue of each practitioner that ultimately protects the internal goods of the practice of public administration from the external goods of organizations. It is the strength of character cultivated through moral processes throughout one's life and career that makes it possible for an individual to stand up to the power of an unethical organization and superiors.

Is this kind of expectation realistic, one may wonder? Yes, if that is finally the last safeguard for a practice. Also, given the number of whistle-blowers who have seen fit to act accordingly, it would seem to be so. Jos, Tompkins, and Hays (1989) found that a significant majority of whistle-blowers would do it all over again, even knowing the cost of their actions in advance, because they were convinced that the evidence showed that their courageous conduct made a real difference in the organization.

The young police officer described in Chapter Seven paid a severe price for his conduct, but when asked if he would do it again said, "Damn right!" without a moment's hesitation. Why? "Because," he replied, "I couldn't live with those scumbags doing what they were doing and getting away with it." He had succeeded in putting the chief and a member of his command staff in prison, and although he and his family had suffered terribly, they had survived and he had done well in the department once new leadership was employed. His courage in taking on the chief at considerable cost to himself also provided a powerful role model for other officers about the meaning of integrity in law enforcement.

Similarly, Marie Ragghianti, as chair of the Tennessee Board of Pardons and Paroles, discovered that the governor and members of his staff were selling paroles and pardons, extraordinarily serious felonious actions. Although she was a single parent with two children and vulnerable to quick termination, Ragghianti reported her observations and evidence to the FBI. The result was the immediate loss of her job, followed by several years of hellish harassment, accusations, rumors, and death threats. However, in the end Ragghianti won back her job in a civil suit, and Governor Ray Blanton was convicted and sentenced to three years in prison (Hejka-Ekins, 1992). When asked later at an ASPA conference panel on whistle-blowers why she brought such pain on herself and her children, she responded that she did so because it was the right thing to do. This kind of courage is the manifestation of virtue in action, the strength of character necessary to maintain the internal goods of any practice.

Individual Ethical Autonomy in Organizations

William H. Whyte Jr. outlined the fundamental problem for individual autonomy within organizations in *The Organization Man* (1956).

The Problem of Organizational Dominance

Whyte recognized that the age of organization was upon us and that it embodied an ethic that he variously termed "the social ethic," "an organization ethic," and "a bureaucratic ethic" (1956,

p. 6). According to Whyte, the essence of this ethic is a commitment to resolve the tension between individuals and organizations by encouraging a primary identification with the organization, "a belief in belongingness as the ultimate need of the individual" (p. 6). It serves the purpose of making "morally legitimate the pressures of society against the individual" (p. 7).

Although Whyte took a dim view of this tendency to absorb individuals into organizational structures and replace their autonomy with collective determination of goals and values, he recognized that the solution was not to be found in a flight from organizational society. Such notions amounted to "misplaced nostalgia," which only confused the issue. Rather, Whyte understood the problem as maintaining "individualism within organization life" (1956, p. 11). Organizations as such are not inherently evil; organizations "can be changed by man," he insisted (p. 13).

Whyte argued that the evil lies in our unwillingness to acknowledge the conflict that must exist between individuals and collectivities and in our failure to provide for that conflict within organizational life. In fact, not only do we refuse to face this necessary antipathy and divergence of interests, but we actively work at suppressing individual values and behavior that are at odds with those of organizations. From this perspective, establishing, reestablishing, and maintaining boundaries between individuals and the organizations they participate in are essential if proper limits are to be established for administrative responsibility.

As is sometimes the case with social critics, Whyte's analysis of the problem was more thorough than his prescriptions for coming to grips with it. Essentially, *The Organization Man* was an exhortation to resist organizational domination of one's values, worldview, and conduct. It was a clarion call to fight the organization's seduction into the security and passivity of its all-encompassing web, a cry for resistance to the temptation to abdicate individual responsibility, a reassertion of the primacy of individuality in the face of pressure to conform to the organization's needs and goals.

This tendency of hierarchical organizations to suppress individual ethical autonomy grows out of the conditions of modern society. (See Chapter Three for a full discussion of modern society.) If the desirable outcomes of ethics education and training are the ability to identify ethical issues, skill in reasoning one's way to a decision, and the ability to act on that decision, modern society and its characteristic form of organization create certain hindrances to independent thought and action (see Figure 8.1). These conditions include role multiplication and fragmentation, diverse value systems, the separation of work from the rest of life, and the prevalence of bureaucratic organizations.

The accumulation of roles that are not related to each other by a common tradition leaves us in the position of being pulled and tugged by a constellation of roles that often conflict and compete for priority. The individual is left to the exigencies of deciding which role must receive primacy at any given moment. The diversity of value systems in modern society compounds this problem, as one is left feeling that because there is no one absolute set of correct values, there is no place to stand to defend a preferred set. The separation of work from the rest of life in modern society attenuates the balancing and buffering effects of other roles and leaves one highly vulnerable to the role demands of one's employing organization.

When we focus on the nature of bureaucratic organizations, we can see that they exhibit a number of characteristics that impede ethical autonomy (Figure 8.1). They structure authority from the top down, thus leaving subordinates at the mercy of superior power and legitimated authority. They focus that authority through rules, regulations, and sanctions down through the ranks of the organization to individuals carrying out particular tasks. They separate instrumental from substantive rationality, reserving substantive thinking about what should be done to those at the top, restricting those lower down to instrumental thinking about the means to efficiently accomplish the ends adopted by their superiors. In addition to these rather intimidating conditions, one's social status and source of support are tied to the employment role, making the consequences for placing it at risk serious indeed.

Taken together, the conditions of modern society and the characteristics of bureaucratic organizations paint a picture of individual employees whose ethical confidence is undermined by the cultural uncertainty inherent in modernism. These ethically challenged modern men and women then have to face an organizational structure well designed to dominate them in their morally weakened state.

Figure 8.1. Hindrances to Ethical Decisions

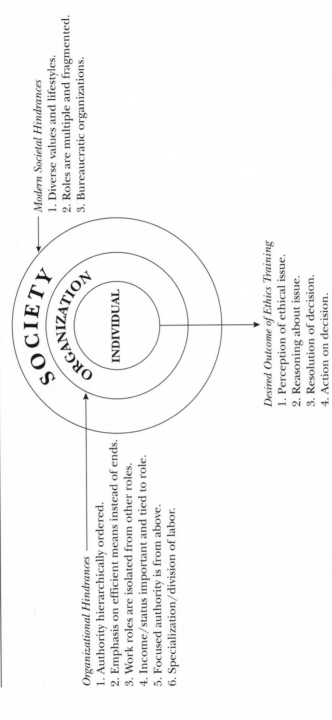

Modern Societal Hindrances
1. Diverse values and lifestyles.
2. Roles are multiple and fragmented.
3. Bureaucratic organizations.

Desired Outcome of Ethics Training
1. Perception of ethical issue.
2. Reasoning about issue.
3. Resolution of decision.
4. Action on decision.

Organizational Hindrances
1. Authority hierarchically ordered.
2. Emphasis on efficient means instead of ends.
3. Work roles are isolated from other roles.
4. Income/status important and tied to role.
5. Focused authority is from above.
6. Specialization/division of labor.

During the 1970s and 1980s, this concern for the pervasive subordination of the individual to the organization was renewed, and recommendations were offered to control the dominance of organizations. William Scott and David K. Hart (1979) have written about the "organizational imperative" that in their view has transformed American values. This imperative assumes that "whatever is good for the individual can only come from the modern organization" and "therefore, all behavior must enhance the health of such organizations" (p. 43). Although they basically restate and elaborate the central themes previously explored by Whyte, Scott and Hart attempt to carry the discussion further by offering an analysis of the "role hierarchy" of the modern organization, made up of a few "significant people" at the top, the larger number of "professional people" in the middle, and the mass of "insignificant people" at the bottom.

They conclude, pessimistically, that "totalitarian America" (p. 211) is not far away and can be turned back only by the "professional people" who can "recognize their historical potential and seize their opportunity to challenge the organizational imperative and reform modern organizations" (pp. 220–221). The villain in the piece, according to Scott and Hart, is current management philosophy, because "the modern organization is value neutral" (p. 223).

In the unlikely event that the professional stratum can and will use its technical scientific leverage, as well as its strategic position, to reestablish the "individual imperative," then modern organizations may be reformed, "totalitarian America" can be forestalled, and "transcendent America" will be brought into being (Scott and Hart, 1979). To accomplish this task, new managerial values are needed that assume that "all individuals have the natural right to the realization of the full potential of every stage of their lives; therefore, all institutions must be predicated upon that right" (p. 226).

Although the overall tone of the argument is colored with an overly dramatic apocalyptic vision of imminent totalitarianism, Scott and Hart have served to remind us again that organizations tend to absorb all individual autonomy into loyalty to the collective goals. However, their reluctant hope that the "professional people" may come riding to our rescue armed with a new philosophy of management is at the same time too hopeful and too pessimistic.

Too much may be expected of the professionals and too little from the insignificant people.

Organization Delimitation and Transcendence

A more sophisticated and theoretically complex approach to the all-consuming dominance of organizations is found in the work of Alberto Guerreiro Ramos (1981). He also is concerned with administrative theory, but views its emergence in the context of a more inclusive economic, social, and political system. In a chapter entitled "Theory of Social Systems Delimitation: A Paradigmatic Statement," Ramos views modern administrative perspectives as the product of a "market-dominated social reality" that places primary value on utility maximization. This means that everything individuals do tends to be considered an occasion for achieving the greatest return for available resources. Instrumental rationality dominates thought about the world and our life in it; substantive rationality unconcerned with the achievement of ends tends to be devalued and ignored. Personal actualization is subordinated to economizing.

Thus Ramos's concern is not limited to organizations, but begins with a comprehensive social analysis that identifies the market mentality as the pervasive and dominant model for political, economic, and social existence. He addresses the problem of organizational theory from this broader theoretical perspective. It is not simply organizations that usurp individuality, but a worldview that provides no room for nonmarket activity.

From Ramos's perspective, administrative theory incorrectly assumes that the economizing behavior created by this kind of socialization is synonymous with human nature. The result of this confusion is an attempt to overorganize individuals under the belief that therein lies the path to self-actualization. Human relations experts and organizational development specialists set about the task of integrating individuals into organizations by employing behavioral science and group dynamics technology. The actual consequence of these misplaced efforts, says Ramos, is "the transformation of the entire society into an operationalized universe in which the individual is always expected to live as an actor with a prescribed role"; hence, the individual is depersonalized and deprived of the conditions for an independent creative personal life: "truly private place and time" (1981, p. 126).

Ramos's approach to dealing with this destructive set of dynamics is one of social systems analysis and design. Briefly, the para-economic model that evolves from this process includes (1) a view of society as a multiplicity of enclaves in which human beings engage in a variety of different but ultimately integrative substantive pursuits and (2) a societal governance system that can develop policies necessary for optimal transaction among those various enclaves. Market behavior is not viewed as illegitimate, but rather it is bounded and relegated to an incidental, secondary role in individual self-actualization. Utility maximization becomes one form of behavior among many others, instead of the dominant one in which individuals are socialized.

Organization delimitation, then, is essential to this model for social systems design. Market-oriented organizations, which include those public and private systems in which employment occurs, must be bounded not simply by attempting to manage individual organizations differently, but by managing the whole society with human self-actualization as the goal (Ramos, 1972). "Parenthetical man" must be allowed to replace the "operational man" of a market-dominated society.

"Parenthetical men" are not integrated into organizations, but make use of them for certain needs. They bracket belief in these ordinary phenomena and "deliberately try to become rootless" in their society in order to establish sufficient distance to understand it. They maintain detachment and a degree of aloofness from the surrounding social conditions, including organizations in which they participate, to avoid being captured and totally assimilated to their limited goals and values.

Organization delimitation is already under way in the United States, according to Ramos. A para-economy is beginning to manifest itself in the neighborhood movement, "nonviolent guerrilla warfare" within organizations, and in the works of A. K. Bierman, Donald Schön, Ralph Nader, John Gardner, Kenneth Boulding, Barry Commoner, and Robert Townsend.

These perspectives advanced by Whyte, Scott and Hart, and Ramos are introduced in this chapter to suggest the importance of bounding organizational loyalties and commitments in a conscious, active, and systematic fashion if we are to maintain any degree of ethical autonomy. Unless we consistently maintain a larger perspective of other roles, other obligations, other personal needs for self-development, and other legitimate enclaves of human activity, the boundaries of administrative responsibility may become all-inclusive. If that occurs, when crises of conscience arise, the limits of administrative loyalty may be impossible to discern because they have become so encompassing that the horizon is too far away to be visible. Worse yet, there may be so little of ourselves remaining beyond the organization's boundaries that these crises are never experienced. This may have been the case with Eichmann, and with some of those involved in Watergate.

All too often I have found myself dealing with practitioners in workshops on administrative ethics who have little ethical autonomy because they allow the organizations that employ them too much importance in the overall pattern of their lives. Work and participation in the organization are their dominant activity and affiliation. Their self-image, self-esteem, and life meaning are tied far too much to the workplace. Consequently they have difficulty finding perspectives from which to evaluate the claims of the organization. They lack values and self-understanding from the other "enclaves" that Ramos considers necessary to prevent being captured by work organizations. Otherwise, when the organization commands, there is only the bureaucratic ethic of obedience to authority and loyalty to the hierarchy to guide ethical judgment.

Organizational delimitation means that we make no total commitments to particular collectivities but maintain a certain tentativeness in dealing with all of them. This degree of detachment should not suggest a lack of seriousness or a life of superficial dabbling. Rather, it represents a recognition of the complexities of human intelligence and identity, as well as the multiple needs of self-expression and association. Simply put, life is not all one thing; to act otherwise is to distort human perception and judgment. It is to make ourselves ethically a prisoner of those aspects of life to which time, effort, and identity have been overcommitted.

To develop this approach a bit further, delimiting an organization implies an ability to transcend its boundaries while working within it. The term *transcendence* is used here to suggest the cultivation of ethical values and principles rooted outside the bureaucratic structure and its inherent norms, the maintenance of sources of identity beyond the work organization, and the adoption of a delimiting view of the organization in relation to other aspects of life.

In order to keep the bureaucratic machine in the service of the public rather than of itself or special interests, values and principles essential to democratic political community must provide constant points of reference from beyond the boundaries of the organization for both the substantive goals and the functional procedures of the organization. At an earlier time, when we assumed the separability of politics and administration and the possibility of limiting administrative discretion to functional decisions, this was the role assigned the political official. The public organization and its administrators were mere tools in the hands of politicians, who were the custodians of the values of the political community. Bureaucratic ethics were constrained by political values determined outside the organization in the legislative process.

However, because we no longer assume that politics and administration can be neatly and clearly understood as discrete processes, we must alter our thinking about how bureaucracy is maintained in the service of the citizenry. Public administrators inside the organization must be understood as bearing an obligation to internalize and cultivate values from the American political community. Their professional values must transcend the limits of the organization and delimit its sway over their professional conduct. The problem, of course, is identifying those values. Addressing it lies beyond the scope of this book, but it is one of the most difficult and important items on the agenda for research and theory development in administrative ethics.

In addition to values drawn from outside the organization, sources of identity beyond its boundaries are also essential. Not only should administrators bring publicly oriented values into the bureaucracy from the political community, but they should also cultivate certain other sources of identity that help to constrain organizational self-service and brake the tendency toward bureaucratic absolutism. At a minimum, public administrators need to develop their professional, political, and community identities.

A professional identity requires continuing professional education and training, involvement in professional associations, regular attention to professional literature, and a sense of responsibility for the public administrative role. Without these, a public administrator is cognitively disadvantaged in dealing with organizational definitions of public problems, appropriate administrative conduct, and the purposes of government. In the absence of professional identity, the organization's definitions tend to occupy the entire field; vision is narrowed to the organization's interests; responsibility shrinks to the boundaries of the organization; obligation is restricted to the chain of command.

A political identity entails active attention to a broad range of issues on the public agenda. It means more than simple membership in a political party, although that certainly might be included in the development of our political profile. More important, public administrators should cultivate independent political judgment on local, state, and national issues. A lively and well-developed sense of personal political position keeps the political process prominently in mind as the larger context within which the organization functions. Active political involvement keeps alive the public administrator's larger obligation as a citizen of the political community.

A community identity suggests that we are engaged with manifestations of public life that occur close to home at the neighborhood, area, and municipal levels. Some might reasonably argue for religious and ethnic identities as well. Attention to neighborhood issues, the efforts of voluntary associations, public school activities, and the affairs of local religious organizations root our mind and self-image in specific human problems and projects. This kind of identity provides a degree of protection from bureaucratic and intellectual abstractions, and vivid points of reference for the aims and purposes of government. Principles such as the public interest, social equity, regime values, and citizenship obligation can be tested in observable social life and personal experience.

A Bill of Rights for the Workplace

A more specific approach to the dilemma of the individual within both public and private organizations is provided by David Ewing's *Freedom Inside the Organization* (1977). Less global than Ramos but consistent with his theoretical perspective, and more thorough and analytical than Scott and Hart, Ewing's concern is that Americans have as citizens enjoyed certain rights that they are required to leave behind when they enter the doors of the organizations in which they work. Freedom of speech, press, and assembly; due process of law; privacy; and freedom of conscience—most Americans are not guaranteed these rights in the workplace.

Ewing argues that "rightlessness" as individuals inside employing organizations is a matter of grave concern because many such organizations are larger in population than the original thirteen colonies. They are, in fact, "minigovernments" (1977, p. 21) that rule over people's lives for forty or more hours per week. The net effect is that individual rights guaranteed by the U.S. Constitution are abrogated for a large portion of a citizen's working years. Ewing argues that "for all practical purposes, employees are required to be as obedient to their superiors, regardless of ethical and legal considerations, as are workers in totalitarian countries" (p. 21).

Why has this domination of organizations over their employees been allowed to exist? Scott and Hart blame modern management philosophy and organizational theory; Ramos identifies the problem with socialization into a market-oriented reality; Ewing finds an additional culprit in the law. The Anglo-Saxon legal principle of freedom of contract has consistently been applied to employer-employee relationships, leading to the view that both enter equally into a voluntary agreement that either can choose to terminate. The employee is free to resign and go elsewhere, just as the employer is free to terminate workers at will. Consequently, the courts have adopted a conservative posture in intervening in these relationships.

Coupled with the law of contracts is an ancient legal tradition that gives the employer the upper hand in determining the conditions of employment. The rights of master and servant, originating in Roman law, were carried over into Anglo-Saxon law as the model of the employment relationship. Thus, modern employer prerogatives in treatment of the worker are rooted in the centuries-old favored status of the master over his servants. According to Ewing, the organizations in which people are employed still retain these prerogatives to a large extent.

In the face of these legal constraints against freedom within organizations, Ewing finds growing inclinations among employees to resist organizational pressures for total loyalty and submission. Far from being an impotent or complacent mass of "insignificant people," Ewing finds mounting rebelliousness, which he explains on the basis of Maslow's hierarchy of needs. Employee demands for greater control over their own lives is a manifestation of a relatively affluent society that has satisfied most of the lower-order survival needs and is now insisting on satisfaction of the higher-level needs for social relationships and self-development.

Ewing's proposals for constraining the power of organizations over individuals reflect his predominantly legal orientation. His essential prescription is organizational constitutionalism, similar to that associated with Elliott Jaques (see Chapter Seven), including an enforceable employee bill of rights. If individuals are to be able to carry out both their rights and their obligations as citizens, they must be protected by clearly defined legal constraints on organizational power and effective institutional procedures for ensuring due process. Ewing argues that these measures are necessary to allow individual conscience to assert itself against self-serving organizations.

Components of Individual Autonomy

It appears, then, that three essential ingredients are required if we are to effectively maintain limits on our administrative responsibility and loyalty to an organization. These ingredients are the components of individual autonomy. First, it is necessary to delimit work organizations and cultivate an identity that transcends their boundaries. Second, it is important to establish legal and institutional mechanisms for constraining organizational power and protecting individual rights to exercise ethical autonomy. Finally, self-awareness concerning values, rights, needs, duties, and obligations within and beyond the organization is required if we are to be able to act as individuals in specific situations. It is this third aspect about which more must be said.

The components of responsible conduct discussed in Chapter Seven are all potential behavior control mechanisms; they can be employed for shaping the conduct of individuals within organizations toward certain desired ends. Societal expectations, individual attributes, organizational structure, and a managed organizational culture are all instruments for directing behavior according to the mandated goals of the organization. However, when the organization appears to be deviating from these legitimate goals or when the preservation of an individual's own integrity conflicts with the organization's demands, the problem becomes one of resisting these behavior controls.

Ethic of Awareness

Perry London (1971) argues that the power to resist behavior controls is to be found ultimately only in human awareness. It is through self-awareness that self-control can be established: "The key to mastery of self is not will, which reduces, even subjectively, to nothing more than our perception of ourselves as struggling, demanding, or insisting. It is awareness, a set of higher processes in the brain with which we recognize ourselves as having self and from which we derive the special human powers of control which animal passions could not supply" (p. 271).

In his call for an "ethic of awareness," London maintains that our attention tends to be directed outward in modern technological society. We become preoccupied with the things around us, to the exclusion of self-awareness. Thus, having no countervailing sense of individual direction and purpose, we become vulnerable to control from sources beyond ourselves, such as organizations. However, he suggests not that we ignore our surroundings and totally withdraw from collective associations, but rather that we focus more on the subjective self in order to expand its contents. If democracy is to be maintained and free society is to prevail, social control must finally be rooted within individuals in the form of a deep awareness of their own values, needs, and aspirations, as well as how they are related to those of others.

When we approach the limits of loyalty to organizational superiors and consider a confrontation or a breach of relations with the organization, this kind of self-knowledge is essential. In fact, it is essential if we are ever to reach that point in the first place. There must be a sense of personal identity that extends well beyond the organization's boundaries, an integrity that is also vested in other roles as well and seeks a larger fulfillment of the self.

Two of Milgram's students, John Sabini and Maury Silver (1982), find this broader identity the essential ingredient in being able to transcend the limited "technical" responsibility of an organization and fulfill "moral" responsibility by questioning its actions. Moral responsibility cannot be confined within institutions and defined by organizational norms alone. One who has the more expansive view afforded by a larger self-identity may perceive the difference between these two kinds of responsibility and be led to question the legitimacy of the organization's authority when it is used unethically; one whose only or primary identity is contained within an organization has no basis for ever recognizing such illegitimacy.

One vivid example of a self-aware public servant struggling to maintain ethical autonomy can be found in Nelson Demille's novel *The General's Daughter* (1992). Warrant Officer Paul Brenner is a criminal investigator for the U.S. Army Criminal Investigation Division (CID) charged with the responsibility of solving the murder of a base commander's daughter, herself a commissioned officer.

As he pursues his investigation, Brenner discovers highly sensitive information about the private lives of a number of high-level officers involving various kinds of indiscretions, all of which would be deeply embarrassing and some of which would severely damage careers and families. The reader follows him through his tortuous efforts to uphold the law, remain faithful to his oath of office, serve the public good, do his duty to the army, protect his agency from unwarranted damage, and fulfill his obligation to protect persons innocent of any crime whose lives may be destroyed in the process of hunting down and prosecuting the killer.

In the fictional Paul Brenner, one sees a public official who transcends his own narrow job description but does not treat it lightly, who has developed an ethical theory by reflecting on his experience, as suggested at the beginning of Chapter Two in the discussion of the vignette from Michener's novel *Chesapeake*. This kind of reflective analysis and ethical imagination is one means for cultivating a sense of the self in its diversity of roles, interest, obligations, and aspirations.

Another form of protection for individual ethical autonomy may be found in the kind of principled thinking at the center of Lawrence Kohlberg's research on cognitive moral development (Kohlberg, 1984). Kohlberg's extensive cross-cultural empirical studies in some fifty countries attempted to discern the different ways in which people think about ethical issues. From his research he developed a six-stage model of how humans develop cognitively with respect to moral decisions across cultures. Kohlberg concluded that all of us move through the same invariant sequence from stage one with obedience and punishment as the main determinants, to stage two where the concern is satisfying one's own needs without regard for others, to stage three with its orientation to social approval, to stage four with an orientation to following the established rules and supporting established authority. Some move on to the final two stages, five and six, which focus on principled thinking that transcends rules, authority figures, the likelihood of punishment or reward, or social approval. Principled approaches to ethical problems look to the great ethical principles such as justice, beneficence, nonmaleficence, prudence, veracity, and the public interest for guidance.

Gilligan (1982) charged Kohlberg's theoretical framework and model with being reflective only of male thought patterns, thus invalid for women. However, Stewart and Sprinthall (1994) report that empirical research by Rest and others has clearly demonstrated that there is no bias against women in Kohlberg's cognitive moral development approach. In fact, women do as well as men in responding to Kohlbergian instruments, and often better.

Another early issue in critiques of Kohlberg was the extent to which moral thinking leads to moral conduct. Research by Blasi (1980), Stewart and Sprinthall, and others indicates that principled thinking does support ethical conduct and therefore can be seen as one kind of protection against organizational dominance. For example, Kohlberg assessed the stage of cognitive moral development of subjects from Milgram's obedience to authority studies, discussed previously in this chapter. He found that only 25 percent of those subjects whose thinking was principled were willing to continue administering electrical shocks to the supposed victim. Other studies reported by Stewart and Sprinthall reflect similar highly significant findings. These authors conclude that the group of studies they review produce "strong evidence to support the relationship between developmental stage and behavior by professionals in such fields as medicine, teaching, counseling, and school administration" (1994, p. 335).

Several instruments are used to assess level of moral development. The two most commonly used currently are the Defining Issues Test, developed by James Rest (1986), and the Stewart

Sprinthall Management Survey (SSMS), designed by Debra Stewart and Norman Sprinthall (1994). All these instruments are built around vignettes presenting ethical quandaries about which the respondent is asked a series of questions. The advantage in the SSMS for public administration is that the vignettes are all from the management setting. This contextual difference from the vignettes used by Kohlberg and Rest does not make a significant difference in the responses, but administrators are more likely to accept the findings as relevant to their professional roles.

It now seems reasonable to suggest that attention to the cultivation of principled thinking is a desirable practical way to protect ethical autonomy from dominant organizations in the hands of malevolent or misguided superiors. We know that this was the case for the subjects in Milgram's studies, and there is no reason to believe it would not have been similar in Zimbardo's.

Stewart and Sprinthall "propose the creation of formal yet practical educational programs to foster ethical reasoning and behavior." They "suggest a seamless connection between graduate and in-service professional training." This training would not focus on the array of moral lapses in government, but would emphasize "extensive experience through dialogue and case studies from a developmental stage framework" (1994, p. 346). One of Stewart and Sprinthall's findings that supports this educational approach is that the more one has had to deal with the principles inherent in a type of situation, the more likely that one establishes a continuing pattern of principled thinking about that class of problems.

Another process that may be helpful when considering the limits of responsibility and loyalty to a particular organization involves an evaluation of the critical role.

Role Evaluation at the Limits of Organizational Loyalty

As we approach crises in our responsibility to the organizations that employ us, we experience the "inescapable tension between interest and duty" that lies at the heart of public life (Tussman, 1960, p. 18). The interests of the self are at odds with the obligations of the organization. Although this potential conflict gives rise to the routine moral dilemmas associated with divergent role demands discussed in Chapters Two through Four, when the tension becomes severe, we experience a profound crisis. Our selfhood is threatened; our ability to maintain a sense of identity and integrity is challenged. We wonder whether we can still look ourselves in the eye, whether we can live with ourselves if we comply with certain orders or fail to oppose particular decisions and activities. These very common clichés reflect the disintegration of the self that we anticipate and fear. Thus, we grope toward the place where the line must be drawn between ourselves as individuals with a larger array of personal interests to be maintained, on the one hand, and the demands of the organization, on the other.

The typical factors involved are certain sources of duty and obligation associated with both arenas. In the administrative role in a public organization, duties and obligations come from laws, a specific government, superiors, peers, subordinates, and the public. Laws mandate certain activities and constrain others. The particular government that employs us projects a set of expectations ranging from the highly formal and explicit to the implicit and informal. Similarly, our organizational superiors prescribe work routines, establish policies, and issue orders that are sometimes broad and general, but at other times specific and detailed. Peers within the organization, as well as professional colleagues beyond its boundaries, create norms, standards, and reciprocal obligations. Supervising and directing the conduct of subordinates toward the goals of the organization imposes another set of responsibilities. Finally, the public or publics with an interest in the organization's function generate a further set of demands and expectations.

In a crisis, one or more of these external, organizationally related forces seriously conflict with the interests of the self, which include our values, beliefs, and self-images. As indicated in Chapter Two, values are beliefs about appropriate behavior and the desirability of end states. Justice, honesty, equal distribution of wealth, and collaboration are examples of values. Beliefs, as used here, would include general ways of viewing the world:

- Human beings tend to be competitive.
- Life is a constant struggle.
- Good people usually win in the end.
- There is purpose in the cosmos.
- Government is the servant of the people.

Self-image has to do with the particular beliefs we hold about ourselves: "I am fair, trustworthy, sensitive, independent, strong, competent, and outspoken."

Whenever we are hard-pressed by role-related duties or obligations to engage in conduct that is highly inconsistent with one or more of these self-interests, we are presented with a problem in maintaining an integrated sense of who we are. It then becomes necessary to resist the demands of the role; alter our values, beliefs, and self-images; or negotiate some kind of compromise. At this point, evaluation of the role may be helpful in identifying the essential problem and determining a course of action.

Role evaluation may be undertaken at three levels (Downie, 1972). Role legitimacy is the level with the most serious potential consequences. The question to be answered is, "Is this particular organizational role legitimate for someone in society to occupy?" More specifically, should there be an environmental impact analyst, or a budget officer, or a prison warden, or a hospital administrator, or a public executioner? Is any one of these a justifiable role? Am I able to condone the ends for which the role in question was established? If I cannot give an affirmative answer to these questions, a breach in my relationship with the organization is highly probable and may be accompanied by a fundamental challenge to its existence. If the role I have been occupying is found to be illegitimate according to my values, beliefs, and self-images, I may well feel compelled to speak out against its being occupied by anyone.

However, if the role is legitimate for someone, the next consideration is its acceptability to me in particular. I might conclude that the role of public executioner is a necessary and justifiable role in society, but find it unacceptable for myself. Perhaps it is consistent with my understanding of justice to execute persons who commit certain types of crimes, but inconsistent with the image I hold of myself as compassionate, sensitive, and forgiving. At this level of role evaluation, the consideration is whether to resign if asked to accept that role, but it probably does not call for an attack on the organization. I am unlikely to challenge the organization's maintenance of the role if I find it unacceptable only for myself.

Role enactment is the next level of evaluation and the least serious in its potential consequences. Even if I am able to condone the role of public executioner and to accept the role for myself, there may still be special circumstances when I cannot carry it out. In a particular case, I may believe that the accused did not receive a fair trial, or I may find that one whom I am to execute is a member of my own family. In instances of this kind, I am likely to seek negotiation with the organization in order to temporarily adjust my role.

An example that may serve to illustrate the distinctions being developed here is the "Saturday Night Massacre" on October 20, 1973, during the events of Watergate. Archibald Cox, the Watergate special prosecutor, had subpoenaed the tape recordings of President Nixon's conversations related to matters under investigation. Nixon responded by ordering Attorney General Elliott Richardson to fire Cox immediately. Richardson refused to comply with the order and resigned. William Ruckelshaus, the deputy attorney general and next in succession, also refused to dismiss Cox and was himself fired. Finally, Robert Bork, the solicitor general, was appointed acting attorney general and carried out the order (Jaworski, 1977; Dean, 1976).

It seems plausible to infer from the information available that both Richardson and Ruckelshaus encountered serious difficulty at the level of role enactment. Apparently neither man had concluded that the role of attorney general had lost its legitimacy, nor were they unwilling to accept the role for themselves under most circumstances. It was carrying out the role in this specific instance that produced an impediment. The presidential order to fire Archibald Cox violated certain self-interests that neither man was willing to sacrifice, so one resigned and the other was fired. Only Bork was willing to accept and enact the role, presumably because his values, beliefs, and self-image were not seriously threatened.

I may run the risk of being fired if I am unable to carry out the orders of my superiors, as happened to Ruckelshaus, but it is more likely that I will only be temporarily reassigned to other duties. Both formal and informal negotiations about the enactment of roles are common modes of organizational behavior. However, if I regularly encounter problems of role enactment, I may need to reevaluate at one or both of the other two levels. Changes in either the way the role is defined by external sources of duty and obligations on the one hand, or in my self-interests on the other, may precipitate an ethical dilemma that calls for such a reevaluation. Self-conscious and systematic management of this process may be helpful in arriving at appropriate modes of action. It is important to be clear about the source of an ethical dilemma: Is it only the circumstances of a specific task? Is the role itself being redefined by the law or superiors so that it is becoming unacceptable? Illegitimate? Are my values, beliefs, or self-image changing in such a way that the role no longer fits me? Am I still able to condone and support the maintenance of the role itself, apart from my own fulfillment of it?

Answers to these questions suggest a range of responses, from negotiating changes in specific tasks on a one-time basis, to seeking more permanent changes in the role, to transferring to another job, to resignation, to challenging the legitimacy of the role and ultimately that of the organization itself. Whistle-blowing and resignation in protest are appropriate responses at this extreme end of the spectrum, when simply leaving the organization and allowing it to continue on its course undisturbed are unacceptable to our conscience. Long argues that as representatives of the citizenry working inside the public bureaucracy, public administrators facing "particularly grievous" cases may "have a duty to resign and go public with the reasons for their opposition to the policy. Frequently, only by such action can the public be informed of facts and arguments that it needs to know if it is to be able to judge the wisdom of the government presently in power" (Long, 1995, p. 4).

However, actions of this kind are probably not appropriate if our values, beliefs, and self-image create only infrequent or minor problems in accepting or enacting the role. (Nader, Perkas, and Blackwell [1972] provide helpful advice on thinking through the possibility of blowing the whistle.)

The limits of organizational loyalty are difficult to identify. Our socialization, the constant organizational pressure to identify with its collective goals and values, and the absence or ineffectiveness of legal and institutional supports for individual autonomy create a murky environment in which it is difficult to discern the boundaries of our obligation. New legislation, new structural arrangements, and a delimiting approach to organizations will help, but without a conscious effort to continuously cultivate self-awareness of the dynamic relationship between the interests of the self and the demands of the role, then laws and organizational safeguards are likely to be of no avail. All three components of individual autonomy are required.

Part Three

The Design Approach

Chapter Nine

Applying the Design Approach to Public Administration Ethics

I began this book with an argument for adopting a design approach to public administration ethics and outlined the specific elements included in Whitbeck's 1996 treatment of that perspective. Now I wish to restate the design approach in terms appropriate for the public administrative role, indicate its general relevance to significant ethical problems, and apply it to a concrete case.

The Design Approach to Public Administration Ethics

Whitbeck's design approach rests on some inherent characteristics of engineering design practice that are relevant in solving ethical problems. As in design, Whitbeck (1996) argues that a "uniquely correct solution or response" (p. 11) to the problem rarely presents itself. In fact, problems can have any number of responses, not some predetermined solution. After one identifies the possible solutions, some will be more acceptable than others, and some problems have several acceptable solutions. The challenge is to find a solution that will "achieve the desired performance or end," "conform to given specifications or explicit criteria," "be reasonable secure against accidents," and "be consistent with existing background constraints" (p. 12). This design approach to ethical problems in public administration includes more than the kind of analysis I discussed in laying out the ethical decision-making model in Chapter Two. While the decision-making model I offered is useful, designing an effective response to an ethical problem of any significance also requires consideration of the social and organizational contexts in which the ethical problem emerges, which Whitbeck's design approach includes. I discussed the social and organizational contexts in Chapters Three and Six through Eight, and they are crucial factors in responsible administration.

In this section, I highlight the important steps of the design approach and then apply them to examples of ethical dilemmas. For our purposes, a design approach has these main elements:

1. *Begin with an assumption of uncertainty, and acknowledge the ambiguities.* In any ethical situation, what appears to be unethical conduct may or may not be. Before rushing to judgment, it is important to gather information from as many of those directly involved as possible, observe behavior over some period of time—unless the situation involves life-or-death urgency—and try to understand the facts of the situation from all sides. Unfounded confidence about our perceptions and interpretations of misconduct can be damaging to relationships, reputations, careers, and organizations. As well, a rush to judgment can raise suspicions about our motives and call into question our judgment.

One of the participants in a training session I conducted presented a case in which he was walking down a long hallway to his supervisor's office and began hearing strange sounds emanating from the open door of the office that seemed to indicate sexual activity. He immediately feared the worst, turned on his heels, and returned to his own office, not wanting to catch the boss in a compromising situation. He was not sure of what to do with his suspicions of unethical conduct by the supervisor, so he decided to keep his own counsel and see what might happen next. A few days later, he overheard the same sounds as he approached the supervisor's office and decided to brazen it out and walk right into the office. When he did so, he discovered that the boss was alone in his office, doing abdominal crunches on the floor. The suspicious worker felt enormous relief that his suspicions had been ill-founded and that he had not acted precipitously based on his impressions of what was taking place. Had the suspicious worker acted on his gut reaction and reported the suspected illicit behavior, he may have done irreparable harm to his supervisor, himself, and his agency. The accusatory nature of his knee-jerk reaction would have ruined his credibility and could have caused ill will between him and his supervisor. Instead of jumping to an unfounded conclusion, the worker's initial reaction was to keep his suspicions to himself. Even so, when he was faced with the possibility of illicit behavior the second time, he rushed to judgment and confronted the supervisor rather than trying to ascertain the facts before confronting him.

2. *Defining the problem too narrowly, simply, or statically may not address the fundamental factors involved in misconduct.* A problem must first be defined, which may require additional information, before a solution can be thoughtfully discovered. Moreover, a hierarchy of ethical problems may exist in what we perceive to be a case of individual unethical behavior. It is important to understand actions and decisions by others that may have contributed to the specific act that captures your immediate attention. For example, although one person may be the one acting unethically, a superior may be pressuring this person to act unethically and this may be a pattern of pressure. Is the individual who seems to be acting unethically actually a member of a subunit of an organization that has isolated itself from the larger organization and gradually evolved its norms toward encouraging unethical ways of getting the job done? Is there a general reluctance in the organization to perceive and deal with ethical problems because the emphasis is on getting the work done on time at the least cost?

As well, ethical problems may change as we attempt to deal with them; they are dynamic in nature. What started out as an ethical problem may turn out to be a legal one also. What seemed to concern the actions of one or a few individuals may be discovered to involve many at all levels of an organization. For example, in a federally funded research laboratory, the executive director and chief financial officer were constantly badgering program directors to use all their federal contract funds—even if they were able to conduct their work under budget—so that the laboratory would not lose any funds. In the case of one program, the director spent nearly twenty thousand dollars on frivolous and unrelated books and resource materials just to spend the budgeted amount. In this case, a gut reaction might be to punish or even fire the program director. However, that narrow definition of the problem would have served a small but incomplete purpose because the motivations and pressures of the executives needed to be addressed as well.

3. *Resolving ethical problems always must be done within certain constraints of time and may require pursuing multiple solutions at once.* Working administrators do not have the luxury of unlimited time to analyze and act on a situation as if they were in a classroom or training exercise. Although I have discouraged precipitous action, at some point action must be taken to deal with an ethical problem, or it will likely be resolved by inaction. Inaction becomes a form of action if events move on under their own momentum. The range of alternatives is always limited to some extent by the nature of the organization, the actions of others, the risk to oneself, possible harm to innocent bystanders, and damage to the organization from certain alternative courses of action. This may suggest the value of a contingency approach to ethical problems. Instead of assuming one must choose only one among a range of alternatives for resolving the problem, consider a sequence of steps that begin with actions that are less drastic, risky, and potentially damaging to the organization and progress as required toward the ultimate course of action. For example, if I recognize what I subsequently confirm to be my supervisor accepting bribes, blowing the whistle by going to the press might be the ultimate course of action but certainly not the first one. Confronting the superior might be the first step, followed by reporting the conduct to my superior's boss.

Another important consideration concerning limits is that sometimes we may not be able to undertake the most ethical course of action we can imagine because it would sacrifice other important values. Compromise in order to balance these values may well be chosen. When this occurs, acknowledging that one has chosen less than the best is a way to preserve ethical autonomy. Taking refuge in an oft-repeated excuse—"I had no other choice"—is tantamount to abandoning ethical autonomy. There are always choices, and it is extremely important to own up to the fact that we sometimes choose less than the most ethical course of action because we cannot tolerate the consequences of the alternatives. We live and act out our ethical commitments in a world of constraints. Ethical perfection always eludes us. In other words, ethical dilemmas and the solutions to them can be messy and uncomfortable.

4. *Ethical problems in public administration almost always take place in an organizational setting that either encourages or impedes ethical conduct, or both. And the ethical problem at hand will certainly give rise to other implications.* To focus only on ethical decision making and courses of action to deal with ethical problems without considering the organizational structure and culture within which they are embedded is to invite failure. The design of a response to an ethical problem requires examining and engaging the structure and culture of the organizational context of a particular ethical problem. If the organization's structure and culture are not supportive of the decision reached about the ethical resolution of a problem, then it will not likely be successful in implementation. This is the point at which ethicists and organizational development specialists need to work together. As ethical problems are identified by managers, some aspect of the organization will likely need to be changed. Of course, the proactive preventive approach would be to regularly conduct an ethics audit or assessment of the structure and culture of the organization. Do members of the organization feel free to discuss the ethical dimensions of their work? Is there a commitment to serious and regular ethics training? Do people working in the organization feel "ethics stress" in trying to conduct themselves appropriately? Do the stories people tell in the organization and the cartoons on the bulletin boards reflect professional ethical values? Is there some kind of dissent channel in the organization through which people can express their conscience when superiors will not listen and respond? Do the members of the organization have any kind of recourse to the chain of command, such as an inspector general or ombudsman? Have people in the organization experienced retribution for calling attention to misconduct? Have they been rewarded? Recall the case of the program director who spent twenty thousand dollars in taxpayer money on frivolous materials for the research lab. To deal only with that specific ethical problem would have meant missing the fact that the culture and leadership of the organization promoted and condoned, however indirectly, such spending. Failure to address the superiors and the culture they created would have meant repeated instances of program directors' misusing taxpayer funds because of the undue pressure they felt to use all monies budgeted.

General Application

One can easily see how the above elements of the design approach could apply to high-profile cases like the abuse of prisoners in the Abu Ghraib prison during the American occupation of Iraq or the NASA space shuttle catastrophes involving the deaths of the crews on *Challenger* and *Columbia*.

In the case of Abu Ghraib, prisoners were regularly mistreated. This was not simply because an individual made a wrong ethical decision, but because a whole series of decisions had created interrogation guidelines (formal and informal) that were ethically questionable and in some cases illegal, and leadership created an environment that failed to stop or report such abuse. Practices rooted in the informal norms of the culture of Abu Ghraib prison encouraged abusive conduct that went even beyond the guidelines.

As a prison general who was troubled by the way prisoners were treated, one might begin with an analysis of alternatives and consequences of the unethical action, followed by finding a fit among various key considerations as recommended in Chapter Two. That would be a useful beginning, but not adequate to deal with the problem over the long haul. Any astute reader of the *Final Report of the Independent Panel to Review DOD Detention Operations* (Schlesinger, 2004) would see that one would need to identify patterns of conduct that included many others who worked in the prison and would need to trace their roots to other places such as the prison at Guantanamo Bay, Cuba, where alleged terrorists were interned. One might investigate where the rules of interrogation and abusive prisoner treatment originated and reflect on what part of this problem involves illegal conduct and what part involves unethical conduct. One also might recommend an examination of the culture and structure of the Abu Ghraib prison. What were the informal norms that led to humiliating prisoners by stripping them naked and forcing physical contact with others of the same sex or intimidating them with vicious guard dogs? One might need to consider the prison's organizational structure and whether there were any effective accountability mechanisms and processes to maintain conduct consistent with official military codes of conduct and international war conventions. Was an inspector general or ombudsman available to whom one could turn for assistance? Were there formal dissent channels that could be used by anyone who felt the abuse of the prisoners was wrong? In short, one would need to try to assess the extent of the problem, how organizational structure and culture contributed to it, and what kind of management interventions would be required to create the conditions to establish and maintain ethical conduct.

Similarly with respect to NASA's two major tragedies with the explosion of the shuttle *Challenger* in 1986 shortly after launch and the destruction of *Columbia* during reentry into the earth's atmosphere in 2003, ethical problems could not be fixed without significant redesigning of the organizational structure and culture. The clearest and most visible case was that of the *Challenger* with Roger Boisjoly, a NASA engineer, discussed in Chapter Eight. Boisjoly had no difficulty reasoning his way to an ethical course of action. He was confident that *Challenger* should not have been launched with the temperatures so low and ice hanging on the launch equipment. However, the culture of NASA at that time had become so oriented toward pleasing President Reagan and demonstrating the commercial viability of the space shuttles that engineering safety standards were overridden by managers. Boisjoly had no dissent channels through which to express his conscience and maintain his engineering integrity. The structure was so hierarchical that Boisjoly was finally told to take off his engineer's hat, put on his manager's hat, and proceed with the launch.

In the case of *Columbia,* seventeen years later, the report on the accident that destroyed that space shuttle reveals there were technical causes for the disintegration of the shuttle during reentry, but the more fundamental reasons had to do with NASA's organizational structure, culture, and management. A large piece of the foam plastic insulation had broken loose due to intense dynamic forces during launch and slammed into the leading edge of one wing. The result was a gash in the wing that allowed super-hot gases to enter the wing, causing the destruction of the shuttle and the death of seven astronauts. This problem had been long identified by the engineers and played down by management. Even on that fateful launch day and during the days that followed, the technical people involved were concerned about possible risk to the *Columbia* and its crew as a result of the impact of the foam insulation on the wing. Management chose to move ahead with reentry with no further investigation. The report identifies the numerous times damage to the shuttle from fragments of the foam insulation had been reported by the engineers but passed over on the way to the next launch. The executive summary of the official report says:

> Cultural traits and organizational practices detrimental to safety were allowed to develop, including: reliance on past successes as a substitute for sound engineering practices (such as testing to understand why systems were not performing in accordance with requirements); organizational barriers that prevented effective communication or critical safety information and stifled professional differences of opinion; lack of integrated management across program elements; and the evolution of an informal chain of command and decision-making processes that operated outside the organization's rules [Columbia Accident Investigation Board, 2003].

Although there were no specific individuals identified in this case similar to Roger Boisjoly in the *Challenger* tragedy, one can discern in the quotation above the blocking of critical safety information and the stifling of professional differences of opinion. Any manager who identified the problem with the foam faced enormous barriers to being heard by those above who had the authority to delay the launch or take emergency measures before reentry. The organization and its structure and culture presented essentially the same problems for the exercise of conscience as existed seventeen years before. Apparently some tried to do the right thing but were prevented from doing so by organizational factors and launch urgency. A design approach to this situation by anyone committed to avoiding future disasters of this kind would necessitate changes in the structure, culture, and role definitions of the key management personnel. This would amount to organizational development in order to create a more ethical organization.

A Specific Application

Most of the readers of this book will likely be thinking that their professional lives are not as dramatic and fraught with serious consequences as these two high-profile cases that involved life and death and major violations of human dignity. So let us look at the implications of the design approach for a situation that might be closer to the experience of the readers of this book.

"The Favorite Contractor"

You are a senior manager of a subunit of the program office of a government agency. Your counterpart in another subunit of the program office is Harold Foster. You both work under the general manager of the agency, Jack Cairn. Annually, your agency contracts out significant amounts of work to private sector firms. Three qualified contractors are available to the office for this work: Alpha Services, Bravo Services, and Charlie Services. Charlie Services has had difficulty delivering on time, but the other two have performed about equally well. Bravo Services is a minority-owned firm that has been a qualified contractor for five years, but has never received more than the small contracts with Foster's and your subunits. The two of you have worked with both Alpha Services and Bravo Services on many of the smaller contracts specific to your units and found them to be fully competent to do the work. However, in the past three years, only Alpha Services has received the large contracts that transcend your separate units. Cairn controls selection of the major contracts, while you and Foster do so for the smaller ones for your own subunits.

Although you and Foster have encouraged Cairn to spread the work between these two contractors to create some beneficial competition and distribute the work equitably, he has consistently refused to do so, insisting that Alpha Services has done fine work and there is no need to change. He regularly espouses his favorite moral rules: "Don't mess with success" and "If it ain't broke don't fix it." When pressed for a more principled response, he talks about continuity and proven performance, but ultimately he defends his actions on the grounds that stability serves the good of the department by reducing transaction costs and thereby increasing efficiency.

You and Foster have argued for including Bravo Services in the major contracts, not only because it does good work but because it is a minority-owned firm that needs government contracts to get well established. You have argued your case based on fairness, maintaining that equals should be treated equally and unequals differently. Both Alpha Services and Bravo Services produce equally well and should receive equal shares of the large contracts. Also, the fact that Bravo Services is minority owned makes it different in that respect from Alpha. You argue that a combination of equally excellent performance and compensatory justice for minority-owned firms that are struggling to compete make it even more deserving of a share of the big contracts if the firms are to be treated fairly in the contracting process.

The boss does not appear to agree because he goes ahead with awarding big contracts solely to Alpha Services. Finally, at the end of one meeting, Foster says to Cairn, "You seem to be ignoring our recommendations for the inclusion of Bravo Services. It appears you have already decided to contract only with Alpha Services." Cairn shrugs off that accusation with, "No, just trying to do what's best for my department."

You and Foster discuss the possibility that Cairn may be racially biased in consistently rejecting Bravo Services out of hand for the bigger contracts. The two of you try to find an alternative explanation for Cairn's conduct, but it is difficult not to interpret his actions as racially motivated. Bravo is fully qualified and has done high-quality work for the two subunits. Whatever the reason for Cairn's resistance to contracting with Bravo for the larger, agency-wide projects, it seems to be unfair treatment of that firm.

As you and Foster begin to design an approach for addressing this serious problem of apparent inequity and perhaps racial bias, you remind yourselves that this is not just an isolated incident; it represents a pattern of practice with potentially serious consequences for the agency and the contractors and implications for the cultural norms of the agency. You decide to proceed through the following steps:

1. *You define carefully and systematically the ethical problem you are facing.* Is it racial bias or unfair treatment for some other reason? Because the act of simply confronting the boss with a charge of racial discrimination is not likely to elicit an honest response if he is biased in that way, you will need to examine other evidence of racism in his conduct. Has he willingly hired, encouraged, and promoted people of minority races and ethnicities? Is there any

other evidence of bias in the stories he tells or the way he favors people in the agency? If there is no other evidence of racial bias, you may have no reason to believe it is such in this case.

If there are no good reasons to believe racism is at work in the selection of contractors, you will need to try to determine why he is consistently favoring Alpha Services. Is he receiving kickbacks from Alpha? Does he have an old friend or relative who is in a key position in that firm? Or is it something else? Does he just feel comfortable staying with a firm he knows and trusts? In order to determine what is influencing Cairn's actions, you may need to talk discreetly with others in the office who have been in the agency for a long time about his relationship to Alpha Services. You may need to carefully talk with people you know at Alpha and Bravo about this by raising indirect questions. Eventually you may need to confront the boss with your concerns and ask him why he does not see the equity problem in excluding Bravo Services from the large contracts that he controls. You should always be open to the possibility that he really believes what he espouses: that continuity and stability best serve the good of the organization.

2. *With a better focus on the nature of the ethical problem, you work through the decision-making model in Chapter Two to identify what you think is the best course of action to address the problem.* Recall from Chapter Two that after you have perceived an ethical problem, the first task is a descriptive one in which you describe the situation and then define the ethical issues. In this case, the facts show that Cairn repeatedly grants agency-wide contracts to Alpha and refuses to consider using Bravo Services, even though it performs well on smaller contracts. The principle at stake is equity and the possibility of Cairn's being racially biased in his administrative decisions. The next step is to identify alternatives. Is there a mechanism within your agency to report your concerns? Is there a proper chain of events for documenting and reporting such things? Is your first step to confront Cairn directly? For each possible solution, you must identify the probable consequences—both negative and positive. Ideally, the positive result would be for larger contracts to be awarded to Bravo. However, you must also consider an end result that is negative. For example, you may be labeled as disloyal or insubordinate if you report on Cairn's actions. Or your relationship with Cairn may suffer, impeding your ability to do well

in your job and succeed in your agency. The next step is to find the most fitting alternative, knowing that you will likely have to defend your actions and perhaps take some blows to your self-image or your reputation among your coworkers. Once this is done, you can select your alternative.

3. *With a course of action identified that provides a fit among the items in the circle at the end of the decision-making model in Figure 2.1, you turn to a consideration of the organizational factors that may encourage or impede what you are proposing to do.* Is the organization so hierarchical that it is difficult to deal with unethical decisions made above your level? Does the culture of the organization support arguing with the boss when that seems to be required? Can one go around the boss to the next person up the chain of command without destroying one's career? Are there dissent channels, either formally established to deal with problems of professional conscience or units with other purposes, that can be used to express concerns about perceived misconduct such as a human resource department?

4. *Having developed an analysis of the organizational structure and culture, the next step in the design approach to administrative ethics is to consider intervention strategies you might employ to make the organization more supportive of the kind of conduct you have decided is consistent with the ethics of the public administrative role.* Much depends on how you have defined the ethical problem. If it is a matter of racism, you might try to get racial sensitivity training sessions established in which the boss would participate. If it is not something that blatant, you might consider pushing for the creation of a contract review committee within the agency to periodically look at all of the contracts awarded during a given period, examine the criteria, and assess the fairness of the distribution of awards. Or you might decide the best way to handle problems of equity in contracting would be to not allow any single person to approve the awards, but to make all such decisions a collective one among top management. Beyond measures of this kind, you might decide to recommend a thorough organizational development project to restructure the organization, clarify its values, institute dissent channels, and create accountability arrangements designed to check favoritism or tendencies to just do the same old thing because it is comfortable to do so.

Conclusion

This is a general sketch of what the design approach entails. It carries our thinking about ethics well beyond analyzing an ethical problem and deciding on the most ethical course of action. It pushes our thinking to the entire organizational environment, including its structure and culture. It calls on us to think creatively and with due consideration to the larger context in which some ethical problem may occur. It does not allow us to think about ethics in some idealized world or some isolated instance, but focuses our attention on the constraints of the real world in which the problem occurs. It requires of us prudent judgment that is rooted in both our ethical reasoning and our character. Not every situation will lend itself to this design approach; however, the responsible administrator will use this approach whenever possible. But be forewarned: addressing an ethical problem can be problematic even at a basic level. The kind of work involved in applying the design approach will be even more complex and difficult. And if agency-wide problems are identified, one might suffer repercussions from coworkers or superiors. Still, the administrative role requires tough decisions and a balancing of one's role and one's commitment to ethical behavior. Administrative responsibility is not an easy task, but it is critical to the work of the practicing administrator.

Chapter Ten

Conclusion
Responsible Administration

Applying Whitbeck's design approach to responsible administration essentially means that focusing only on the analysis of ethical problems and making ethical decisions is inadequate for the work of public administration in the real world. Ethical analysis and decision making do not take place in a vacuum. The situation of the administrator also must be considered, and the resolution of ethical problems must take into account the key elements of the administrator's work environment. To focus more specifically on the administrative role, I suggest that some additional considerations are needed in the process of designing a solution to an ethical problem. These considerations are drawn from the components of responsible conduct I outlined in Chapter Seven (see Figure 7.1):

1. The ethical solution must take into account the organizational setting in which the problem emerges and in which the administrator works. As I have noted throughout this book, organizations can encourage or impede ethical decision making and conduct. Any course of action to address an administrative ethical problem must assess how the organization will support a course of action or try to stop it. That is not to suggest that one should do something about an ethical problem only if the organization is likely to be supportive. Rather, it means a solution must be designed to address resistance and optimize support.

2. In designing an approach for resolving an ethical problem, one must consider both the organizational structure and culture.

The common structural characteristics of bureaucracies in which most public administrators work can create resistance, generate retaliation and retribution, and simply wear down an administrator who is attempting to act ethically. However, the structure can also provide strong support rooted in law and bolstered by formal authority. Still, even if the organizational structure is supportive of one's conduct, the informal culture of the organization may make life difficult and painful—or provide a sense of solidarity in confronting the organization's hierarchical structure.

3. Looking beyond the specific ethical problem, an administrator should think about the kinds of changes in the organizational structure and culture that would be needed to make them more supportive of ethical conduct and less resistant.

4. Considering ethical problems from a management perspective requires thinking strategically. A manager should be thinking about the kinds of interventions that would be appropriate to bring about the desired changes in organizational structure and culture. Identifying the necessary changes, as in the third step, and the best strategy for achieving that change amounts to joining organizational development with ethics, an important aspect of the design approach to ethics. It involves designing courses of action to change the organization to be more supportive of ethical conduct.

Let us now review what has been covered to this point and see how it applies to taking a design approach to ethics.

The Responsible Administrator

The vision that emerges from the previous chapters on the meaning of responsible public administration is that of a juggler managing a multitude of competing obligations and interests. The meaning of responsible administrative conduct under these circumstances is problematic indeed. Public administrators find themselves caught between their objective responsibility and their subjective responsibility. At times they feel and believe themselves to be responsible for acting in ways that are at odds with what the organizational hierarchy or the law holds them accountable for. These conflicts between objective and subjective responsibility are manifested in three types of conflicting responsibility: conflicts of authority, role conflicts, and conflicts of interest. Each confronts public administrators with quandaries about where their ultimate responsibility lies and presents opportunities to engage in unethical conduct.

I began Chapter Two with the assertion that administrators' ethical identities emerge incrementally from the pattern of decisions that they make over the course of a career. More often than not, this is done without much conscious consideration of the ethical dimensions of these decisions. However, without the guidance of a coherent and widely shared tradition, public administrators, like all other modern people, need to cultivate a process of systematic reflection as ethical dilemmas emerge from these contending interests and obligations. Through "contemplating real moral problems in the abstract where character is formed" (Michener, 1978, p. 1049), we may cultivate a working theory of ethical conduct, a sense of intuitive judgment, and integrity of character that are cumulative over time—in short, an ethical identity.

As I explained in Chapter Two, four levels at which we reflect and deliberate about ethical issues were identified: the expressive level, where the response is purely emotional; the level of moral rules, where axioms for conduct from the larger culture and that of the organization are presented; the level of ethical analysis, including a systematic examination of the underlying ethical principles; and the postethical level, where our basic assumptions about human nature, the nature of the universe, and what constitutes knowledge and truth are considered. I argued that it becomes more important to move to levels two and three—moral rules and ethical analysis—as we move higher in organizational responsibility. This enables us to be rationally accountable for our conduct.

A decision-making model was then presented to structure reflection and deliberation at those two levels. It consists initially of linear steps involving defining the ethical problem, describing the context, identifying the range of alternative courses of action, and projecting the probable consequences of each. However, this model also includes a nonlinear process of searching for a fit among several considerations: moral rules, ethical principles, anticipatory self-appraisal, and a rehearsal of defenses. In this final stage of resolving an ethical issue, the fit among these four elements is not a matter of sequential logic leading to an ineluctable conclusion, but more like an aesthetic logic or gestalt.

In Chapter Three, I identified two roles in particular—public administrator and citizen—and the tension between them as worthy of our sustained attention. Both must be maintained and served if a public administrator is to behave responsibly, but they do not always mesh well with each other. The fact that the public administrator wears these two hats—citizen and employee of the citizenry—at times gives rise to conflicts between obligations to the citizenry and the organization established to serve the citizenry.

As I argued in Chapter Four, responsibility is the key component of ethics for the administrative role. When confronted with an ethical problem and how to deal with it, we are also confronting our responsibility in the administrative role. As I noted, we are confronted with two types of responsibility: objective versus subjective. These dual components make our task complex and stressful. And when we consider that we have multiple responsibilities in a single role, compounded by conflicts among many roles, our task becomes that much more complex.

I addressed such role conflicts in Chapter Five. The three most common conflicts of administrative responsibility are conflicts of authority, role conflicts, and conflicts of interest. Most administrators are familiar with and educated about conflicts of interest, such as bribery, gifts and entertainment, and information peddling. What is less familiar to most administrators is a conflict of authority, where two or more authorities, such as the law, our superiors, elected officials, or the public, conflict and impose conflicting objective responsibilities on us. An obvious example is when the law mandates one course of action and our boss dictates another. And our roles can conflict. Each role has values associated with it, and those values may be incompatible at times. For example, we may be confronted in our work with a situation that offends our values as parents. Or we may have conflicts as a supervisor and subordinate. In cases of role conflicts, we must review, clarify, and redefine our roles.

From the managerial perspective, we are concerned with maintaining responsible conduct on the part of these doubly bound individuals. Hence, in Chapters Six and Seven I discussed techniques for shaping the conduct of the members of public organizations toward consistently ethical conduct—internal and external controls as general approaches in Chapter Six and specific techniques in Chapter Seven. If responsible conduct is to be maintained, managers must pay attention to four sets of techniques: individual attributes, organizational structure, organizational culture, and societal expectations.

But as I argued in Chapter Eight, we also worry about the self-serving tendencies of large, bureaucratic structures. We fear that if public organizations begin to run amok, our fellow citizens within them may fail to act on our behalf and in our interests, either because they have lost sight of the legitimate goals of these organizations or because they are intimidated into silence by unethical superiors. We are apprehensive that the struggle may not take place at all, with the inherent conflict between individuals and organizations being resolved too decisively in favor of the organizations, or that the struggle may assume a dominant position, consuming the time and resources of the organization. In either case, the public's intended work may never get done.

Thus, in Chapter Eight I identified the elements that are necessary to preserve individual ethical autonomy within public organizations. I identified organizational remedies for the protection of whistle-blowers, assessing them as imperfect but offering some help for those who feel compelled to exercise their conscience about misconduct within their organizations. Individual responsibility was seen as the final protection against organizational corruption. The means of supporting individual responsibility by encouraging autonomy include (1) the conscious delimitation of commitment to an employing organization and the cultivation of identities that transcend its boundaries, (2) legal and institutional protection for individual rights and conscience, (3) an ethic of awareness, and (4) the cultivation of principled thinking. A systematic process for evaluating one's role at the limits of organizational loyalty was outlined as one means for determining a course of action in crises.

Finally, in Chapter Nine I restated Whitbeck's design approach in terms appropriate for public administration and highlighted the four basic elements of that approach. I showed how the approach could be applied to the case of the Abu Ghraib prison scandal and the cases of the *Challenger* and *Columbia* space shuttles. I ended that chapter with a hypothetical case in which two subordinates were concerned that their superior was granting contracts based on racial motivations. In doing so, I showed how the design approach impels us to think creatively and with due consideration to the larger context in which ethical problems occur.

It seems, then, as Whyte observed five decades ago, that an inherent tension exists between individuals and the organizations in which they are employed. This is certainly true for individuals who attempt to take seriously their ethical responsibility as both citizens and employees of the citizenry. Some means of managing this conflict therefore is in order—some way of preserving a desirable level of individual autonomy while maintaining the collective goals for which public organizations are created. The elements necessary for this kind of balancing of interests have already been identified and discussed. It now remains to combine these two perspectives to complete a design template for responsible administration or ethical conduct in public organizations.

A Model of Responsible Administration

I am often asked for a blueprint or model of responsible administration. Designs are graphically represented in blueprints. In this case, a model serves the function of a blueprint. It is intended as a guide for managers attempting to construct, or reconstruct, an organizational environment conducive to responsible conduct and supportive of professional ethics. It should be emphasized that analyses that use this model do not involve ethical reflection as it is usually understood by moral philosophers. Rather, it is a template for designing an environment in which one can not only engage in ethical analysis but act accordingly. Although philosophers might well exclude such considerations, administrative ethics must address these contextual concerns to have any practical impact.

A general model for responsible administration that acknowledges the necessary and legitimate role duality of the public administrator may be developed by combining the components of responsible conduct, discussed in Chapter Seven, and the components of individual autonomy, outlined in Chapter Eight. Such a model recognizes the obligations of the organizational and the citizen roles; however, it is assumed here that the priority of the citizen role must ultimately be maintained. When our obligations as a citizen to our fellow citizens are clearly in conflict with the demands of a public organization, the more fundamental duty is to the citizenry (see Cooper, 1991, for a complete discussion of this).

Table 10.1 displays the model for responsible administration. The left column represents the organizational and individual threats to responsible administration. These threats are counterbalanced by both organizational and individual responsible administrative actions. The underlying basis for the organization-related actions are the components of responsible conduct I outlined in Chapter Seven—for example, individual attributes, organizational structure, organizational culture, and societal expectations. The corresponding individual actions are based on the components of individual ethical autonomy I outlined in Chapter Eight, including organizational delimitation and transcendence, legal and institutional mechanisms for constraining organizational power, and self-awareness.

It should be clear that the two sets of components and the actions that follow from them are not inherently, necessarily, or continuously in opposition. All or some of the components of responsible conduct may be more or less in conflict with all or some of the components of individual ethical autonomy, depending on the extent to which both the organization and any given administrator are responsive to the legally mandated mission of the organization. If an agency deviates from the accomplishment of its mission while an administrator remains committed to it, conflict will follow. Also, if an administrator deviates from an organization's mission through either misconduct or perceived obligations to the public while the organization remains devoted to it, conflict will result. Incongruence between administrative obligation and de facto or de jure organizational goals will produce tension and conflict.

The model proposed therefore is not a simple balancing of neatly opposing elements; rather, it identifies elements that together can provide corrective forces if incongruence occurs, as it surely will in any organization. It represents a field of forces that can create checks and balances on organizational corruption, self-service, and tyranny on the one hand, and individual corruption, self-service, and arrogance on the other. Because these two sets of

Table 10.1. Model of Responsible Administration

Threats	Responsible Administrative Actions Organizational	Individual
Corruption	Maintain and develop knowledge of the organization, its mission, and policy arena	Maintain and develop knowledge of one's own values, beliefs, convictions, worldview, and life priorities
	Make decisions consistent with the legally mandated mission of the organization	Offer proposals for legislative change in the organizational mission based on public preferences, demands, and interests
	Comply with the organization's informal norms and procedures	Propose changes in norms, rules, regulations, and procedures based on public preferences, demand, and interests; professional judgment; or personal conscience
	Work within the specialized structure of the organization	Encourage collaboration among units with other organizations, elected officials, and the public
Tyranny/hubris	Act within the provision of current codes and ethics legislation	Act within the values of the political community and personal conscience
	Acknowledge accountability to hierarchical structure of organization	Question, resist, and challenge orders inconsistent with the mission of the organization, professional codes, or values of the political conscience and offer proposals for legal and institutional protection from retaliation

(continued)

Table 10.1. Model of Responsible Administration *(continued)*

| | *Responsible Administrative Actions* | |
Threats	*Organizational*	*Individual*
Self-service	Maintain and enhance the knowledge of the professional field systems	Maintain and develop current knowledge of the social, political, and economic systems
	Commit energy and time to the work of the organization, its mission, and policy arena	Maintain and cultivate family, social, and community relationships
	Exercise best technical judgment	Provide for regular and accessible public participation

components have been dealt with at some length in Chapters Seven and Eight, they will not be discussed here. However, it may be useful to comment briefly on each of the juxtaposed pairs of actions that should flow from them.

Maintaining and developing knowledge of the organization, its mission, and its policy arena is essential for adequately carrying out our responsibilities as an employee of a particular public organization. Cultivating this knowledge that transcends our specific job tasks is the way we move beyond being simple instrumental functionaries and carry a share of responsibility for the overall functioning of the organization and the creative solving of public problems. The necessary complements to this job-related knowledge are our personal values, beliefs, convictions, worldview, and life priorities. To appropriately bound the demands and influence of the organization and maintain some degree of ethical autonomy, we must consciously develop self-awareness through regularly reflecting on our position in relationship to job-related issues and on where we stand on a broad range of political, social, and philosophical concerns. This is the means by which we develop an identity apart from the employment role.

The young officer described in Chapters Seven and Eight who blew the whistle on his chief for stealing at crime scenes is an example of this constructive tension between one's own ethical convictions and knowledge of the organization. Even as a probationer, he knew well the nature of his department's culture with respect to "ratting" on a fellow officer. He also understood the chain-of-evidence procedures requiring property taken from crime scenes to be recorded in the evidence log. Furthermore, he understood his organizational alternatives: he could go to the chief himself with his findings or to the internal affairs unit within the department, but neither of those alternatives would lead to an ethical outcome. He also knew that the district attorney was the next step in the established hierarchy outside the department. He knew the character of the officials in that office well enough to trust them with his highly sensitive information. Finally, it was his own self-awareness and conscience that would not allow him to simply walk away from the corruption and ignore it. Clarity about his own ethical priorities pushed him in the direction of using his organizational knowledge to resolve a course of action.

Making decisions congruent with the legally mandated mission of the organization is fundamental to the fulfillment of the employment role and the proper functioning of the hierarchical system of the public organization. This commitment provides a discipline of purpose and a constraint on the personal biases and preferences of the individual administrator and on the tendencies of superiors in the hierarchy to turn public organizations into their own private power fiefdoms. Everyone in the hierarchy must be reminded regularly of what the law adopted by the elected representatives of the citizenry has mandated as the goals and objectives of its work. But we should not presume that the law is perfect and simply to be served mechanically and mindlessly at any given moment. Public administrators are obligated to offer proposals to their organizational superiors, elected officials, and the people for changes in the law and in the mission of the organization as they learn more about public preferences and the nature of the problems to be solved.

The case of the highway in need of widening for the safety of young pedestrians discussed in Chapter Four can be used to elucidate these competing obligations. Although the law requires an environmental impact statement to infringe on parkland, a responsible administrator must feel some obligation to do more than simply plod along for two years while children are left at risk. In this position, one might initially vigorously pursue an expedited EIS process, seek an administrative exemption for this special case, or turn to the courts for special treatment. However, over the long haul, this kind of situation deserves an administrator's proactive attention to seek changes in rules and legislation to handle instances where safety is a serious consideration.

Complying with the organization's informal norms and procedures is ordinarily required of a responsible public administrator. These are the specific organizational means for structuring and maintaining work that is consistent with the organization's legitimate mission. Because not everything can be written down formally and recognizing that informally evolved norms give cohesion and identity to an organization, these unofficial patterns of practice play an essential role.

However, at times these controls may subvert the mission or detract from its achievement, as in goal displacement. A truly responsible administrator will bear an obligation to propose changes when they become problematic for the wishes of the public, inconsistent with professional judgment, or in conflict with personal conscience. It is irresponsible to simply ignore or circumvent inappropriate norms and procedures on the one hand, or reluctantly comply with them on the other.

An example of problematic informal norms that have been confronted in recent years are those concerning relationships between men and women in the workplace. For decades it had been common practice for men to assume that women working with them would do such things as make coffee for the staff or take notes in meetings, though these were not included in their official duties. More seriously, men assumed that it was acceptable to make passes at women in the workplace or harass them sexually in other ways. These informal norms have now been recognized generally as unacceptable and in some cases explicitly prohibited in law and rules. Addressing informal norms of this kind that demean workers, infringe on their privacy, and fail to respect their professionalism is an ethical obligation.

Public administrators must work within the specialized structure of the employing organization; that is their most immediate obligation and deserves their initial loyalty and effort. That particular piece of the public's property is entrusted to their care and use. Nevertheless, responsible administrators should also bear a larger obligation to encourage collaboration rather than competition with other units, organizations, elected officials, and the public.

Suboptimization does not enhance the work of the government as a whole; it wastes resources. Most complex problems require the effective cooperation of various governmental units, as well as the citizenry.

This set of balancing obligations requires no specific illustrative example, because the problems of keeping organizational loyalty and collaborative accomplishment of goals are pervasive. Law enforcement agencies tend to be extremely turf conscious and only reluctantly share information on important cases. Branches of the armed forces suffer the same organizational provincialism. Health agencies and welfare departments tend to ignore each other. State highway planners and local governments find it difficult to work cooperatively for the public good. Federal and state agencies find it easier to deal with each other legalistically and distantly. Responsible administration calls for a balance between doing one's duty to the employing organization and seeking collaboration for more important public values and objectives.

Acting within current codes of ethics and ethics legislation provides the routine points of reference for what is deemed to be ethical conduct for public administrators. Together these represent the generalized formal judgments of the political and professional communities about acceptable and unacceptable conduct. Both leave large areas of interpretation and judgment to practicing administrators in concrete situations. However, this process of interpreting and applying the specifications of ethics legislation and codes of ethics should be informed by the core values that represent the foundations of the political tradition, sometimes referred to as regime values, as well as by the developed conscience of the administrator. These encourage compliance with the spirit of the law and codes rather than merely the letter. Also, internalized political values and developed conscience provide a check on self-protective and self-serving codes, which professional associations have been known to adopt. They also establish a broader point of reference from which to evaluate the legitimacy of any particular piece of ethics legislation.

For example, although there are federal regulations concerning conflict of interest that would apply to the case of Linda and George in Chapter Two, Linda's supervisor should consider the importance of individual dignity and respect for privacy that are highly important values in our political tradition. The question then is not whether the supervisor should observe the regulations or be responsive to Linda's wishes. Rather, it is a matter of how the intent of the regulation can be upheld and show respect for Linda's dignity and privacy. The tension between these two obligations is a healthy one for any supervisor to address and reflect on. Simply ordering Linda to stop seeing George would be treating her in a mechanical and disrespectful manner, but simply giving in to her would run the risk of accepting real or perceived conflicts of interest. Thus, one solution might be to talk it through with her, offering assurance that you understand her dilemma and want to be helpful. You might then discuss the various alternatives for protecting her dignity and privacy while fulfilling your duty to the law. The alternatives outlined in Chapter Two would be likely ones to include. You are searching for a win-win solution that does not punish her for having a private life outside work.

Responsible public administrators generally should acknowledge their accountability to the hierarchical structure of the organization. When functioning properly the hierarchy is, as Appleby (1952) suggests, the structure of responsibility; it is the means for managing different levels of responsibility for the mission of the organization and the appropriate delegation of authority. However, being accountable to superiors does not necessarily mean simply following orders that are illegitimate. Administrators are also obligated to question, resist, and challenge orders that are inconsistent with the mission of the organization, established professional codes, the values of the political community, or their own conscience. Ultimately they must maintain accountability to the citizenry, professional colleagues, and their own principles. Superiors who deviate seriously from these touchstones should be confronted with the administrator's best judgment and reasons for believing that orders are not legitimate. This responsibility includes contributing to the development of institutional arrangements that will provide reasonable protection for administrators offering such challenges to superiors. Individual responsibility needs to be buttressed with supportive mechanisms for whistle-blowers when such action becomes necessary.

The case of Marie Ragghianti discussed in Chapter Eight provides an illustrative example for this balancing set of obligations. When Ragghianti began to suspect that pardons were being sold by someone on Governor Blanton's staff, she approached his general counsel, Eddie Sisk, and Blanton's assistant, Charlie Benson. They assured her that there was no such practice going on within the governor's office. Subsequently, as she began to experience pressure from Sisk and Benson to engage in questionable activities, Ragghianti met with the governor himself. His cool and unresponsive reaction to her suspicions of misconduct within his own inner circle finally confirmed in her mind that she had exhausted all recourse within her organizational hierarchy. Ragghianti had been scrupulously accountable to her superiors and reluctant to circumvent the established chain of command. However, even while doing so she did not hesitate to question suspicious conduct by those above her, resist their improper requests, and ultimately take her concerns about the governor himself to the FBI. She upheld her oath of public office in defiance of corrupt superior authority after having been careful to be accountable to the duly established hierarchy. Furthermore, Ragghianti did not view her duty as fulfilled with Blanton, Sisk, and Benson sentenced to prison. She did not rest until reforms for the Board of Pardons and Paroles of the State of Tennessee were enacted into law.

Maintaining and enhancing knowledge of the professional field makes public administrators responsible for having a competent basis from which to perceive a range of alternative courses of action when confronting an ethical issue. It also provides the necessary basis for evaluating the performance of themselves and others. However, that kind of professional knowledge needs to be complemented by a more comprehensive understanding of the social, economic, and political systems. This broader knowledge discourages a narrowly professional perspective and overcommitment to an employing organization. It encourages carrying out public administration as an integral part of the larger political, economic, and social context. It confronts us with obligations to a democratic society with a diverse social fabric and makes us more aware of the economic consequences of our administrative actions.

Illustrative of the importance of this tension between acting within current codes and legislation and a comprehension of the broader social, economic, and political environment might be the case of Mrs. Carmichael in Chapter Four. As assistant project director for the Municipal Redevelopment Agency (MRA) in the

Victoria area, you would be acting entirely within the law to just go ahead and move Mrs. Carmichael out of her home to some other location and demolish it. However, the power of a more complex set of values in addition to the law has a constraining effect on your conduct. You know that redevelopment agencies have been accused of being insensitive to those with little power, especially the elderly and the poor, both of which characterize Mrs. Carmichael's status. If you are not careful in seeing that her needs are met as fully as possible, there may be litigation against the MRA that could stimulate political pressure on the agency and possibly affect its budget. You know personally how you are inclined to act, but without a rich understanding of the broader values of your work context, you might be tempted to simply act in accordance with the law. Thus, the tension between acting within the current codes and laws and keeping your antenna tuned to the big picture provides a useful balance for working out ethical problems.

Commitment of energy and time to the work and purposes of the organization is clearly required of anyone who presumes to accept the role of a fiduciary of the citizenry. This role requires us to set aside private projects and interests and engage seriously and actively in the work of the public. This includes bringing our best creative insights to bear on public problems. Our responsibility includes maintaining physical health, clarity of mind, and focused attention while on the job. However, maintaining family, social, and community relationships is equally essential. Public administrators cannot effectively carry out the role of fiduciary citizen without ongoing experience with and commitment to these other enclaves of life. Without these dimensions of life, the organization may become too dominant in our thinking; we may lose other points of reference. A citizen administrator must also be a citizen who is consistently involved in private life.

The vignette from Michener's novel *Chesapeake* that opens Chapter Two can be used to elucidate this essential balance between organizational commitment and maintaining a well-rounded life outside of work. One wonders about the Pusey Paxmores and the Owen Steeds who were so caught up in devotion to the Nixon White House that they became unidimensional people. Every presidential administration runs the risk of so consuming its staffers that they lose the balancing effects of family life, community involvement, and social activities not directed toward some political purpose, but just for the value of being with others. Tunnel vision that makes the work organization seem disproportionately important in the scheme of things can cause people to act in unethical ways in any organization, as occurred in the Nixon White House and other political administrations.

Administrators of the public's business should exercise their best technical judgment when tackling complex problems. Their technical knowledge and skills are tools for which they are being paid; they are the specific justification for the fiduciary role on behalf of the people. However, technical judgment must be complemented with intelligence gathered from the citizenry through regular and effective opportunities for participation. Technical expertise alone does not guarantee that government will be of and by the people as well as for them. Technical efficiency and even effectiveness should be subordinated to the will of the citizenry. In this way, professional values are regularly informed by the public. Responsible administrators bring their expertise to bear on problems and do their best to educate the citizenry about the technical considerations in an issue, but ultimately they accept the right of the people to influence the decision and action—even the right of the people to be wrong.

An example of the importance of this set of relationships might be the case of the contaminated lake in Chapter Two. The response of your supervisor that the risk of human infection was low at the current level of bacterial contamination is a narrow technical judgment. Even if this assessment of risk is accepted at face value, it does not take into account the likely reactions of the citizenry. In short, there will surely be a general public outcry over the lake situation. Our social values are highly sensitive to the loss of human life even if the numbers are small, especially if the deaths could have been prevented. The potential legal consequences are enormous if the truth comes out, as it usually does sooner or later, and an avalanche of litigation lands on the department. The likely economic and political fallout from neglecting to deal with the contamination is equally serious. Thus, if the supervisor had had the benefit of both technical knowledge and a lively sense of the citizenry from regular contact with them, his response might have been different when he first discovered the contamination. He might not have fallen into the trap of relying solely on technical considerations that may make sense in isolation but much less when viewed through the eyes of the people. The vivid prospect of dire consequences for human life, followed by the resultant uproar from the public, might have enlivened his moral sense and moved him to seek more ethical alternatives.

This line of thought also illustrates the way in which deontological (duty-oriented) and teleological (consequentialist) ethical perspectives need to be held together in actual practice. The duty to preserve and respect human life cannot be separated from the consequences of not dealing with the contaminated lake water. Some people will die, and the consequences of that include moral, legal, political, social, and economic outcomes that are very undesirable.

These two sets of components may be used as a template or guide for organizational diagnosis and design. They suggest the essential ingredients that we ought to look for in existing organizations, as well as those that ought to be built into new ones. This model for the sustenance of responsible administrators is an ideal type in the Weberian tradition. It is a construct that will never be fully actualized in any specific, concrete organizational manifestation. Nevertheless, it indicates the complexity of maintaining responsible administration and responsible administrators, and identifies the areas of organizational life to which we should direct our research, analysis, training, and organizational development.

This model is consistent with Ralph Kilmann's admonitions to avoid "quick fixes" (1984). Attention to any one or even several of the essential components will not be adequate to maintain the precarious balance between citizenship and the organization. Only a comprehensive review and treatment of the relevant aspects of an organization's structure, its personnel, training programs, formal rules and policies, prevailing informal norms, relationship to the citizens, and the laws under which it operates will be fully sufficient. A long-term commitment to a plan for organizational and personnel development based on such a review will produce far more significant results than sporadic efforts.

However, it is also true that no particular public organization can fully accomplish the task on its own. Elected officials, citizens' organizations, professional associations, and academic institutions will be required to contribute in significant ways as well. Some portion of the work to be done lies beyond both the capacity of public agencies and their perceived interests. Thus, although much can and must be addressed entirely within public organizations, some of the work will entail partnership arrangements, and still other tasks will have to be undertaken outside and apart from these public organizations. Responsible administration is not just the task of those who practice public administration. It is the work of all who strive for a democratic society in an administrative state.

References

Aberbach, J. D., Putnam, R. D., and Rockman, B. A. *Bureaucrats and Politicians in Western Democracies.* Cambridge, Mass.: Harvard University Press, 1981.

Aiken, H. D. *Reason and Conduct.* New York: Knopf, 1962.

Alford, C. F. *Whistleblowers: Broken Lives and Organizational Power.* Ithaca, N.Y.: Cornell University Press, 2001.

American Society for Public Administration. "Whistle Blowing: A Time to Listen . . . A Time to Hear." Policy statement, Dec. 2, 1979.

American Society for Public Administration. "Code of Ethics and Implementation Guidelines." Washington, D.C.: American Society for Public Administration, 1985.

American Society for Public Administration. "Code of Ethics." Washington, D.C.: American Society for Public Administration, 1994.

"Appearance of Success Is Key to Tax Audit System." *Los Angeles Times,* Dec. 21, 1979.

Appleby, P. H. *Morality and Administration in Democratic Government.* Baton Rouge: Louisiana State University Press, 1952.

Appleby, P. H. "Public Administration and Democracy." In R. C. Martin (ed.), *Public Administration and Democracy: Essays in Honor of Paul Appleby.* Syracuse, N.Y.: Syracuse University Press, 1965.

Arendt, H. *Eichmann in Jerusalem.* New York: Viking Penguin, 1963.

Arthur D. Little. *Effective Citizen Participation in Transportation Planning.* Washington, D.C.: U.S. Department of Transportation, 1976.

Association of the Bar of the City of New York, Special Committee on the Federal Conflict of Interest Laws. *Conflict of Interest and Federal Service.* Cambridge, Mass.: Harvard University Press, 1960.

Bailey, S. K. "The Relationship Between Ethics and Public Service." In R. C. Martin (ed.), *Public Administration and Democracy: Essays in Honor of Paul Appleby.* Syracuse, N.Y.: Syracuse University Press, 1965.

Banton, M. *Roles: An Introduction to the Study of Social Relations.* New York: Basic Books, 1965.

Barnard, C. I. "A Definition of Authority." In R. K. Merton and others (eds.), *Reader in Bureaucracy.* New York: Free Press, 1952.

Barnard, C. I. *The Functions of the Executive.* Cambridge, Mass.: Harvard University Press, 1964.

Bates, S. "My Lai and Viet Nam: The Issues of Responsibility." In P. A. French (ed.), *Individual and Collective Responsibility: The Massacre at My Lai.* Cambridge, Mass.: Schenkman, 1972.

Baucus, M. S., and Beck-Dudley, C. L. "Designing Ethical Organizations: Avoiding the Long-Term Negative Effects of Rewards and Punishments." *Journal of Business Ethics,* 2005, *56,* 355–370.

Baumhart, H. "How Ethical Are Businessmen?" *Harvard Business Review,* 1961, pp. 6–9.

Beard, E. "Conflicts of Interest and Public Service." In J. T. DeGeorge and J. A. Pichler (eds.), *Ethics, Free Enterprise and Public Policy.* New York: Oxford University Press, 1978.

Beard, E., and Horn, S. *Congressional Ethics: The View from the House.* Washington, D.C.: Brookings Institution, 1975.

Becker, H. "Whose Side Are We On?" In *Annual Editions Readings in Social Problems, 1973–74.* Guilford, Conn.: Dushkin, 1973.

Bellah, R. N., and others. *Habits of the Heart: Individualism and Commitment in American Life.* Berkeley: University of California Press, 1985.

Bellah, R. N., and others. *The Good Society.* New York: Knopf, 1991.

Bennis, W. *Beyond Bureaucracy: Essays on the Development and Evolution of Human Organizations.* New York: McGraw-Hill, 1966.

Bentley, A. F. *The Process of Government.* San Antonio, Tex.: Principia, 1949.

Benveniste, G. *The Politics of Expertise.* (2nd ed.) San Francisco: Boyd & Fraser, 1977.

Berger, P., Berger, B., and Kellner, H. *The Homeless Mind: Modernization and Consciousness.* New York: Vintage Books, 1973.

Berger, P., and Luckman, T. *The Social Construction of Reality.* New York: Doubleday, 1966.

Berger, P., and Neuhouse, R. J. *To Empower People: The Role of Mediating Structures in Public Policy.* Washington, D.C.: American Enterprise Institute, 1977.

Berman, E. M., and West, J. P. "Managing Ethics to Improve Performance and Build Trust." In *Public Integrity Annual.* Lexington, Ky.: Council of State Governments, 1997.

Berman, E. M., West, J. P., and Cava, A. "Ethics Management in Municipal Governments and Large Firms: Exploring Similarities and Differences." *Administration and Society,* 1994, *26,* 185–203.

Berry, J. M., Portney, K. E., and Thompson, K. *The Rebirth of Urban Democracy: Making Democracy Work in a Complex World.* Syracuse, N.Y.: Syracuse University Press, 1991.

Blasi, A. "Bridging Moral Cognition and Moral Action." *Psychological Bulletin,* 1980, *88*(1), 1–45.

Blitz, M. *Duty Bound: Responsibility and American Public Life.* Lanham, Md.: Rowman and Littlefield, 2005.

Boisjoly, R. M. "Personal Integrity and Accountability." *Accounting Horizons,* 1993, 7(1), 59–69.

Bok, S. *Secrets: On the Ethics of Concealment and Revelation.* New York: Vintage, 1984.

Bowie, N. E., and Freeman, R. E. (eds.). *Ethics and Agency Theory.* New York: Oxford University Press, 1992.

Bowman, J. S. "Ethical Issues for the Public Manager." In W. B. Eddy (ed.), A *Handbook of Organization Management.* New York: Marcel Dekker, 1981.

Bowman, J. S. "Ethics in Government: A National Survey of Public Administrators." *Public Administration Review,* 1990, 50(3), 345–353.

Bowman, J. S., and Ensign, D. (eds.). *Public Integrity Annual.* Lexington, Ky.: Council of State Governments, 1997.

Bowman, J. S., and Williams, R. L. "Ethics in Government: From a Winter of Despair to a Spring of Hope." *Public Administration Review,* 1997, 57(6), 517–526.

Brenner, S., and Mollandar, E. "Is the Ethics of Business Changing?" *Harvard Business Review,* 1977, 55(1), 57–71.

Bruce, W. "Ethics and Administration." *Public Administration Review,* 1992, 52(1), 81–83.

Buchanan, J. M., and Tullock, G. *The Calculus of Consent: Logical Foundations of Constitutional Democracy.* Ann Arbor: University of Michigan Press, 1962.

Burke, J. P. *Bureaucratic Responsibility.* Baltimore, Md.: Johns Hopkins University Press, 1986.

Caiden, G. E., and Truelson, J. A. "Whistleblower Protection in the USA: Lessons Learnt and to Be Learnt." *Australian Journal of Public Administration,* 1988, 47(2), 119–129.

Calhoun, J. C. *A Disquisition on Government and Selections from the Discourse.* (G. Post, ed.). New York: Liberal Arts Press, 1953.

Caro, R. A. *The Power Broker: Robert Moses and the Fall of New York.* New York: Vintage, 1975.

Catron, B., and Denhardt, K. G. "Ethics Education in Public Administration." In T. L. Cooper (ed.), *Handbook of Administrative Ethics.* New York: Marcel Dekker, 1994.

Chandler, R. C. "The Problem of Moral Reasoning in American Public Administration: The Case for a Code of Ethics." *Public Administration Review,* 1983, 43(1), 32–39.

Chandler, R. C. "The Public Administrator as Representative Citizen: A New Role for the New Century." In H. G. Frederickson and R. C. Chandler (eds.), "Citizenship and Public Administration." *Public Administration Review,* 1984, 196–206.

Cleveland, H. *The Future Executive*. New York: HarperCollins, 1972.

Columbia Accident Investigation Board. "Executive Summary." In *Report*, Vol. 1. Aug. 2003. http://www.caib.us/news/report/default.html.

Cooper, T. L. "The Hidden Price Tag: Participation Costs and Health Planning." *American Journal of Public Health*, 1979, *69*(4), 368–374.

Cooper, T. L. "Hierarchy, Virtue, and the Practice of Public Administration: A Perspective for Normative Ethics." *Public Administration Review*, 1987, *47*(4), 320–328.

Cooper, T. L. *An Ethic of Citizenship for Public Administration*. Upper Saddle River, N.J.: Prentice Hall, 1991.

Cooper, T. L. "Author's Response to Willa Bruce's Review of *The Responsible Administrator: An Approach to Ethics for the Administrative Role*." *Public Administrative Review*, 1992a, *52*(3), 311–313.

Cooper, T. L. "Conclusion: Reflecting on Exemplars of Virtue." In T. L. Cooper and D. N. Wright (eds.), *Exemplary Public Administrators: Character and Leadership in Government*. San Francisco: Jossey-Bass, 1992b.

Cooper, T. L. (ed.). *Handbook of Administrative Ethics*. New York: Marcel Dekker, 1994.

Cooper, T. L. "The Paradox of Responsibility: An Enigma." *Public Administration Review*, 1996, *52*(6), 599–604.

Cooper, T. L. (ed.). *Handbook of Administrative Ethics*. (2nd ed.). New York: Marcel Dekker, 2001a.

Cooper, T. L. "The Emergence of Administrative Ethics as a Field of Study." In T. L. Cooper (ed.), *Handbook of Administrative Ethics*. (2nd ed.). New York: Marcel Dekker, 2001b.

Cooper, T. L. "Big Questions in Administrative Ethics: A Need for Focused, Collaborative Effort." *Public Administration Review*, 2004a, *64*(4), 395–407.

Cooper, T. L. "Organization Structure and Culture Strike Again!" *Ethics Today*, 2004b, *7*(1), 1–2. http://www.unpan.org/namerica-aspa-ethics.asp.

Cooper, T. L. "Ethical Norms of Organization Culture." Unpublished manuscript, n.d.

Cooper, T. L., and Wright, D. N. (eds.). *Exemplary Public Administrators: Character and Leadership in Government*. San Francisco: Jossey-Bass, 1992.

Cooper, T. L., and Yoder, D. E. "The Meaning and Significance of Citizenship in a Transnational World: Implications for Public Administration." *Administrative Theory and Praxis*, *21*(2), 1999, 195–204.

Crozier, M. *The Stalled Society*. New York: Viking Penguin, 1973.

Davis, K. C. *Discretionary Justice: A Preliminary Inquiry*. Baton Rouge: Louisiana State University Press, 1969.

Davis, M. "Conflict of Interest." *Business and Professional Ethics Journal*, 1982, *1*(4), 17–27.

De George, R. T. "Agency Theory and the Ethics of Agency." In N. E. Bowie and R. E. Freeman (eds.), *Ethics and Agency Theory*. New York: Oxford University Press, 1992.

Dean, J. *Blind Ambition*. New York: Simon & Schuster, 1976.

Dees, J. G. "Principals, Agents, and Ethics." In N. E. Bowie and R. E. Freeman (eds.), *Ethics and Agency Theory*. New York: Oxford University Press, 1992.

Demille, N. *The General's Daughter*. New York: Warner Books, 1992.

Denhardt, K. G. *The Ethics of Public Service*. Westport, Conn.: Greenwood Press, 1988.

Dennard, L. F. "The Democratic Potential in the Transition of Postmodernism." *American Behavioral Scientist*, 1997, *41*(1), 148–162.

Dewey, J. *Human Nature and Conduct*. New York: Holt, 1922.

Dewey, J. *The Public and Its Problems*. Chicago: Swallow Press, 1927.

Downie, R. S. *Roles and Values: An Introduction to Social Ethics*. London: Methuen, 1971.

Downie, R. S. "Responsibility and Social Roles." In P. A. French (ed.), *Individual and Collective Responsibility: The Massacre at My Lai*. Cambridge, Mass.: Schenkman, 1972.

Drews, E. M., and Lipson, L. *Values and Humanity*. New York: St. Martin's, 1971.

Durkheim, E. *Professional Ethics and Civic Morals*. (C. Brookfield, trans.). New York: Routledge & Kegan Paul, 1957.

Dvorin, E. P., and Simmons, R. H. *From Amoral to Humane Bureaucracy*. San Francisco: Canfield Press, 1972.

Egger, R. "Responsibility in Administration: An Exploratory Essay." In R. C. Martin (ed.), *Public Administration and Democracy: Essays in Honor of Paul Appleby*. Syracuse, N.Y.: Syracuse University Press, 1965.

Emmet, D. *Rules, Roles and Relations*. New York: St. Martin's Press, 1967.

Ewing, D. *Freedom Inside the Organization: Bringing Civil Liberties to the Work Place*. New York: Dutton, 1977.

Farrell, B. J., Cobbin, D. M., and Farrell, H. M. "Can Codes of Ethics Really Produce Consistent Behaviours?" *Journal of Managerial Psychology, 17*(6), 2002, 468–490.

Federal Personnel Manual. Washington, D.C.: U.S. Government Printing Office, 1972.

Finer, H. "Better Government Personnel." *Political Science Quarterly*, 1936, *51*(4), 569–599.

Finer, H. "Administrative Responsibility in Democratic Government." In F. Rourke, *Bureaucratic Power in National Politics*. (2nd ed.) Boston: Little, Brown, 1972. (Originally published 1941.)

First Annual Report to the Congress on the Activities of the Office of Special Counsel. Washington, D.C.: U.S. Government Printing Office, 1979.

Flathman, R. E. *The Public Interest: An Essay Concerning the Normative Discourse of Politics.* Hoboken, N.J.: Wiley, 1966.

Fleishman, J. L., Liebman, L., and Moore, M. H. (eds.). *Public Duties: The Moral Obligations of Government Officials.* Cambridge, Mass.: Harvard University Press, 1981.

Ford, R. C., and Richardson, W. D. "Ethical Decision Making: A Review of the Empirical Literature." *Journal of Business Ethics,* 1994, *13,* 205–221.

Foster, G. D. "Law, Morality, and the Public Servant." *Public Administration Review,* 1981, *41*(1), 29–33.

Fox, C. J., and Miller, H. T. *Postmodern Public Administration.* Thousand Oaks, Calif.: Sage, 1996.

Frederickson, H. G. "Toward a New Public Administration." In F. Marini (ed.), *Toward a New Public Administration: The Minnowbrook Perspective.* Scranton, Penn.: Chandler, 1971.

Frederickson, H. G., and Hart, D. K. "The Public Service and the Patriotism of Benevolence." *Public Administration Review,* 1985, *45*(5), 547–553.

Frederickson, H. G. "Minnowbrook II: Changing Epochs of Public Administration." *Public Administration Review,* 1989, *49*(2), 95–100.

French, P. "Nuremberg Trials: The Jodl Defense." In P. French (ed.), *Individual and Collective Responsibility: The Massacre at My Lai.* Cambridge, Mass.: Schenkman, 1972.

Friedrich, C. J. "Responsible Government Service Under the American Constitution." In C. J. Friedrich and others (eds.), *Problems of the American Public Service.* New York: McGraw-Hill, 1935.

Friedrich, C. J. "Some Observations on Weber's Analysis of Bureaucracy." In R. Merton (ed.), *Reader in Bureaucracy.* New York: Free Press, 1952.

Friedrich, C. J. (ed.). *The Public Interest.* New York: Atherton Press, 1962.

Friedrich, C. J. "Public Policy and the Nature of Administrative Responsibility." In F. E. Rourke (ed.), *Bureaucratic Power in National Politics.* (2nd ed.) Boston: Little, Brown, 1972. (Originally published 1940.)

Gabris, G. T. "Beyond Conventional Management Practices: Shifting Organizational Values." In J. S. Bowman (ed.), *Ethical Frontiers in Management: Seeking New Strategies for Resolving Ethical Dilemmas.* San Francisco: Jossey-Bass, 1991.

Gaus, J. M. "The Responsibility of Public Administrators." In J. M. Gaus, L. D. White, and M. Dimock (eds.), *The Frontiers of Public Administration.* Chicago: University of Chicago Press, 1936.

Gilligan, C. *In a Different Voice: Psychological Theory and Women's Development.* Cambridge, Mass.: Harvard University Press, 1982.

Goffman, E. *The Presentation of Self in Everyday Life.* Woodstock, N.Y.: Overlook Press, 1973.

Goodnow, F. *Politics and Administration.* New York: Macmillan, 1900.

Goodsell, C. T. "Public Administration and the Public Interest." In G. L. Wamsley and others (eds.), *Refounding Public Administration.* Thousand Oaks, Calif.: Sage, 1990.

Gorney, R. *The Human Agenda.* New York: Simon & Schuster, 1972.

Graham, G. A. "Ethical Guidelines for Public Administrators: Observations on Rules of the Game." *Public Administration Review,* 1974, *34*(1), 90–92.

Grojean, M. W., Resick, C. J., Dickson, M. W., and Smith, D. B. "Leaders, Values, and Organizational Climate: Examining Leadership Strategies for Establishing an Organizational Climate Regarding Ethics." *Journal of Business Ethics,* 2004, *55*(3), 223–241.

Grosenick, L. E., and Gibson, P. A. "Governmental Ethics and Organizational Culture." In T. L. Cooper (ed.), *Handbook of Administrative Ethics.* New York: Marcel Dekker, 2001.

Grunebaum, J. O. "What Ought the Representative Represent?" In N. E. Bowie (ed.), *Ethical Issues in Government.* Philadelphia: Temple University Press, 1981.

Gustafson, J. "Notes on Theology and Ethics." In D. Jenkins (ed.), *The Scope of Theology.* Cleveland, Ohio: World Publishing, 1965.

Guttman, A. "The Virtues of Democratic Self Constraint." In A. Etzioni (ed.), *New Communitarian Thinking: Persons, Virtues, Institutions, and Communities.* Charlottesville, Va.: University Press of Virginia, 1995.

Guy, M. E. "Minnowbrook II: Conclusions." *Public Administration Review,* 1989, *49*(2), 219–220.

Haque, A. "Ethics and Administrative Discretion in a Unified Administration: A Burkean Perspective." *Administration and Society,* 2004, *35*(6), 701–716.

Hardin, G. "The Tragedy of the Commons." In G. Hardin and J. Baden, *Managing the Commons.* New York: Freeman, 1977.

Harel, I. *The House on Garibaldi Street.* New York: Bantam Books, 1975.

Harmon, M. "Administrative Policy Formulation and the Public Interest." *Public Administration Review,* 1969, *29*(5), 483–491.

Harmon, M. "Normative Theory." In F. Marini (ed.), *Toward a New Public Administration: The Minnowbrook Perspective.* Scranton, Penn.: Chandler, 1971.

Harmon, M. *Responsibility as Paradox: A Critique of Rational Discourse on Government.* Thousand Oaks, Calif.: Sage, 1995.

Hart, D. K. "The Virtuous Citizen, the Honorable Bureaucrat, and 'Public' Administration." *Public Administration Review,* 1984, *44*, 111–120.

Hart, D. K. "The Moral Exemplar in an Organizational Society." In T. L. Cooper and D. N. Wright (eds.), *Exemplary Public Administrators: Character and Leadership in Government.* San Francisco: Jossey-Bass, 1992.

Hart, D. K. "Administration and the Ethics of Virtue: In All Things Choose First for Good Character and Then for Technical Expertise." In T. L. Cooper (ed.), *Handbook of Administrative Ethics.* New York: Marcel Dekker, 2001.

Heclo, H. "OMB and the Presidency: The Problem of Neutral Competence." *Public Interest,* 1975, *38*(2), 80–98.

Hejka-Ekins, A. "Teaching Ethics in Public Administration." *Public Administration Review,* 1988, *48*(5), 885–891.

Hejka-Ekins, A. "Marie Ragghianti: Moral Courage in Exposing Corruption." In T. L. Cooper and N. D. Wright (eds.), *Exemplary Public Administrators: Character and Leadership in Government.* San Francisco: Jossey-Bass, 1992.

Held, V. *The Public Interest and Individual Interests.* New York: Basic Books, 1970.

Isenberg, D. J. "How Senior Managers Think." *Harvard Business Review,* Nov.–Dec. 1984, *62,* 81–90.

Jackall, R. "Moral Mazes: Bureaucracy and Managerial Work." *Harvard Business Review,* Sept.–Oct. 1983, pp. 118–130.

Jackson, R. *The Case Against the Nazi War Criminals.* New York: Knopf, 1946.

Jackson, R. *The Nurnberg Case.* New York: Knopf, 1947.

James, H. S. "Reinforcing Ethical Decision Making Through Organizational Structure." *Journal of Business Ethics,* 2000, *28,* 43–58.

Janis, I. L., and Mann, L. *Decision Making.* New York: Free Press, 1977.

Jaques, E. *A General Theory of Bureaucracy.* New York: Halsted Press, 1976.

Jaworski, L. *The Right and the Power.* New York: Pocket Books, 1977.

Johnson, R. A. *Whistle-Blowing: When It Works—and Why.* Boulder, Colo.: Lynne Rienner Publishers, 2003.

Jones, W. J., Sontag, F., Becker, M. O., and Fogelin, R. *Approaches to Ethics.* (2nd ed.) New York: McGraw-Hill, 1969.

Jos, P. H., Tompkins, M. E., and Hays, S. W. "In Praise of Difficult People: A Portrait of the Committed Whistleblower." *Public Administration Review,* 1989, *49*(6), 552–561.

Jun, J. S., and Rivera, M. "The Paradox of Transforming Public Administration: Modernity Versus Postmodernity Arguments." *American Behavioral Scientist,* 1997, *41*(1), 132–147.

Kernaghan, K. *Ethical Conduct: Guidelines for Government Employees.* Toronto: Institute of Public Administration of Canada, 1975.

Kilmann, R. H. *Beyond the Quick Fix: Managing Five Tracks to Organizational Success.* San Francisco: Jossey-Bass, 1984.

King, G. D. "Commentary on Codes of Ethics of the International Association of Chiefs of Police." In I. Hill (ed.), *The Ethical Basis of Economic Freedom.* Chapel Hill, N.C.: American Viewpoint, 1976.

Kneier, A. "Ethics in Government Service." In I. Hill (ed.), *The Ethical Basis of Economic Freedom.* Chapel Hill, N.C.: American Viewpoint, 1976.

Kohlberg, L. *Essays on Moral Development.* New York: HarperCollins, 1984.

Kohn, S. M. *Concepts and Procedures in Whistleblower Law.* Westport, Conn.: Quorum Books, 2001.

Leahy, P. J. *The Whistle Blowers: A Report on Federal Employees Who Disclose Acts of Governmental Waste, Abuse and Corruption.* Prepared for the Committee on Governmental Affairs, U.S. Senate. Washington, D.C.: U.S. Government Printing Office, 1978.

Lieberman, J. K. *How the Government Breaks the Law.* New York: Viking Penguin, 1973.

Lifton, R. J. *The Protean Self: Human Resilience in an Age of Fragmentation.* New York: Basic Books, 1993.

Lippmann, W. *Public Opinion.* Orlando, Fla.: Harcourt, 1922.

London, P. *Behavior Control.* New York: HarperCollins, 1971.

Long, N. E. "The Ethics and Efficiency of Resignation in Public Administration." *Administration and Society,* 1995, *25*(1), 3–11.

Lowi, T. J. *The End of Liberalism: The Second Republic of the United States.* (2nd ed.) New York: Norton, 1979.

Luebke, N. R. "Conflict of Interest as a Moral Category." *Business and Professional Ethics Journal,* 1986, *6*(1), 66–81.

Lynch, T. D., Lynch, C. E., and Cruise, P. L. "Productivity and the Moral Manager." *Administration and Society,* 2002, *34*(4), 347–369.

MacIntyre, A. *After Virtue.* (2nd ed.) Notre Dame, Ind.: Notre Dame University Press, 1984.

Margolis, J. "Conflict of Interest and Conflicting Interests." In T. L. Beuchamp and N. B. Bowie (eds.), *Ethical Theory and Business.* Upper Saddle River, N.J.: Prentice Hall, 1979.

Marini, F. (ed.). *Toward a New Public Administration: The Minnowbrook Perspective.* Scranton, Penn.: Chandler, 1971.

Martin, M. W. *Everyday Morality: An Introduction to Applied Ethics.* (2nd ed.) Belmont, Calif.: Wadsworth, 1995.

Marx, F. M. *Public Management in the New Democracy.* New York: HarperCollins, 1940.

Mathews, D. "Afterthoughts . . ." *Kettering Review,* Winter 1985, pp. 60–63.

Mayer, R. T. "Minnowbrook II: Conclusions and Reflections." *Public Administration Review,* 1989, *49*(2), 218.

McKeon, R. "The Development and the Significance of the Concept of Responsibility." *Revue Internationale de Philosophie,* 1957, *2*(39), 3–32.

Means, R. *The Ethical Imperative.* New York: Doubleday, 1970.

Meier, K. J. *Politics and the Bureaucracy.* Boston: Duxbury Press, 1979.

Menzel, D. C. "Teaching Ethics and Values in Public Administration: Are We Making a Difference?" *Public Administration Review,* 1997, *57*(3), 224–230.

Menzel, D. C. "Ethics Management in Public Organizations: What, Why, and How?" In T. L. Cooper (ed.), *Handbook of Administrative Ethics.* (2nd ed.) New York: Marcel Dekker, 2001.

Merit Systems Protection Board. *Blowing the Whistle in the Federal Government: A Comparative Analysis of 1980 and 1983 Survey Findings.* Washington, D.C.: U.S. Government Printing Office, Oct. 1984.

Mertins, H. (ed.). *Professional Standards and Ethics: A Workbook for Public Administrators.* Washington, D.C.: American Society for Public Administration, 1979.

Mertins, H., and Hennigan, P. J. (eds.). *Applying Professional Standards and Ethics in the Eighties: A Workbook Study Guide for Public Administrators.* Washington, D.C.: American Society for Public Administration, 1982.

Merton, R. K. "Bureaucratic Structure and Personality." In R. K. Merton (ed.), *Reader on Bureaucracy.* New York: Free Press, 1952.

Michener, J. A. *Chesapeake.* New York: Random House, 1978.

Mihm, J. C. *The Federal Workforce: Observations on Protections from Discrimination and Reprisal for Whistleblowing.* Washington, D.C.: U.S. General Accounting Office, 2001.

Milgram, S. *Obedience to Authority: An Experimental View.* New York: Harper-Collins, 1974.

Miller, H. T. *Postmodern Public Policy.* Albany: State University of New York Press, 2002.

Moore, M. *Creating Public Value: Strategic Management in Government.* Cambridge, Mass.: Harvard University Press, 1995.

Morgan, D. F. "The Public Interest." In T. L. Cooper (ed.), *Handbook of Administrative Ethics.* (2nd ed.) New York: Marcel Dekker, 2001.

Mosher, F. *Democracy and the Public Service.* New York: Oxford University Press, 1968.

Nachmias, D., and Rosenbloom, D. H. *Bureaucratic Government USA.* New York: St. Martin's Press, 1980.

Nader, R., Perkas, P. J., and Blackwell, K. *Whistle Blowing.* New York: Grossman, 1972.

National Association of Schools of Public Affairs and Administration, Commission on Peer Review and Accreditation. "Self-Study Report Instructions." Washington, D.C.: National Association of Schools of Public Affairs and Administration, 1996.

National Education Association. "Code of Ethics of the Education Profession." 1975. http://www.nea.org/aboutnea/code.html.

Nelson, W. E. *The Roots of American Bureaucracy, 1830–1900.* Cambridge, Mass.: Harvard University Press, 1982.

Ornstein, N. J., and Elder, S. *Interest Groups, Lobbyists and Policymaking.* Washington, D.C.: Congressional Quarterly Press, 1978.

Ostrom, V. *The Intellectual Crisis in American Public Administration.* (2nd ed.) Tuscaloosa: University of Alabama Press, 1974.

Parenti, M. "Power and Pluralism: A View from the Bottom." *Journal of Politics,* 1970, *32*(3), 501–530.

Peace Officer Standards and Training Commission of the State of California. "Career Ethics/Integrity Training Approved." *POST Scripts,* 1988, *22*(3), 6.

Perrow, C. *Complex Organizations: A Critical Essay.* Glenview, Ill.: Scott, Foresman, 1972.

Peters, T. J., and Waterman, R. H. *In Search of Excellence: Lessons from America's Best-Run Companies.* New York: Warner, 1982.

Pfiffner, J. P. "Torture as Public Policy." *Public Integrity,* 2005, 7(4), 313–329.

Pincoffs, E. L. *Quandaries and Virtues.* Lawrence: University Press of Kansas, 1986.

Porter, D. O. "Minnowbrook II: Conclusions." *Public Administration Review,* 1989, *49*(2), 223.

Pranger, R. *The Eclipse of Citizenship: Power and Participation in Contemporary Politics.* New York: Holt, 1968.

Preimsberger, D. T., and Block, S. "Values, Standards and Integrity in Law Enforcement: An Emphasis on Job Survival." *Journal of California Law Enforcement,* 1986, *20*(1), 10–13.

Preston, N. *Understanding Ethics.* Sydney: Federation Press, 1996.

"Proposed Civil Service Changes May Encourage Whistle-Blowers." *Los Angeles Times,* Jan. 5, 1978.

Ramos, A. G. "Models of Man and Administrative Theory." *Public Administration Review,* 1972, *32*(3), 241–246.

Ramos, A. G. *The New Science of Organizations: A Reconceptualization of the Wealth of Nations.* Toronto: University of Toronto Press, 1981.

Rawls, J. *A Theory of Justice.* Cambridge, Mass.: Belknap Press of Harvard University Press, 1971.

Rest, J. *Moral Development.* New York: Praeger, 1986.

Rezaee, Z., Elmore, R. C., and Szendi, J. Z. "Ethical Behavior in Higher Educational Institutions: The Role of the Code of Conduct." *Journal of Business Ethics,* 2001, *30*(2), 171–185.

Rohr, J. "The Study of Ethics in the P.A. Curriculum." *Public Administration Review,* 1976, *36*(4), 398–406.

Rohr, J. *Ethics for Bureaucrats.* (2nd ed.) New York: Marcel Dekker, 1989.

Rohr, J. A. *Public Service, Ethics, and Constitutional Practice.* Lawrence: University Press of Kansas, 1998.

Rokeach, M. *Beliefs, Attitudes and Values.* San Francisco: Jossey-Bass, 1970.

Rosener, J. B. "Citizen Participation: Tying Strategy to Function." In P. Marshall (ed.), *Citizen Participation for Community Involvement: A Reader on the Citizen Participation Process.* Washington, D.C.: National Association of Housing and Redevelopment Officials, 1977.

Rushdie, S. "India at Five-0." *Time,* Aug. 11, 1997, pp. 34–37.

Sabini, J., and Silver, M. *Moralities of Everyday Life.* New York: Oxford University Press, 1982.

Sappington, D.E.M. "Incentives in Principal-Agent Relationships." *Journal of Economic Perspectives,* 1991, *5*(2), 45–66.

Schein, E. H. *Organizational Culture and Leadership: A Dynamic View.* San Francisco: Jossey-Bass, 1985.

Schlesinger, J. R. *Final Report of the Independent Panel to Review DOD Detention Operations.* Washington, D.C: U.S. Government Accounting Office, 2004.

Schmidt, W., and Posner, B. *Managerial Values in Perspective.* New York: American Management Association, 1983.

Schmidt, W., and Posner, B. "Values and Expectations of Federal Service Executives." *Public Administration Review,* 1986, *46*(5), 447–454.

Schnebel, E., and Bienert, M. A. "Implementing Ethics in Business Organizations." *Journal of Business Ethics,* 2004, *53,* 203–211.

Schultz, D. "Professional Ethics in a Postmodern Society." *Public Integrity,* 2004, *6*(4), 279–297.

Schutz, A. *On Phenomenology and Social Relations.* Chicago: University of Chicago Press, 1970.

Scott, W. G., and Hart, D. K. *Organizational America.* Boston: Houghton Mifflin, 1979.

Selznick, P. *TVA and the Grass Roots: A Study in the Sociology of Formal Organization.* New York: HarperCollins, 1966.

Selznick, P. *The Moral Commonwealth: Social Theory and the Promise of Community.* Berkeley: University of California Press, 1992.

Sennett, R. *The Fall of Public Man.* New York: Vintage Books, 1974.

Sherman, L. "Learning Police Ethics." *Criminal Justice Ethics,* 1987, *1*(1), 10–19.

Small, J. "Political Ethics: A View of the Leadership." *American Behavioral Scientist,* 1976, *19*(5), 543–566.

Smith, H. *The Power Game: How Washington Really Works.* New York: Ballantine, 1988.

Srivastva, S., and Cooperrider, D. L. "The Urgency for Executive Integrity." In S. Srivastva and Associates, *Executive Integrity: The Search for High Human Values in Organizational Life.* San Francisco: Jossey-Bass, 1988.

Stahl, G. O. *Public Personnel Administration.* (7th ed.) New York: Harper-Collins, 1976.

Stein, J. *Fiddler on the Roof.* New York: Crown, 1971.

Stewart, D. W., and Sprinthall, N. A. "Moral Development in Public Administration." In T. L. Cooper (ed.), *Handbook of Administrative Ethics.* New York: Marcel Dekker, 1994.

Storing, H. (ed.). *The Complete Anti-Federalist.* Chicago: University of Chicago Press, 1981.

Thompson, D. F. *The Democratic Citizen.* Cambridge: Cambridge University Press, 1970.

Thompson, D. F. "The Possibility of Administrative Ethics." *Public Administration Review,* 1985, *45*(5), 555–561.

Thompson, V. A. *Without Sympathy or Enthusiasm: The Problem of Administrative Compassion.* Tuscaloosa: University of Alabama Press, 1975.

Truelson, J. A. "Whistleblower Protection and the Judiciary." In T. L. Cooper (ed.), *Handbook of Administrative Ethics.* New York: Marcel Dekker, 2001.

Truman, D. B. *The Governmental Process.* New York: Knopf, 1951.

Tullock, G. *The Politics of Bureaucracy.* Washington, D.C.: Public Affairs Press, 1965.

Tussman, J. *Obligation and the Body Politic.* New York: Oxford University Press, 1960.

U.S. House of Representatives and U.S. Senate. *Code of Ethics for Government Service.* 85th Cong., 2nd sess., 1958.

U.S. Office of Special Counsel. *A Report to Congress from the U.S. Office of Special Counsel Fiscal Year 1996.* Washington, D.C.: U.S. Government Printing Office, 1997.

U.S. Senate. Subcommittee of the Committee on Labor and Public Welfare. *Ethical Standards in Government.* Washington, D.C.: Government Printing Office, 1951.

Van Wart, M., and Denhardt, K. G. "Organization Structure: A Reflection of Society's Values and a Context for Individual Ethics." In T. L. Cooper (ed.), *Handbook of Administrative Ethics.* New York: Marcel Dekker, 2001.

Vartabedian, R. "IRS Admits It Ranked Staff Members by Aggressiveness." *Los Angeles Times,* Jan. 1998, pp. D1, D10.

Wakefield, S. "Ethics and the Public Service: A Case for Individual Responsibility." *Public Administration Review,* 1976, *36*(6), 661–666.

Waldo, D. *The Administrative State: A Study of the Political Theory of Public Administration.* New York: Ronald Press, 1948.

Waldo, D. "Public Administration and Culture." In R. C. Martin (ed.), *Public Administration and Democracy: Essays in Honor of Paul Appleby.* Syracuse, N.Y.: Syracuse University Press, 1965.

Waldo, D. "Reflections on Public Morality." *Administration and Society,* 1974, *6*(3), 267–282.

Walzer, M. *Obligations: Essays on Disobedience, War and Citizenship.* Cambridge, Mass.: Harvard University Press, 1970.

Wamsley, G. L., and Zald, M. M. *The Political Economy of Public Organizations: A Critique and Approach to the Study of Public Administration.* Bloomington: Indiana University Press, 1973.

Warren, R., and Weschler, L. "The Costs of Citizenship." Unpublished manuscript, 1975.

Watkins, B. T. "Few Colleges Found to Offer Ethics Courses." *Chronicle of Higher Education,* June 30, 1980.

Weber, M. *From Max Weber: Essays in Sociology.* (H. H. Gerth and C. W. Mills, eds.) New York: Oxford University Press, 1946.

Weisband, E., and Franck, T. M. *Resignation in Protest: Political and Ethical Choices Between Loyalty to Team and Loyalty to Conscience in American Public Life.* New York: Grossman, 1975.

Whitbeck, C. "Ethics as Design: Doing Justice to Moral Problems." *Hastings Center Report,* 1996, *26*(3), 9–16.

White, L. D. *Introduction to the Study of Public Administration.* New York: Macmillan, 1926.

Whyte, W. H., Jr. *The Organization Man.* New York: Simon & Schuster, 1956.

Wilensky, H. *Organizational Intelligence.* New York: Basic Books, 1967.

Wilson, W. "The Study of Administration." *Political Science Quarterly,* 1887, *2*(1), 197–220.

Winter, G. *Elements for a Social Ethic.* New York: Macmillan, 1966.

Wittmer, D. "Ethical Work Climates: Comparing Top Managers in Public and Private Organizations." *Journal of Public Administration Research and Theory,* 1996, *6*(4), 559–572.

Wittmer, D. P. "Developing a Behavioral Model for Ethical Decision Making in Organizations: Conceptual and Empirical Research." In H. G. Frederickson and R. K. Ghere (eds.), *Ethics in Public Management.* Armonk, N.Y.: M. E. Sharpe, 2004.

Wolin, S. "The Age of Organization and the Sublimation of Politics." In S. Wolin, *Politics and Vision: Continuity and Innovation in Western Political Thought.* Boston: Little, Brown, 1960.

Wright, D. *The Psychology of Moral Behavior.* Baltimore, Md.: Penguin, 1971.

Yankelovich, D. *New Rules: Searching for Self-Fulfillment in a World Turned Upside Down.* New York: Random House, 1981.

Yankelovich, D. *Coming to Public Judgment: Making Democracy Work in a Complex World.* Syracuse, N.Y.: Syracuse University Press, 1991.

Yoder, D. E., and Cooper, T. L. "Public-Service Ethics in a Transnational World." In H. G. Frederickson and R. K. Ghere (eds.), *Ethics in Public Management.* Armonk, N.Y.: M. E. Sharpe, 2005.

Yoder, D. E., and Denhardt, K. G. "Ethics Education in Public Administration and Affairs: Preparing Graduates for Workplace Moral Dilemmas." In T. L. Cooper (ed.), *Handbook of Administrative Ethics.* New York: Marcel Dekker, 2001.

Zimbardo, P. *Quiet Rage: The Stanford Prison Experiment.* New York: Harper-Collins, 1992. Video.

Index